Australian Television

AND

International Mediascapes

for Jo, Ben and Hugo
and
for Katherine, a constant television companion

Australian Television

AND

International Mediascapes

STUART CUNNINGHAM
Queensland University of Technology
and
ELIZABETH JACKA
University of Technology, Sydney

CAMBRIDGE
UNIVERSITY PRESS

Published by the Press Syndicate of the University of Cambridge
The Pitt Building, Trumpington Street, Cambridge CB2 1RP, UK
40 West 20th Street, New York, NY 10011–4211, USA
10 Stamford Road, Oakleigh, Melbourne 3166, Australia

Printed in Australia by Australian Print Group

National Library of Australia cataloguing-in-publication data

Cunningham, Stuart.
Australian television and international mediascapes.
Bibliography.
Includes index.
1. Television broadcasting – Australia. 2. Television
programs – Australia. 3. Television broadcasting – Social
aspects – Australia. 4. Television broadcasting – Social
aspects. 5. Television programs – Social aspects.
I. Jacka, Elizabeth. II. Title.
384.550994

Library of Congress cataloguing-in-publication data

Cunningham, Stuart.
Australian television and international mediascapes/Stuart
Cunningham and Elizabeth Jacka.
p.   cm.
Includes bibliographical references (p.   ) and index.
1. Television broadcasting – Australia. 2. Television programs,
Foreign. I. Jacka, Elizabeth. II. Title.
HE 8700.9.A8C86 1996
384.55'0994–dc20   95–38851

A catalogue record for this book is available from the British Library.

ISBN 0 521 47003 X Hardback
ISBN 0 521 46974 0 Paperback

Contents

Illustrations

FIGURES

TABLES

Preface

Neighbours, a cheap and unpretentious suburban soap opera that took some time to build audiences in Australia, has been an unprecedented success in Britain, reorienting television schedules, opening the way for a much closer co-operative relationship between the British and Australian industries, and creating a whole social field of audience and fan response around it. *The Flying Doctors*, with its outback community spirit, was perceived as a model of social democratic values in The Netherlands, where it was voted most popular imported program in 1992. If we listen to concern expressed about the commercialisation of European or New Zealand television, we hear that Australian models of commercial programming are as worrying as United States models, and are simple recycled versions of the hegemonic master texts of the dominant exporting nation. Such impacts on mass audiences or intellectuals are complemented by beguiling examples of Australian television's power to charm all sorts of different sub-communities: *Neighbours* has been mined for its use in developing English-language skills (as a kind of *Sesame Street* for older persons), in Mauritius; lesbian and gay communities on the west coast of the US made *Prisoner Cell Block H* a cult hit; and audiences in the Midlands of the United Kingdom campaigned for its retention when it was in danger of being pulled from the schedule in 1990.

These are some of the ingredients we wish to mix into a study of Australian television in the international market-place. Media, communications and cultural studies research has not developed robust traditions for bringing such peripheral cultural and industry contra-flow into visibility. At the same time, the traditional paradigms for understanding cultural exchange and domination have come under increasing strain in recent years. In a rapidly globalising and diversifying world they have seemed less and less capable of describing the ramifying patterns that characterise contemporary audiovisual culture, and of accounting for audience negotiation with dominant meanings and products. Most theorists of globalisation have tended to over-emphasise the centrality of the US in the audiovisual industries and to be preoccupied with audience negotiation of the dominant US product. They have viewed cultural exchange through a peculiarly metropolitan prism.

During the 1980s and 1990s, Australia developed a sizeable international profile for its film and television product – what the French felicitously call *l'audiovisuel*. With blockbusters like *Crocodile Dundee* (1986) and its US-backed sequel, and *The Piano* (1993) and *Schindler's List* (1993), Australian or Australian-connected films consolidated the international reputation first established in the 1970s. In this book, however, we are concentrating on product made for television. We do this for a variety of reasons. While film and television drama are for most intents and purposes two parts of the same industry, the methods of studying them have developed different protocols because of their different modes of consumption. Television finds itself embedded in the routines of everyday life for the great majority of people, while film continues to be an occasioned and occasional activity, with foreign film particularly finding its audiences across a much narrower stratum of international communities. Thus, television programs are much more appropriately understood as product – produced, acquired and screened not for their intrinsic or individual worth but for their ability to fill schedules, to 'feed the monster'. Whereas it is appropriate to study the international circulation of foreign films as discrete aesthetic objects, for that is precisely how they are marketed across the world's art-cinema circuits, the same protocols are impossible to apply to television programs. Also, while there is now a substantial literature on the careers of Australian films overseas (Hamilton and Matthews 1986; Lewis 1987; O'Regan 1988), this is the first book to bring together the collective international career of Australian television.

Our study examines both the international and the domestic aspects of the phenomenon of Australian program export. We first of all consider it in relation to international debates on globalisation and so-called 'borderless markets', on convergence of technologies and ownership across communications media; on market structure including theories of post-fordism; and on cross-cultural exchange (Chapter 1 and Chapter 2). In doing this, our work can be regarded as an extended and carefully situated case study of an audiovisual producer and exporter on the periphery of world trade flows, which has nonetheless come to exert an impact and profile disproportionate to the size of its industry and its domestic market.

In this, Australian program export is an excellent illustration of the contemporary multi-directional flow of contemporary world television trade (Chapters 6–11).

In tracing the reasons for this, we are led to the other side of the equation – the domestic structure and operations of the Australian television industry (Chapters 3–5). We concentrate primarily on patterns and developments since the mid-to-late 1980s, when the story traced by Elizabeth Jacka and Susan Dermody in *The Screening of Australia* (1987; 1988) and in *The Imaginary Industry* (1988, Parts 1 and 2) ended. There are obvious patterns of internationalisation which pre-date this as a starting point – it would probably be fair to say that Australia has had an in-built orientation to export for most of the history of the film industry, and certainly since the mid-1970s in television.

The decade we have studied, 1985–94, represents new departures in the process of globalisation of audiovisual industries. By globalisation we mean an ever greater process of inter-linking once separate industries, trans-border program consumption and the diversification of cultural exchange, with many more sources of cultural expression gaining the attention of international audiences. The dominant themes of this period include the changing policies governing audiovisual support mechanisms, for example the Australian Film Finance Corporation's demands for 'market attachment' (usually overseas) for projects it funds; the growth of co-productions and co-ventures as the norm for high-budget drama and, increasingly, documentary; the financial crises of the commercial networks, which accelerated the need to seek off-shore finance for an ongoing production slate; and the domestic policy debates that have shifted to reflect Australia's growing transparency to economic, political and cultural internationalisation.

What of our method in our approach to these themes? We seek to present a middle-range approach that integrates industry and cultural analysis and is informed by contemporary debates in political economy, media, communication and cultural studies, sociology, and policy studies about globalisation and cross-cultural communication. Chapter 1 begins by canvassing these debates, while Chapter 2 and Chapter 3 use industry analysis to introduce the international and domestic context within which Australian television operates. The main players are profiled in Chapter 4 and Chapter 5.

The question of how cultural and reception analysis can be adequately performed on the careers of Australian programs in several major overseas territories is examined in Chapter 1. The results are followed through in

Chapter 3 and in Chapters 6–11, where we examine how the television systems and culture of various major territories act as the prism through which Australian programs are filtered. Throughout this part of the book, detailed discussions of the international careers of programs and services such as *Neighbours, Sylvania Waters, The Flying Doctors, Paradise Beach, Beyond 2000, Brides of Christ, Shortland Street, Mini-Dragons* and Australia Television, the Australian Broadcasting Corporation's international satellite service, demonstrate the industrial and cultural specificity of reception contexts for television that is Australian or has crucial Australian connections. Finally, in the concluding Chapter 12, we use cultural policy studies approaches to examine the effects of internationalisation on the domestic mediascape.

Acknowledgements

The logistical magnitude of the research entailed in the preparation of this book has meant that we have incurred lasting debts of gratitude to numerous people and organisations for their assistance. The fundamental funding was provided in 1992–4 by an Australian Research Council Large Grant entitled 'Global Trends in Audiovisual Media – Effects on Australian Industrial and Cultural Development'. We are pleased to record from the outset that our undertaking would have been impossible without such support. It enabled travel to conduct several field investigations of the industrial and social environment into which Australian programs are being introduced. It also enabled us to access the valuable research assistance of Maree Delofski, Amanda Hickie and Kiernan Fitzpatrick in Sydney; Julie Morrison, Rea Turner and John Ritchie in Brisbane; Julie Anderson in New York; and Miranda van den Brock in Amsterdam.

Ancillary funding that supported the research was provided by the Faculty of Business and the School of Media and Journalism, Queensland University of Technology; the Department of Industry, Technology and Regional Development (DITARD); the School of Humanities, University of Technology, Sydney, which housed the Sydney base for the project; Christchurch Polytechnic; and the University of Waikato. Elizabeth Jacka's research in Europe was partly supported by the Association of Commonwealth Universities' Howard Thomas Fellowship in Media Studies. This was held at Goldsmiths' College, University of London; the assistance of Ivor Gaber, head of the Department of Communications and his staff is gratefully acknowledged. Preliminary findings from the research were presented at a wide variety of venues: we would like to thank the receptive audiences at Goldsmiths' College, University of London; the School of Journalism amd Communication, Carleton University, Canada; the College of Journalism, University of Maryland; the Department of Cinema Studies, New York University; the Screen Producers Association of Australia; Institute for International Research conferences; the Department of English, University of Queensland; the Australian Communication Association; the Institute for Cultural Policy Studies, Griffith University; and the Centre for International Research on Communication and Information Technologies.

Individual chapter writers Geoff Lealand (Chapter 10) and Helen Wilson (Chapter 11) have made a valuable contribution to the overall coverage of the book. Our editor at Cambridge University Press, Phillipa McGuinness, has been patient and helpful. The School of Media and Journalism, Queensland University of Technology, and the School of English, Linguistics and Media, Macquarie University provided hospitable environments for our writing.

A significant amount of the primary research for this book has been based on substantial interviews with a wide range of industry personnel and analysts. Often, this meant an hour or more of time away from busy schedules, and follow-up exchanges of documentation to update and correct information and perspective. For some, it meant much more: hosting visits by us, providing references or helping set up contacts and/or interviews for us. Instead of referencing each and every source when background information has been offered in the context of interviews, we here list the positions and institutional affiliations of these people, which were current at the time of interview. Only when we directly quote such sources do we reference them.

To the following, then, we extend our thanks.

In Australia: Rod Watson, Program Scheduler and Dominic Stone, Program Scheduler and Acting General Manager, Australia Television; David Marshall, University of Queensland; Jock Given, Policy Advisor, Sue Murray, Director, Marketing, Rosemary Curtis, Research Manager, Kate Gilroy, Research Officer and Peter Langmead, Research Officer, Australian Film Commission, Patricia Edgar, Executive Director and Jenny Buckland, Director of Marketing, Australian Children's Television Foundation; Chris Gunn, General Manager, Beyond Distribution; Ian Holmes, Managing Director, Grundy Worldwide; Nick McMahon and Greg Coote, Village Roadshow/Warner Roadshow; Kim Vecera, General Manager Business Affairs, Roadshow Coote and Carroll; Errol Sullivan, Southern Star/Sullivan; Bruce Moir, Managing Director, Film Australia; Des Monaghan, Network Program Development Director, Seven Network; Terry Ohlsson, Managing Director, and Don Samulenok, Director of Sales, Crawfords Australia; Peter Sainsbury, Co-production Consultant, Australian Film Commission; Juliet Grimm, Head Program

Development, BBC Enterprises Sydney; Marena Manzoufas, Head of Program Sales and Acquisitions, ABC International; Yulena Chernachev, George Patterson Advertising.

In Britain: Richard Collins, Senior Research Fellow and Jason Copley, honours student, Goldsmiths' College, University of London; Bill Allen, Director of Sales, Central Television Enterprises; Liz Cook, Director International Sales and Judith Bland, Managing Director, Eaton Films; Jeremy Boulton, Director of Acquisitions, BSkyB; Victor Glynn, Portman Productions; Colin Leventhal, Director Acquisitions, Channel Four; Gary Mitchell, Sales Manager, Richard Price Television Associates; Charles Denton, Chief Executive, Zenith; Mike Phillips, Managing Director Thames International, Thames TV; Sue Elliot, Head Program Regulation, Independent Television Commission; Mike Frost, Deputy Head Program Acquisition, British Broadcasting Corporation; Jeremy Coopman, Head of Publicity, Grundy Organisation UK.

In Ireland: Bill Harpur, Head of Acquisitions and Tony Fahey, Head of Research, Radio Telefis Eireann; Derry O'Brien, International Services Department, The Irish Trade Board/An Bord Trachtalta.

In France: Waddick Doyle, Université de Paris; Pascal Volle, media consultant; Pascal Bensoussan, Managing Director, F Productions; Annie Belet, Quartier Latin; Simone Halberstadt-Harari, President and Director General, Tele Images; Marie Pierre Moulinjeune, Head of Acquisitions, France 2.

In The Netherlands: Bert Van Der Veer, Program Director, RTL4; Louis Heinsmann, Head International Relations and Louise Tolen-Worth, Head Program Purchasing, Nederlandse Omroepprogramma Stichting; Hedy van Bochove, Director Acquisitions and Development, Joop van den Ende TV – Produkties BV; Ria van Essen, Head of Programming, Vara Televisie.

In Germany: Joerg Hermes, Assistant Head of Acquisitions, RTL Plus; Manfred Schutze, Head of Acquisitions, ZDF; Dr Gottfried Langenstein, Deputy Director, International Affairs, ZDF; Michael Schmidel, Production Department, Taurus Films.

In the United States: Jonathan Levy, Federal Communications Commission, Washington; Lynne Gross, California State University at Fullerton; Toby Miller, New York University; Marjorie Ferguson, University of Maryland; Brooke Bailey Johnson, Senior Vice President, Programming and Production, Arts and Entertainment Network; Fred Cohen, President, Kingworld International; Fred Gaines, Los Angeles entertainment lawyer; Nelsa Gidney, American Program Services; Barbara Kreisman, Chief, Video Services Division, Mass Media Bureau, Federal Communications Commission; Stephen Fields and Bruce Rider, Acquisitions, Disney

Channel; Anthony I. Ginnane, International Sales Agent, Fries Distribution; Carol Martz, Program Manager, KCOP; Russell J. Kagan, International Program Consultants; Carolanne Dolan, Senior Manager of Acquisitions, National Geographic Television; Sandra Pastoor, Director of Programming and Operations, WCDA; John Grant, Managing Director and Stephen Ashley, Director, Scheduling and Planning, Public Broadcasting Service; Tammi Crystal, Program Scheduling, Discovery Networks; James McNamara, Chief Executive Officer and President and Thea Diserio, Senior Vice President, New World International; and Phil Oldham, Executive Vice President, Genesis Entertainment.

In Canada: Dan Johnson, Vice President, Production, Finance and Distribution, Alliance Communications; Paul Attallah and Sandy Forbes, Carleton University; Katka Selucky, Telefilm Canada; Wendy McGrath, Anglophone Coproductions, Communications Canada; Debbie Rudka, CTV Toronto; Bill Morgan, CBC Toronto; D. Hoover, Global TV; Ted Riley, Atlantis Productions.

In New Zealand: Bettina Hollings, Manager of Programming, Channel 2; Caterina de Nave, television producer/director; Sam Fairhall, Manager Pacific Service, and Christine Fenby, Manager Pacific Operations, TVNZ.

In Papua New Guinea: Lindsay Jorgenson, Manager HiTron; Sean Dorney, ABC correspondent, Port Moresby; Sir Alkan Tololo, Chairman NBC; Lindsay Lailai, Secretary, PNG Department of Communications; Saroriba Nash, Lecturer in Journalism, University of Papua New Guinea; Bill Kuha, Secretary, PNG Department of Home Affairs and Youth; Julian Jalal, PNG Chief Censor; Isikeli Taureka, Managing Director, Post and Telecommunication Corporation, PNG; John Taylor, Chief Executive Officer, EM TV.

In Fiji: Nick Samitz, Manager Fiji One; Nii-K Plange, Lecturer in Sociology and Andrew Horne, Professor of English, University of the South Pacific.

For permission to reproduce copyright material we would like to thank the following: Arts & Entertainment Network; Hearst/ABC/NBC; the Australian Film Commission; Film Australia; the Grundy organisation; the *New Zealand Herald*; the *New Zealand Listener*; Roadshow, Coote and Carroll; *Shout Magazine*; *Television Business International*; *TV Times* (UK); *TV World*; VARA Television and Crawfords Media International; *Variety*; *Woman* (UK). All reasonable efforts were made to secure permission for illustrative material used but the publishers would be glad to hear from anyone we have been unable to contact.

Stuart Cunningham and Elizabeth Jacka

Abbreviations

ABA	Australian Broadcasting Authority
ABC	Australian Broadcasting Corporation
ACDO	Australian Cultural Development Office
AFC	Australian Film Commission
AFI	Australian Film Institute
AFM	American Film Market
APEC	Asia Pacific Economic Council
ARD	Arbeitgemeinschaft der Öffentlichrectlichen-Rundfunkenstalten der Bundesrepublik Deutschland
ASEAN	Association of South East Asian Nations
ATV	Australia Television
A&E	Arts and Entertainment
BARB	British Audience Research Board
BBC	British Broadcasting Corporation
BIG	Beyond International Group
BTCE	Bureau of Transport and Communications Economics
CBC	Canadian Broadcasting Corporation
CER	Closer Economic Relations
CIRCIT	Centre for International Research on Communication and Information Technologies
CIT	Central Independent Television
CNBC	Cable National Broadcasting Corporation
CNN	Cable News Network
CTV	Canadian Television
DASET	Department of Arts, Sport, the Environment and Territories
DITARD	Department of Industry, Technology and Regional Development
EC	European Community
EFSA	Export Film Services Australia

ESPN	Electronic Sports Programming Network
EU	European Union
FCC	Federal Communications Commission
FFC	Film Finance Corporation
GATT	General Agreement on Tariffs and Trade
HBO	Home Box Office
IIR	Institute for International Research
ITN	Independent Television Network
ITV	Independent Television (Network)
MIPCOM	International Market for Television, Video, Cable and Satellite Films and Programs
MTV	Music Television
NATPE	National Association of Television Programming Executives
NBC	National Broadcasting Corporation
NHK	Nippon Hoso Kyokai
NIP	National Interest Program
NOS	Nederlandse Omroepprogramma Stichting
NZOA	New Zealand On Air
PBS	Public Broadcasting Service
QTV	Queensland Television
RAI	Radio-televisione Italia
RCC	Roadshow Coote and Carroll
RCTI	Rajawali Citra Televisi
RTE	Radio Telefis Eireann
RTM	Radio and Television Malaysia
SBS	Special Broadcasting Service
SIN	Spanish International Network
SMATV	Satellite Master Antenna Television
SNS	Subscriber News Service
STB	System Televisyen Berhad
SVT	Sveriges Television
TBI	Television Business International
TCI	Tele-Communications Incorporated
TVNZ	Television New Zealand
TVO	Television Ontario
TVRI	Television Republik Indonesia
TVS	Televisi South
UK	United Kingdom
US	United States [of America]
YTV	Youth Television
ZDF	Zweites Deutsches Fernsehen

Global Mediascapes:
Theory and Industry

1

Theoretical Perspectives

The last ten years have seen profound changes in the television cultures of many countries. Technological innovation, industrial realignments and changes in regulatory philosophy have transformed a collection of comparatively self-contained systems into one of increasingly international patterns of ownership and increasingly global flows of programming. Australia has been the slowest of the developed countries to change; at the time of writing it still has virtually no television other than the traditional free-to-air channels, nevertheless it has not been cut off from the changing patterns of world television. In particular, as it has developed for its size a robust and efficient program-production industry, nurtured by years of government intervention, Australia has begun to become a significant middle-sized exporter of programming. Its best and most lucrative market remains the UK but Australian programs now turn up virtually in every television market in the world.

In this book we trace how Australia came to occupy that position within what we can call the world television system. In the process we analyse how this system has itself evolved, how it operates both as an industrial system and a system of cultural exchange, and what the political, economic and cultural effects of these patterns might be. In doing so we investigate current debates about globalisation, cultural imperialism, the nation and cultural identity. We examine the local history of the development of the Australian program production industry and show how state policies of industry development have evolved and how they have been conceptually sustained. We analyse why traditional arguments for intervention, which have depended on notions of protecting national identity and cultural integrity, are giving way to new rationales framed in terms of international competitiveness and the cultivation of export markets, and what the limits and problems of these shifts are.

3

We also look at the effects the changing geo-political patterns within the world system – most notably the partial dismantling of national boundaries in Europe, the demise of Communism and the rise of the Asian economies – are having on cultural ecologies and the consequent receptiveness of many regions of the world to new cultural influences, including new sources and kinds of television. This will help us to understand how and why Australian programs have been able to find acceptance in international markets. We argue that the reasons for this are industrial as much as cultural since, in many places where Australian-originated programs act as filler material, they would not be perceived as falling into any category other than foreign. In order to show the broad industrial and cultural reasons for the appearance of Australian programming across the world, we develop a middle-range methodology, which steers a course between the 'total' explanations of political-economic theories and the narrow 'micro-situational' audience analysis informed by ethnography.

Europe and North America historically have been the richest television markets and they are also the largest sources of program export revenue for Australia. We examine the flow of programs from Australia to five European countries (the UK, Ireland, France, Germany and The Netherlands) and to the US and Canada, and analyse the complex factors – industrial, regulatory, cultural, historical, linguistic and aesthetic – that influence the receptiveness of these television cultures to Australian programs.

In recent years, Asian television has seen a proliferation of new commercial services and a dismantling of many of the state-imposed barriers to inward cultural flows, including television programs. Australia has a unique position as a multicultural nation of European heritage but an increasing Asian character. Geographically positioned in the region, it has many historical, economic and cultural links with Asia and with Asian broadcasting institutions. Government policy explicitly targets the further development of trading and economic planning links with Asia; the national broadcaster, the Australian Broadcasting Corporation (ABC), has begun a free-to-air satellite service to the region. We review the changing Asian media landscape and the progress of the ABC's service.

If Australia has traditionally been a net importer of programs from the rest of the world, especially the US and the UK, and thus in the discourse of cultural imperialism is a 'victim', it has acted more like an imperialiser in its own immediate region of the Pacific. New Zealand has always had a particularly acute sense of its own subordination to its bigger trans-Tasman first cousin (rather like Canada's attitude to the US), and indeed, following the radical de-regulation of the New Zealand broadcasting system that occurred in the late 1980s, Australian programs appeared to flood New Zealand screens. In tiny Pacific nations like Papua New Guinea, Australia has had a determining influence on the fledgling television system and has been a major source of programming.

CULTURAL IMPERIALISM

The rhetoric for the policies of cultural protection and support followed by Australia since the mid-1960s has been sustained by a version of the cultural imperialism thesis. This dominant media studies paradigm has also shaped most of the debate about international cultural flows since the 1970s, when key interventions such as the research of Kaarle Nordenstreng and Tapio Varis on international television flows, the work of Herbert Schiller on the US domination of the international communications industries, and the theorisations of dependency and cultural domination by Latin American scholars and the UNESCO movement for a New World Information and Communication Order (NWICO) set the paradigm firmly in place (Nordenstreng and Varis 1974; Schiller 1976; Mattelart 1979; MacBride 1980).

As John Tomlinson (1991) has established, the cultural imperialism thesis is not actually one thesis but a complex and often contradictory set of views, which have been increasingly seen as both conceptually flawed and insufficiently supported by empirical evidence. In the classic formulation by a scholar such as Herbert Schiller, the thesis sees the US domination of international audiovisual flows as part of a strategy to reinforce US economic and political domination of the rest of the world. As recently as 1991, in an article tellingly entitled 'Not yet the post-imperialist era', Schiller restates his position:

> Media-cultural imperialism is a sub-set of the *general* system of imperialism. It is not free-standing; the media-cultural component in a developed, corporate economy supports the economic objectives of the decisive industrial-financial sectors ... what is regarded as cultural output also is ideological and profit-serving to the system at large (Schiller 1991, p.14).

While there is plenty of evidence to show that the US often consciously used the mass media as a diplomatic instrument (Guback 1969; Swoch 1993; Curtin 1993) to further political and economic interests, it cannot be assumed, as Schiller does, that this process was actually effective; in other words, that mere exposure to US product leads automatically to the cultural effect assumed.

In his 1991 article, Schiller is responding to a growing body of work that began to appear as early as 1980 and that started to question the validity of the cultural imperialism thesis. A number of critics began to examine its conceptual soundness (for example, Lee 1980; Fejes 1981), to question the empirical basis on which it was founded (Tracey 1985, 1988) and to challenge the theorisation of audience response on which it rested (Ang 1985; Katz and Liebes 1985). The usefulness of Tomlinson's critique is to show that at least one reason why the debate has been so unresolvable is that the thesis is actually composed of a complex of at least four distinct discourses: cultural imperialism can be equated with media imperialism; it can operate as a discourse of nationality; it can operate as a discourse of global capitalism; and/or it can stand as a critique of modernity (Tomlinson 1991, p.19ff.). Separating out these strands is the first task of beginning to engage with and test the thesis in ways that are adequate to the current historical phase.

Tomlinson, following Chin-Chuan Lee's account (1980), discusses the distinction between cultural imperialism and media imperialism and argues that left-wing scholars like Herbert Schiller conflate them. In this view, the undoubted dominance of the US in certain areas of mass *media* export (film, television, recorded music, publishing, advertising, video games) leads automatically to *cultural* domination. The next step then is to assume rather than demonstrate an automatic connection between cultural domination and domination in the political and economic arena.

The most obvious flaw in this argument is the assumption that media exhaust culture. Culture is much more than media even if media are part of culture. The second problem is the failure to conceptualise sufficiently the connection between the economic, political and cultural domains. Work in cultural studies and in other disciplines, especially that done from a post-modernist and post-colonial perspective, has clearly established the inadequacy of this marxist topology of base and superstructure (Hall 1977; Bennett 1982). A further flaw is the inadequacy of the way in which media effects are theorised. Textual and audience studies since the 1970s indicate that individual texts can be read in a multiplicity of ways, and empirical research is required to determine what role imported media products actually do play in formations of culture in any particular localities and moments. The final critique of media imperialism is based on historical grounds. In its classic form, the thesis was developed in the 1960s and early 1970s when the US still dominated the world system and when it was easier to demonstrate that television exchange was characterised by a one-way flow of media products from the US to other Western countries with very little in the way of exchange or flows from one peripheral country to another. Since then, however, things have changed (Sinclair *et al.* 1995).

The US is no longer as dominant in the world economy as that economy has globalised; for one thing the growth of global media firms means it is no longer necessary for them to be located in any one place. Economies once considered peripheral are developing rapidly, which is leading to new flows of people, money, goods and cultural products in new directions. As a consequence the model of the world that envisages a single centre of power and a number of peripheral societies on the receiving end can no longer be sustained.

GLOBALISATION OF THE MEDIA

> Globalization as a concept refers both to the compression of the world and the intensification of consciousness of the world as a whole (Robertson 1992, p.8).

The term 'globalisation' is difficult to escape; it has become almost a cliche in contemporary theoretical and policy debates, and myths about it abound (Ferguson 1992). Its meaning is certainly no less ambiguous than the notion of cultural imperialism it has tended to displace. Marshall McLuhan's visionary concept of the 'global village' is the most famous early notion of a global culture (1964; *see also* McLuhan and Powers 1989), but the concept has gained increased currency since the mid-1980s. It remains unresolved whether globalisation is a new phenomenon or whether the present era is simply a new stage of a process that has been proceeding over centuries.

As Immanuel Wallerstein has shown, the globalising processes are as old as capitalism itself (Robertson 1992, p.9). Since the sixteenth century at the latest, exploration and colonisation had begun to link points on the entire globe; transport and communications technology had always played a crucial role in this linking and in the consequent spread of the capitalist mode of production and of cultural modernity. Navigation is the first such technology but what Harold Innis called the 'control of empires' accelerated enormously in the nineteenth century with the invention of the telegraph and the telephone and even more in the twentieth century with the arrival of the mass media, especially television, with its capacity to 'bind' space and 'compress' time (Carey 1989, p.160). The technology that presents us with the next large leap in space-binding and time-compressing capabilities is the satellite; it is the advent of satellite television, which can address a global community in real time, that has precipitated the latest round of concern about globalisation and the media.

The cultural significance of communication technologies is their ability to 're-spatialise' the globe, to create new cultural geographies, that is, to link already existing communities or even create new ones (Morley and Robins 1989, p.22). Until recently, the communities the mass media created were largely national or sub-national ones; both commercial and public service media were constructed along national lines and addressed national audiences, playing their role in various sorts of nation-binding ideological projects. Certainly since their inception the media have had globalising elements: the growth of international news agencies, owned by the US and Europe since the nineteenth century (Tunstall and Palmer 1991, p.46ff.), the world-wide pre-eminence of Hollywood since the First World War (Thompson 1985) and the dominance of the US as a supplier of television programs (Wildman and Siwek 1988, p.26). But the satellite era undoubtedly introduces new elements into the globalisation picture, namely the ability to address trans- and cross-national communities.

In the spirit of Tomlinson's disaggregation of cultural imperialism, we can similarly disaggregate the concept of global media. There are global media *events*, when virtually everyone with access to a television set is able to witness major events at the same time (for example, the Gulf War, the crackdown in Tienanmen Square, the fall of the Berlin Wall, the Bosnian conflict). Then there is the regional and potentially global spread of *service delivery platforms* (for example, Star TV, CNN, BBC World TV). On a broader scale, it can mean the formation of global media *firms*, which own and/or control media outlets in most regions of the world (News Corporation, Time-Warner, Sony or Matsushita). Finally, the concept can refer to the global *distribution* of media, including television programs.

While the first of these is not our major concern (global media events have been extensively analysed by other commentators (Wark 1994a; 1994b)), we shall have cause to examine each of the other three. Global distribution is not new – television programs have been exchanged since television began in the 1950s – but in the last ten years this phenomenon has increased exponentially due to the great proliferation of services worldwide, and because the sources from which programs come have widened. We shall be exploring the unfolding of this process and the place that Australia is playing within this diversification of world television flows. Global media firms and service delivery platforms are qualitatively new phenomena which have come into existence only since the profound re-configuration of world television, which occurred during the 1980s.

The debate about the cultural effects of globalisation bears similarities to the arguments forwarded by proponents of the cultural imperialism thesis against the earlier modernisation paradigm. On the one hand, an emerging global culture can be celebrated as bringing peoples together in a new cosmopolitanism and internationalism, taking the world beyond sectarian nationalisms, 'Cold Warrior' power blocs and the old imperium of first-, second- and third-world divisions. New communities of interest will emerge to displace the old world order: 'Afro-Caribbeans in Brixton could have more in common with Moroccans in Paris than with their upper-class neighbours in Dulwich' (Mulgan and Warpole 1986, p.113). On the other, commentators like Herbert Schiller see globalisation as leading to an intensification of cultural imperialism.

> The role of television in the global arena of cultural domination has not diminished in the 1990s. Reinforced by new delivery systems – communication satellites and cable networks – the image flow is heavier than ever. Its source of origin also has not changed that much in the last quarter of the century (Schiller 1991, p.15).

We shall argue against both the utopian and dystopian views of globalisation – a new cosmopolitan internationalism versus the further homogenisation of culture. Rather, the concept of globalisation is a myth precisely in the sense of a powerful grid of understanding that outstrips the evidential basis for it (*see* Ferguson 1992). And the power of the myth may already be passing. As Ien Ang (1994, p.325) has argued, talk about globalisation may have been 'part of a short-lived rhetoric which coincided with a precise historical moment' during the late 1980s and early 1990s. This was a period when major political transformations (such as the end of the Cold War, the breakdown of Communism and the advent of the European Union) were carried by and to the world through media such as CNN, with global reach. These developments coalesced to 'produce an apocalyptic sense of globalised reality'. She suggests that our present and immediate future can be characterised as a '*post*-globalised world rife with regional realignments and fracturings, nationalist and ethnic separatisms,

everywhere • every day • anytime • around the world

STOLEN LIVES
93-minute movie plus 11 one-hour series
(Also available as a 13-hour maxi series)

New high quality filmed drama. An
intriguing mystery with a strong appeal
to female audiences. STOLEN LIVES is
about a woman who lived a despicable
lie. Only after her death was her secret
revealed with its legacy of shame. A
brand new GRUNDY offering from Ivan
Hall Productions.

MISSION: TOP SECRET
The largest international co-production of a children's
programme ever. 24 half-hours or six family movies
available this year. A European Film Corporation
production, a joint venture between GRUNDY
WORLDWIDE and The Quartier Latin Group, in
association with France 3 and Canal J (France); NDR,
NDR Intl. and Rive Gauche (Germany); Yorkshire TV
(U.K.); Telewizja Polska and Dzielnica Lacinska (Poland);
TVE and Coral Europa (Spain); RTSI (Switzerland);
Reteitalia (Italy); and Channel 10 (Australia).

UNSEEN TREASURES
OF THE WORLD
52-minute documentary special

A world first! An exclusive look at
the riches and treasures of the
Golden Age of Russia long hidden
under lock and key behind the Iron
Curtain. Magnificent and exclusive!
A superb, high quality production
for a family documentary slot.

PRISONER-CELL BLOCK H
692 one-hour episodes. The incredible record-breaking
"cult" series. When a leading British ITV station came to
the last episode of PRISONER, hundreds of protesters
demanded the series be repeated. The first time in
television history a programme has been so popular.
Now PRISONER-CELL BLOCK H is licensing

**Grundys' key globalising strategy is dubbed 'parochial internationalisation' by
company founder, Reg Grundy. (Advertisement in *Variety*, 5 April 1993.)**

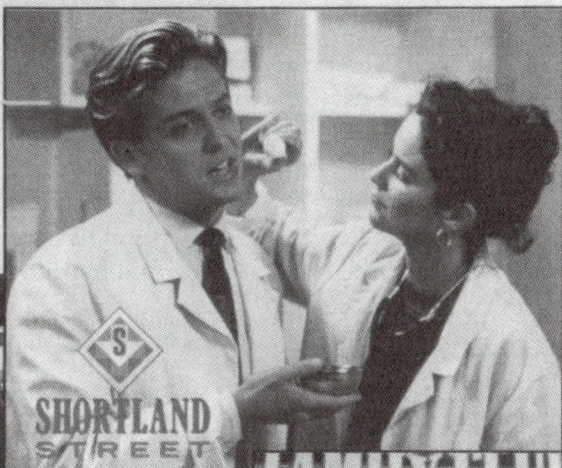

and, in parallel, a proliferation of overlapping and criss-crossing media vectors, which undermine a unified and singular notion of the "global"'. In the rest of this section, we explore some of the limits of the dystopian view of globalisation, while the problems with the utopian side are examined in the next.

Global culture is seen by its critics as imposed and inauthentic while local culture is organic and authentic (Smith 1990, p.178–9). Those critics who equate globalisation with homogenisation bewail the uniformity of architecture, urban design, fashion, consumption styles, consumer brands, transport systems and, eventually, media that can be observed in so many regions of the world; CNN becomes the perfect bad object for this position. Television is a principal source of this appearance of homogenisation: television schedules from Dublin to Moscow, from Copenhagen to Sydney are replete with programs with names like *Santa Barbara*, *Melrose Place*, *LA Law*, *Oprah Winfrey*. As new types of services are opened up in Asia, the Pacific, Eastern Europe and now South Africa (and therefore the rest of Africa) it is safe to predict that more American programming will be shown. Does this mean that fears about cultural homogenisation are justified?

Ironically, the globalisation as homogenisation thesis, though appearing to speak for the Third World, is filtered through a particularly Western optic. It over-emphasises those societies where there is or has been a high level of US imports, and overlooks the fact that large sections of the globe do not participate in the 'global village' for political and/or economic reasons. Some parts of the Middle East would come into this category, where there are political barriers to the entry of television material from the West. Most of Africa, parts of Latin America, the Indian sub-continent, what used to be called Indo-China and China itself are areas in which relative poverty and a huge gulf between the urban middle class and the rural poor mean that access to global television is extremely restricted and confined to elite groups.

Another weakness or blind spot of the media imperialism thesis is to give too much weight to the importance of imported television. Television has always been and remains primarily a domestic medium. According to figures from 1989, the volume of purely domestic material is 29 times higher than that which is traded (O'Regan 1993). Television remains a gloriously hybrid medium, with a plethora of programming of an inescapably and essentially local, untranslatable nature. While US programs lead the world in their transportability, and even manage to dominate schedules on some channels in some countries, they are rarely the most popular programs where viewers have a reasonable menu of locally produced material from which to choose.

In more economically advanced parts of the world, as well as having homogenising tendencies, the new global television regime paradoxically seems to offer new possibilities for diversification of program sources. The advent of satellite and other kinds of new services, which can address niche audiences both within and across national boundaries, has led to the development of exportable specialised services and programming from sources other than the traditional dominant exporters – the US and the UK. As well as making global television possible, satellite technology strengthens regional sub-markets by allowing the exchange of programs and services between culturally and linguistically proximate territories – so a Latin American 'audiovisual space' based on Spanish, a Middle Eastern one based on Arabic, and an east Asian one based on Chinese languages, can emerge (Sinclair *et al.* 1995). The growing strength of these regionally based services is leading to increasing flows from the peripheries back to the core. So services originating in Mexico are broadcast to Spanish-speaking communities in the US; *telenovelas,* popular Latin American soap operas, dominate schedules of some of the new privately owned services in Europe, especially but not exclusively in Spain, Italy and Portugal; Chinese-language services are seen in Europe and North America; and countries hitherto largely on the receiving end of the export flow, including Australia, are making real inroads into the schedules of the dominant television cultures. The new patterns in world television do not represent a one-way march towards globalisation in the sense of homogenisation or a deepening of American hegemony.

In a very volatile international television regime we see at present globalising, regionalising and localising forces working simultaneously and in overlapping ways – a set of phenomena which Roland Robertson (1994) attempts to capture in the awkward neologism 'glocalisation'. Within this complex system we are addressed at different times as part of a global community, a regional one, a national one and even a local one – on a city or locality-wide basis. So while there are homogenising forces operating in the sense that it is at least theoretically possible for the whole globe to tune in to the same broadcast at the same time, or for *Beverly Hills 90210* to turn up on most countries' television schedules, there are also new indigenising forces at work, as well as new regional television communities being formed by trans-border services of various kinds. To see what is currently happening as an inexorable march towards cultural homogeneity is to collude in myth-making.

THE NATION AND NATIONAL CULTURE

> If the nation can no longer be defined by ethnicity, because the civil society is made up of many groups, nor by exclusion, because the nation-state needs to incorporate all significant groups, what is its basis? (Castles 1990, p.20)

Utopian accounts of globalisation embrace its potential for moving the world beyond the nation-state. Globalisation is seen to threaten national sovereignty by taking a degree of economic control away from national economies and into multi-national or global corporations, and therefore the globalisation of media will undermine the ability of national governments to maintain political control and a sense of national unity. The de-colonisation process that occurred after the Second World War led to huge waves of migration, which created new diasporic communities in virtually every part of the developed world. Up to this point, there were higher degrees of congruence between economy, polity and culture (Gellner 1983, p.43). Economies were largely organised along national lines, although with increasing amounts of international trading and a large degree of centre-to-periphery economic control through branch plants and foreign investment. Political structures were organised virtually exclusively around the nation-state and the ideology of nationalism enforced a high degree of cultural uniformity within the nation.

For post-national critics, the acceleration of trans-national flows across the globe that began after the Second World War has gradually led to an erosion of the appearance of congruity between economy, polity and culture within the nation-state. The increased flow of people (immigrants, guest workers, refugees, tourists), of technology, of finance (through increasing de-regulation of financial markets), of communication (telecommunications, information and media) and of ideologies such as the spread of 'Western' ideas of democracy (Appadurai 1990, p.296) has increasingly undermined the primacy of nation-states and of a world whose human geography could be understood as a collection of discrete and independent nations, which interacted along the lines of the liberal democratic model of citizens – the model that is designated by such terms as 'the community of nations'.

The picture is even more complicated on the cultural level. The situation in a post-colonial world is one where diverse cultures exist within national borders, either because of high levels of migration (as in settler societies like Australia, the US, Israel or Canada) or because national borders were historically drawn in a way that pulled together people of diverse ethnic and linguistic origin (as in the case of former Yugoslavia). These movements of peoples around the globe have of course created cultural, ethnic, racial and religious linkages across borders – diasporic Chinese and Jewish communities are the longest established and best known – but virtually every other ethnic group can point to diasporic communities across the globe (Castles 1990, pp.4–5).

The implications of this for the media are apparent: they can no longer address an entirely culturally uniform audience. As Wallerstein says, these days minorities are in the majority (1991, p.192). As well as national media, which address the audience as citizens of the nation, there are also significant splinterings within the national community, which call for the media to address specific cultural, racial, ethnic, and linguistic groups. Multicultural television (such as Australia's public broadcaster, the Special Broadcasting Service) is one solution to this; another is the development of narrowcast services, which appeal to niche markets within the national community. Yet another is to develop global niche market services, which satellite technology makes feasible. The fracturing of the nation-state clearly is another reason for questioning the media-imperialism thesis as an explanatory mechanism for understanding international power relations in the domain of communication. If we can no longer so clearly regard nations as culturally homogeneous and politically united, the success of this explanation is undermined.

However it is important not to announce the death of the nation prematurely. One of the limitations of theories of globalisation is that they have been produced out of the North Atlantic information corridor, and bear distinct traces of a Western, metropolitan bias, which takes as its template for progressive change the nature of the societies of Western Europe, the US, Canada and possibly Japan – in other words, 'G7' nations with pre-eminent economic and political power. It is these societies for which supra-national globalisation makes most sense, because it is the process which they are undergoing most strongly and from which they stand to gain most.

It is a peculiarly Eurocentric notion as well to assume that the history of nationalism in its twentieth-century guises has been uniformly violent, suppressive and destabilising. Any account of national culture from the optic of a peripheral nation like Australia must take its distance from these theories of globalisation in respect to the post-modern *construction* of a national culture and the positive role the state plays in buttressing these cultures. It is the post-colonial cultures of those states peripheral to the metropolitan power blocs that have most to gain from a 'strategic nationalism'. Such a stance welcomes the poly-cultural, poly-ethnic nature of their societies and holds to the central role that a nation-building state can perform in shoring up the cultural as well as the jurisprudential, political and economic integrity of small countries in the context of globalisation. In this way, they at least have some possibility of sharing some of the benefits as well as bearing some of the burdens of globalisation. While perfectly understandable, justifications for seeking to move beyond nationalism in Europe have little purchase in peripheral countries like Australia.

As our study demonstrates, there is something very persistent about the nation as a point of cultural identification and allegiance, even by those sections of the national community that might be considered marginalised by dominant modes of national self-definition. Although an exploration of the reasons for the durability of the national at the ideological level lies beyond our scope, our observations of television cultures where Australian programs have travelled have revealed that in spite of superficial resemblances between them – not least because of the presence of the same US programs – the audience still continues to be constructed largely as a national audience and there are very significant markers of national difference.

Theories of media globalisation emphasise those aspects of the television landscape undergoing rapid change. The counterpoint to this transformation is in those aspects of television culture that are slow to change and that are attached to the persistence of the national as a primary point of identification for audiences. How else can we explain the fact that domestic services and domestic programs still attract the greatest audience allegiance even when services and programs from other sources are also watched?

TELEVISION ECOLOGY

> Broadcast TV is the private life of the nation state (John Ellis, quoted in Hartley 1992, p.101).

The television culture, or what we shall call the 'television ecology' of a country, is a complex mix of factors. We prefer the term 'ecology' because it helps to give a sense of the delicate balance of interlocking factors – if one element is changed it will have effects throughout the whole system. The economic dimension of television ecologies is the most studied and best understood. For example, it is obvious that the introduction of new services in competition with existing ones changes the economic balance and, all other things being equal, reduces the ability of each service to pay for programs. This could lead to the disappearance of certain kinds of programs that might be considered desirable for social and cultural reasons. There is a range of other factors that affect the economic ecology of television, including advertising restrictions, local quotas, cross-media and foreign-ownership rules and state subsidies.

But an ecological optic draws us beyond pure industry analysis toward the relationship between broadcasters and audiences and the general cultural milieu in which television exists. This cultural milieu includes patterns of everyday living such as the rhythms of work time and leisure time, the division between the country and the city, traditions of leisure, the popular cultural forms that exist in that society and their relationship to dominant forms of (usually American) modernity, domestic relations and rituals and divisions between the public and the private. These are some of the factors captured in Arjun Appadurai's notions of 'mediascape' and 'ideoscape' and his suggestion that we can only understand global patterns of difference by considering the overlapping or disjunctural relations between them (Appadurai 1990, p.301).

The tradition of the Spanish siesta and the propensity of Spaniards to go out of the house late at night means that scheduling television in Spain is a different task from that in Germany, a more 'privatised' society (Rogge and Jensen 1988). It is the strong tradition of cabaret and music hall in France that makes variety programs so prominent on French television. The ubiquity and popularity of *telenovelas* in Latin America has its roots in popular literary forms and in radio serials. The German tradition of *Heimatfilm* (films extolling the country as homeland) since the 1930s and a fondness for *Arztfilme* (films about doctors) makes a program like *Die Schwarzwaldklinik* ('Black Forest Clinic') particularly attractive to German viewers (Kruetzner and Seiter 1991, p.160). The inextricable link between television and the struggle for national development in Asian nations like Singapore and Malaysia makes understandable their ambivalent responses to Western interest (welcoming investment while suspicious of incursions of Western content).

In pursuit of the concept of television ecologies, as soon as we look beyond simple inquiries on the amount of imported programming, we are reminded how underdeveloped such comparative or cross-cultural perspectives are. These examples are dangerously close to crude national stereotypes – the French like cabaret, the Germans like *Heimatfilm* – and we don't wish to suggest that television ecologies can be reduced to such simple formulae. There are of course class, gender, generational and ethnic differences within countries that make nonsense of such stereotypes, as many audience studies have pointed out (for example, Barrios 1988; Gillespie 1991). As previously argued, the advent of trans-national television of various kinds, both nationally-based niche services and true trans-border services, has changed the national character of television and fostered new trans-national television communities. However, even where alternative services are available in superabundance, as in the US, it is still the case that old-fashioned terrestrial national television is watched for upward of 60 per cent of the time.

Most studies of international television markets look only at economic and perhaps demographic factors; there is a kind of blindness towards other more cultural aspects of television systems, which give them their particular local character. To conceptualise television ecologically is to see the way it both creates and reinforces various kinds of communities, even if they are communities that exist only for the life of particular programs. Although watching television is primarily a domestic activity, the very act of watching with other households across the region, nation or globe makes it a social act. As David Morley notes about the simultaneous viewing of the evening news across a nation: 'the fact of watching and engaging in a joint ritual with millions of others can be argued to be at least as important as any information content gained from the broadcast' (Morley 1992, p.81).

The television discourse 'knows' this and continually interpellates its imagined audience as members of that community. It does this as much between the programs as it does within them. It is the local address contained in the space between programs that is the key to television's cultural specificity. Compare it with cinema, which has no voice that speaks in the first person and addresses the audience in the second person. Television also interacts with the extra-televisual events that are important for particular societies. Roger Silverstone – who has gone further than most in attempting to theorise the articulation of television and every-day life – says, '[b]roadcast national events articulate calendar time: at Christmas, Thanksgiving, Coronation or Royal Wedding, Cup Final or Superbowl' (Silverstone 1994, p.20).

The television discourse is that continuous flow first commented on by Raymond Williams in his pioneering book, *Television: Technology and Cultural Form* (1974). It consists not only of programs but of all the ways in which the audience is addressed, invited in, made accomplices. It includes station identifications, advertisements, previews, voice-overs and the bodily and aural presence of personalities as guides and presenters. Despite the pervasiveness of the US style of schedule, as commercial television spreads throughout the world, this television discourse and its embodiment, the local television guide, are different in different places, and they, more than the programs themselves, mark a television service as local.

For example, it may not be only our lack of familiarity with the Italian language that makes trying to read an Italian program guide such a foreign experience. Commentators like Williams himself, John Caughie (1990) and John Ellis (in Hartley 1992, p.101–04) have commented on the strangeness of other people's television. The mix of programs, the favoured genres, the way they are grouped into time slots and blocks, can differ markedly from one television culture to another even when the same program is shown (like the ubiquitous *Santa Barbara*). The television schedule is a code in the Barthesian sense. The time slot is the paradigmatic aspect; it is a space into which something must go – the cartoon spot, the news, the game show, or the slot where they do the Lotto draw or give a preview. The sequence of program elements flow is the syntagmatic element – current affairs after the news, talk show after the movie. This code governs both the program flow on the screen itself and the way the television guide works.

When this code is interrupted, as when people move to another television system, there is disruption and confusion and frustration until the new code is learnt. Just as cultures are proximate so are television systems. The Australian commercial system is near enough to the US system and the ABC used to be like the British system. The last two have moved further apart between 1985 and 1995 as the ABC has moved to a more commercial schedule (at least to the extent that the programs begin on the hour or half hour), while the BBC and the European public-service broadcasters have programs at 10 minutes to or 25 minutes past the hour.

Roger Silverstone notes the way in which styles of narrative, forms of story-telling and, particularly, resonant forms of myth-making condition the nature of television:

> Television may have provided a new content for domestic and national rituals, but it essentially preserved both their traditional form and their function. Preserved, too, were and are the familiar and barely disguised forms of narrativity within television programs which, in both factual and fictional expressions, provide a secure framework for the representation of the unfamiliar or threatening. This mythic character of television has often

been noted. It refers to the persistence of familiar oral forms of story-telling – to the structured narratives of folklore present in news drama and documentary; to the particular functional significance of forms of story-telling as articulating the endemic and irresolvable contradictions of the host society; and it refers also to the ideological character of images and stories which naturalise and disguise the reality of the historical and the man-made (Silverstone 1991, p.38).

This account emphasises what is deeply embedded and slow to change about a television culture. Silverstone, following Anthony Giddens, says that television gives 'ontological security' (Silverstone 1994, p.5). Such conservatism underlines why traditional television moves slowly to accommodate the challenge of the changing cultural mix of its audiences. There has been very little international research done on how immigrant communities use the television services of their new countries (but *see* Naficy 1993). There is some evidence, however, that the entertainment needs of diasporic communities have traditionally been dealt with by other means, notably the video cassette recorder (O'Regan 1991). This same conservatism confounds the move towards globalisation in television and the appearance of what Simon During calls 'the global popular' (During 1992, p.341). It also flies in the face of all the utopian rhetoric of new media – of audiences' willingness to junk old-fashioned forms of media like broadcast television in favour of new-fashioned media like video games and the Internet (Wark 1994).

Which vision of the media future is the correct one? Clearly both. However the advent of new media does not seem yet to have made serious inroads into the audience for broadcast television. We must assume that the young males who play video games are doing it instead of some other activity forgone, perhaps playing sport. Experience in the US seems to indicate that even in a multi-channel environment most of the time most people watch the same few familiar channels, which offer them the 'ontological security' that Silverstone talks about. And by and large, in spite of a quantity of imported programming being watched and enjoyed, it is a local (national) form of ontological security that is sought.

It is against this background that we must consider the questions of how, why and with what impacts Australian programs are received by their international audiences. Do they find a way of enmeshing themselves within television ecologies or are they simply unimportant and barely noticed fragments that float by the viewer? Is their only function to fill the schedule or to help the station meet cultural obligations in a particular area, for example, that of children's programming?

The answers, as we shall see, differ in each territory. In the UK, Australian programs do appear to have provoked a strong if ambivalent series of post-colonial responses. In New Zealand, an equally strong but markedly different response may be based on perceptions of Australia as a somewhat imperious and overly commercial television provider. (English-speaking) Canada would seem a fertile recipient of Australian programming; this is however by no means the case. In Europe, especially France, there is a history of mythologisation of the Australian wilderness as exotic and threatening. Thus Australian programs might be inserted into this grid of interpretation. Other connections with European traditions are less obvious, although Australian models of production have been looked to as alternatives to US models during the profound shifts toward commercialisation experienced since 1985. Certainly Australia, like the US and Canada, is a favoured place for migration from Europe. But this connection is not exploited in Australian television programs with very few exceptions, such as *The Magistrate*. In the United States a relatively large number of Australian programs are shown but, on balance, have little cultural impact given the huge multi-channel environment into which they are inserted. In the Asian region, Australian programs are as yet a rare event. They can sometimes make an impact beyond their prominence in the schedule, however, because they touch on cultural and diplomatic sensitivities.

To trace the intrication of television with everyday life is one way of analysing the cultural impacts of international program flows. A more obvious way is to engage with various traditions of audience analysis. In the next section we consider what such traditions can offer in providing ways of understanding the cross-cultural impact of Australian television programs in various situations.

CROSS-CULTURAL AUDIENCE ANALYSIS

In his examination of the discourses of cultural imperialism, John Tomlinson points out that in studies of media flows 'there is a definite sense of ... "the moment of the cultural" being forever deferred' (1991, p.40) in favour of the more solid evidence that seems to be delivered by political economy. In other words, there has been very little detailed analysis of the specific means by which domination, resistance and negotiation work in the transfer and reception of cultural meaning. Recent critiques of the 'innoculation' theory of cross-cultural transfer assumed by much cultural imperialism literature have advocated micro-situational audience studies, influenced by ethnographic methodologies, as the appropriate way to register the diverse ways in which this domination, resistance and negotiation work (Fiske 1987).

While some studies in this vein have been extremely fruitful, most notably Marie Gillespie's study (1991) of the way in which Punjabi youth in a London suburb interacted with *Neighbours*, we argue that when we track the fortunes of the television export of a peripheral nation like Australia, such approaches are incapable of capturing all the intermediate factors at work. Methodological protocols central to such studies would need substantial modification to account for peripheral program reception. Researchers have often been most interested in the atypical or sub-culturally specific response to programs and, to achieve the depth of qualitative analysis desired, they have had to sacrifice breadth of audience coverage. Such studies rarely weigh the relative importance of industrial or social contingencies in explaining the acceptance or otherwise of programs by audiences. When studies are restricted to reporting and analysis of the self-understanding of selected audience respondents, wider factors affecting the impact of programs are often bracketed out.

Instead, we propose an approach that is situated between political economy and micro-situational reception studies – a middle-range approach – that looks at the broader context of viewer reception set by the television ecology; the professional practices of trading in, marketing and scheduling programs; and the strategic role played by the gatekeepers of the television industries, including managers, commissioning editors and program buyers, and popular media criticism. Let us consider how this approach might differ from one prominent example of cross-cultural reception analysis, Liebes and Katz's *The Export of Meaning* (1990).

This book is an account of audience decodings of *Dallas* on three continents; the authors argue that the key reasons for the international popularity of US prime-time television, and especially serial/soap formats like *Dallas*, lie in:

> (1) the universality, or primordiality, of some of its themes and formulae, which makes programs psychologically accessible; (2) the polyvalent or open potential of many of the stories, and thus their value as projective mechanisms and as material for negotiation and play in the families of man; and (3) the sheer availability of American programs in a market-place where national producers – however zealous – cannot fill more than a fraction of the hours they feel they must provide (1990, p.5).

However, it is clear that universality and primordiality are features of the genre as a whole, rather than peculiar to US soap opera. Even a cursory examination, for example, of Mexican and Brazilian *telenovelas* or Malaysian soap opera makes this clear; thus they cannot account for the international success of US serials. The third reason that Liebes and Katz adduce to account for global popularity is the one they least explore, yet it is far more significant than they allow. Indeed, there is something strangely decontextualised about the detailed recording and elegant analyses of their selected respondents in Israel, Japan and the United States. 'Vigorous marketing,' they say, 'is certainly a reason for the international success of *Dallas*' (1990, p.4), but they pay almost no attention to this level of explanation.

Liebes and Katz offer an intriguing chapter on the reasons for the *failure* of the program in Japan. They point out that Japanese viewers had a broader prime-time range from which to choose, compared especially to the Israelis; that they had and preferred their own soap tradition, the 'home' drama; that social modernisation has led the Japanese away from imported US models of entertainment; and, most importantly, that *Dallas* may simply have been incompatible with indigenous tastes and values. But the authors include no discussion of the scheduling, promotional, marketing and purchase practices involved in the (short-lived) introduction of *Dallas* into the Japanese market.

This treatment should be compared with the analyses of the program's introduction into foreign markets presented by Jean Bianchi (1984) and the *East of Dallas* research team led by Alessandro Silj (1988, pp.36–8), which indicate that factors like scheduling, program philosophy and cultural environment prior to program reception militated against its success in countries such as Peru and, for unexpected and surprising reasons, enhanced its success in countries such as Algeria. In the last, a one-party nation with one state-owned television station, *Dallas* was a popular success. 'One wonders,' says Silj, 'why the television of an anti-imperialist, anti-capitalist state, the guardian of a social and family morality deeply marked by the Islamic religion, a pioneer of collective values ... should wish to put out a program so imbued with antagonistic, "American" values' (1988, p.36).

The explanation offered is an amalgam of social and political contextual factors. In the Peruvian case, where *Dallas* was not successful – it ran for less than a year – Silj's explanation is industrial and cultural. *Dallas* became the losing card in a ratings battle between the two leading commercial channels when it was pitted against a local comedy program. This seems to bear out a maxim of international television, that successful local programming will tend to relegate US material to second or lower place. However, Silj is careful to remind us that the situation in Peru was a contingent one – had the local program been of lesser quality, the outcome might well have been reversed. Bianchi and Silj's conclusions are that viewer reception is a dynamic process, governed by the cultural identities of audiences and the 'sedimentation of other social practices' (Silj 1988, p.40); we can take this to mean the industrial, institutional and cultural conditions obtaining prior to any audience seeing any foreign program – the television ecology.

Many cross-cultural studies promote the variability and specificity of international audience response, and are imbued with a sense of the viability and integrity of the cultures of peripheral or small nations. So it is somewhat ironic, because of the structured dominance of American programs at highly visible places in schedules, that such studies should focus on US programs almost exclusively. As Ellen Seiter strongly argues with regard to the theoretical field from which this position draws, 'in our concern for audiences' pleasures ... we run the risk of continually validating Hollywood's domination of the world-wide television market' (Seiter *et al.* 1989, p.5).

The success or otherwise of peripheral export nations like Australia is far more reliant than the US on factors outside those captured by audience studies. This explains why so little reception research has been possible on their product in international markets and, equally, why such analysis must take the middle-range course foreshadowed here. The middle-range between political economy approaches and reception analysis involves a number of mediating factors. How are Australian programs acquired overseas? Who engages in their appraisal and acquisition, and what perceptions have these 'primary audiences' formed of Australian material? These people are the major gatekeepers, who regulate (in the widest sense) the flow of Australian programming in international markets. And what are the characteristics of the major territories that influence the success or failure of Australian programs internationally? All these mediating factors embody legitimate, indeed central, aspects of cultural exchange, as virtually all the significant research on non-dominant nations' television production and reception indicates (Lee 1980; Hjort 1985; Silj 1988; de la Garde *et al.* 1993). These themes will be sketched in the next chapter, and elaborated in detail in Part 3.

2

Globalisation and International Television Trade

Television, like film, has always been an international industry in the sense that both films and television programs have always been exported. The dominant presence has of course been the US but other countries have also had export industries of various sizes. Britain has been a significant television exporter for many years, various European countries have successfully marketed art cinema internationally, India has been a source of film and television product for the sub-continent, and Hong Kong is a major producer and exporter of film and television.

There has long been a debate about the reasons for US domination of international television trade. Explanations have included tracing the long history of strategic US state and industry activity to perpetuate its dominance (Guback 1969; 1984), together with a contemporary focus on its need to maintain its positive balance of trade in the audiovisual arena against losses in other areas of export (Collins 1990, p.7). US innovations in technology and production style, or what economists call 'first mover advantage' (Guback 1969; Hoskins and McFadyen 1991); the size of its home market, or economies of scale (Hoskins and Mirus 1988; Wildman and Siwek 1988); the low 'cultural discount' of US product (Hoskins and Mirus 1988); and production in the English language – the 'language of advantage', in Richard Collins' memorable phrase (Collins 1989a) – have all been used to account for US pre-eminence.

Notwithstanding the outcome of this debate, it was predicated on the nature of the world audiovisual market as it existed until the mid-1980s. But this market has begun to change in the years since 1985, that is, since the major data on international audiovisual flows were collected. These transformations can be attributed to technological change and the growth of commercialism and a de-regulatory spirit in many parts of the world. There are already signs that as new television markets mature, the balance of trade is slipping away from the US (Amdur 1993). Certainly it is no

25

longer possible even for the US to finance programs completely in the domestic market, so the US too is forced to become more dependent on international partnerships. Hoskins and McFadyen (1991) argue that the historical comparative advantages of the US are being eroded, as potential competitors either develop features similar to the US model or outdo it (for example, through technical innovation).

CHANGES IN WORLD TELEVISION

During the 1980s the term 'world television' began to be used in recognition that something had changed in the international character of the television industry. Whereas previously distribution had an international aspect, now the production side of television began to be internationalised as well. The notion is similar to terms like 'global television' or 'international television', but each gives a particular emphasis to the object of study. The term 'international' has the oldest currency; a notion familiar from disciplines like international relations or international trade; it presupposes a situation where nations are more or less self-contained entities, and refers to the relations into which those entities enter – whether economic, political or diplomatic. International trade in television programs has existed since the beginning of television. The Nordenstreng and Varis studies (1974; 1984) examined that trade in the 1970s and early 1980s and pointed out its nature as a 'one-way street' from core to peripheral nations.

In this earlier phase, program production was largely carried out for and financed within the country of origin and was intended largely for domestic audiences. This was even true in the US, notwithstanding the importance for its economy of the export trade in audiovisual material. Television-importing countries would go to the television markets and buy what was available and suitable that year; the world in fact was divided into a number of national markets. From the mid-1980s the changes that transformed this picture have three aspects: technological, regulatory and industrial. While these forces are interrelated and are part of larger changes in economy, society and culture, we will separate them for analysis.

The technological changes are the ones that seem the most compelling and which receive the most breathless media attention. However, as critics of technological determinism have pointed out for decades, technological innovation and diffusion only occur when other factors are in place. The two innovations that have been most significant for broadcasting since the mid-1980s are satellite technology, and the convergence of broadcasting and telecommunications technologies made possible by digitalisation. The first is significant because it enables the near-instantaneous exchange of image and sound across any distance, thus abolishing the significance of distance alone as an economic factor in broadcasting. As we have seen, the cultural significance of satellites is that they can enable the linking of new broadcasting communities across traditional borders and boundaries, thereby changing relations between geography and identity.

On a more basic level, satellites enable services to be delivered to viewers in new ways. By overcoming distance, they encourage suppliers other than the traditional nationally-based ones. They have also been used to supply services on a subscription basis (although terrestrial frequencies can also be used to do this, as is the case in France and New Zealand), thus changing the basis of the relationship between supplier and consumer, with significant regulatory consequences. The development of new transmission technologies such as satellite and the extension of cable television – part of the growing ability of telecommunications media of carriage to double as media of content – can undermine the traditional basis of heavy government regulation of the content of broadcasting services as well as restrictions on foreign and cross-media ownership. Because these technologies take broadcasting from the realm of scarcity to the realm of plenty, they undermine the notion that the electromagnetic spectrum is held as a public trust, and therefore requires regulation by the state in the public interest (Michael 1990).

During the 1980s, there was an accompanying change in the ideologies that informed government policy in the developed world, especially in the countries of Anglo-Saxon origin (UK, US, Anglophone Canada and, to a lesser extent, Australia). There was a move from a Keynesian framework for economic policy embracing government oversight of the economy and a commitment to the welfare state, toward the free market as a more efficient way of allocating goods and services. This affected broadcasting alongside other industries and, in particular, led to a preference for private over public ownership of media organisations. This was found in its most explicit form in the UK with the ideology of Thatcherism (Collins 1989b), but was also seen in the regulatory philosophy in the US under Reagan (Gomery 1989). The combination of technological potential and de-regulatory and anti-statist thinking in several leading countries of the industrialised world fostered profound changes in broadcasting regimes in these countries – the most important of which was the proliferation of new services.

At the same time as these technological and regulatory changes were occurring, the trend toward a broader globalisation of the economy was being mirrored in the media industries. The privatisation of the media in Europe fostered the appearance of new media moguls in television, with Berlusconi as the most obvious example (Tunstall and Palmer 1991). Often, those who had been already active in publishing took leading roles in ownership and control of the new media. Building synergies among media was seen as the way forward – progress toward a single market in Europe fostered the growth of media conglomerates with trans-national holdings in newspapers, publishing, film and television production and distribution, and cable service provision. Similar moves in the US towards cross-media holdings and the development of pay services led to the appearance of major US media conglomerates also (Time-Warner, News Limited, TCI, Turner Television) and these interests began to position themselves in Europe and later in other parts of the world, such as Australasia and Asia. Change in the Asian region was more dramatic than that in Europe or North America. Extremely rapid economic development (as much as 8 per cent a year in places like Korea, China and Indonesia) has led to an enormous expansion in the availability of television. The number of television households in Asia increased by 70 per cent in the five years to 1993, compared with 4.3 per cent in the UK and 6.7 per cent in the US (Hugh Leonard 1993).

Many discussions of world television focus almost exclusively on the growth of global media firms and the extent of their trans-national control. However to concentrate purely on ownership would be to see the matter in an unduly superficial way. The changes we wish to focus on are due less to new technologies, or even to the growth of global media conglomerates – though they of course play an enabling role – than to a move from the dominance of state-run and public-service broadcasting to market-driven systems, which changes the television ecology at many levels.

Alessandro Silj, writing on what he calls the new television in Europe, describes the transformation in these terms:

> The small screen has lost the magical aura of its early days; it is now an integral part of everyday life. Only occasionally does television still speak with the 'Master's Voice', as a pedagogical instrument of the state. And nowadays it occupies by far the most important position in the economics of leisure (1992, p.1).

Only a small number of regions of the world – Canada, Australia and Latin America – have had a truly mixed system since the inception of television. Elsewhere the model has been exclusively public service (or virtually so, as in the UK), or state-controlled media as in Asia and the former Communist regimes. But now those regimes are loosening and being opened to competition. Virtually everywhere in the developed and developing world we can see the gradual replacement of tightly controlled state-run or heavily regulated broadcasting systems, by market-driven systems less concerned with transmitting the master's voice and more concerned with the ordinary market mechanisms of maximising audiences and advertising or subscription revenue.

In Asia, where there is not a strong tradition of media independence, the concept of television as the master's voice is particularly apposite. Television culture has been highly controlled and centralised, with a restricted number of services and tight state censorship. The growth of privatised and cross-border services has begun to loosen these ties. While many Asian governments, for example those of Singapore, Malaysia, China and to a lesser extent Indonesia, continue to see television's role as fostering national development goals and thus still subject to state control, the free-enterprise drive for audience maximisation, advertising revenue and profits here, as elsewhere, undermines the government's ability to continue to exert tight controls over what is being watched (Shoesmith 1993, p.155).

The commercialisation of television can be seen in the dramatic trans-formation of the television schedule. The public-service schedule is being replaced by the American model. The former eschews stripping (program episodes screened daily at the same time), has programs commencing at odd times, not strictly on the half-hour or hour, does not have standard-ised slots for the same kind of program at the same time each week, and pays little or no attention to what is available to viewers on other channels. It is a style of schedule appropriate in a non-competitive environment. It would, however, be wrong to infer from this tendency towards the uni-versalisation of the commercial television model any automatic transition to global television in the sense of programming. In discussions of world television, the three levels – ownership, style of service and programming sources – are very often confused. The global spread of one of these levels does not automatically extend to the others.

A NEW DIVERSITY IN PROGRAM SOURCES

As we mentioned in Chapter 1, although US films dominate the box office in most countries, for free-to-air television the picture is different. Up to

90 per cent of television fare in many countries is locally originated and imports, mostly from the US, have traditionally been confined to the area of drama – that is, movies, telemovies, mini-series, situation comedies (sitcoms) and most importantly, in terms of volume and longevity, series and serials, including soap operas. In news, current affairs, sport, game shows, information programming and variety, the content has been overwhelmingly local. However, the amount of local programming depends partly on the size of the home country and the degree of cultural proximity it has to nearby countries with bigger production industries. For example Ireland, New Zealand, Belgium, Bulgaria, Chile and Australia have high levels of imported content, some considerably more than 50 per cent. These screens are full of product from either the US or from culturally proximate countries: the UK for Ireland, Russia for Bulgaria, Mexico and Brazil for Chile (Tracey 1985; Sinclair 1990).

Has this situation changed as we move from the domination of state broadcasting monopolies towards a multi-channel environment? New commercial services, both advertiser-supported and subscription, and delivered by terrestrial, cable and satellite technologies, have commenced in most Western European countries in the last decade and increasingly are appearing in Eastern Europe. Advertising-supported satellite services, such as Star TV, have rapidly developed in Asia, with the Indian sub-continent and China as particularly fertile areas of growth. When new services are in start-up mode, they at first depend heavily on imported programming, usually from the US, although in India it is also from the UK and in China it is mostly Chinese-language programming from Hong Kong. The appeal of US programming to service operators is partly its bulk and cheapness but also because US programming is the televisual *lingua franca* of the world. It is therefore readily accepted by audiences in virtually any territory, even if it is not the most popular television.

However new services do not automatically bring more American programs, as critics fear. The growth of new services, and the comparative cheapening of the means of production and distribution outside the high-budget drama area, has stimulated local production and new regional centres of production and export potential. As the new services gain audience and thus revenue, their demand for locally-made programming that rates with audiences increases. There is also an increase in format sales where the scripts of successful soaps or game shows are purchased from the US or other countries like the UK or Australia, and then adapted to the local conditions and culture and re-made with local actors.

In Germany, for example, as the new commercial services become more robust, they are fostering the growth of a new soap opera industry. The Germans had considerable experience producing high-budget costume drama on film, and with a film-like mode of production. But Germany had no tradition of mass producing cheap serial drama on tape. They have learnt this from the Australian production company Grundys, among others, and have now begun to produce a great number of cheaper format serials. As we will describe in later chapters, the Grundy organisation has successfully sold formats to both Germany and the Netherlands and is pursuing similar strategies in other territories.

Expanded production and export industries are also stimulated by new international 'ethnoscapes', in Appadurai's terminology (1990), which occur through migration, exile and the movement of refugees and guest workers. Hindi programming is seen by Indian guest workers in the Middle East and immigrants in Africa, Asia and the Pacific. Mandarin programs are seen by the Chinese diaspora all over the world but especially in South East Asia; Arab-language programs are watched all over the Middle East; Spanish-language programs made in Mexico are seen in Latin America, by Spanish-speaking immigrants in the US, and are imported back to the mother country of Spain itself; Portuguese-language programs made in Brazil are seen in Latin America, Portugal, and the ex-Portuguese territories of Africa, where they are transmitted via satellite from Portugal. Mexican and Brazilian *telenovelas* are also shown widely in culturally proximate cultures like Italy and their popularity is also extending to other countries. A Brazilian *telenovela* has occupied the number-one spot in Moscow – a Brazilian *Dallas* evidently (Sinclair *et al.* 1995).

Australia is also a significant centre of audiovisual production for international television markets. However, unlike the examples of Egypt, Mexico and Hong Kong, Australia does not serve a geo linguistically defined regional sub-market. A central element of its comparative advantage as a producer comes from sharing a language with the US. Australia is thus able, at least theoretically, to produce for the same market as the US (Collins 1989a). There is some evidence that Australian programs can operate as substitutes for US programs in the UK, Europe, New Zealand and Asian satellite television. While some programming is sold into the US market it has made little impact culturally, but in that it is no different from any other supplying country. The fact that Australia is an English-language production centre is becoming increasingly important because the more internationalised television becomes, the more crucial the language of production becomes. With English the *lingua franca*

Energetic and raw youth series, *Heartbreak High* – a multicultural working class counterpart to *Beverly Hills 90210* – is shown on BSkyB's Sky One channel along with other Australian soaps. (Advertisement in *TV World*, Mid-Market MP-TV Edition 1994, p.8) throughout the world (de Swann 1991), an English-language production centre automatically lowers costs and potentially increases markets (Silj 1992, p.32).

Also, as it is characterised by high levels of American imports, Australia has learnt, both as a production centre and as a viewing culture, a great deal from and about American television style. Australia can generate product not unlike American material, but with a cultural difference that at certain times and places makes a difference for program purchasers and viewers. However, it is also heavily influenced by the British public-service model. So the Australian television system is a hybrid; its culture is partly an amalgam of the world's major internationally transferable production centres, and this stands it in good stead to deal with differing international market requirements.

What emerges from this sketch of world television is the sense of a multi-layered set of structures and a complex set of programming flows, none of which can be explained under the traditional media imperialism model. That model saw the US at the centre of a system of one-way audiovisual flow, with recipient nations at the periphery as passive consumers. The picture that emerges from a contemporary analysis is a veritable post-imperialist or post-colonial one, with no single centre and no automatic peripheries. As Michael Tracey aptly puts it: 'The very general picture of TV flows ... is not a one-way street; rather there are a number of main thoroughfares, with a series of not unimportant smaller roads' (1985, p.23).

POST-FORDISM AND THE AUDIOVISUAL INDUSTRY

The changes in the television cultures of many countries are part of a broader set of industrial, political and geographic patterns that have been theorised as the transition from fordism to post-fordism. The characteristics of fordism include centralised large corporations, vertical integration, a stable and permanent work force, standardised products, a stable level of consumption, a welfarist approach to social life and a stable aesthetic. Post-fordism, by contrast, is characterised industrially by flexible specialisation or vertical disintegration, decentralised decision-making, product differentiation, and outsourcing (Askoy and Robins 1992, pp.3–4). The last has led to the growth of specialised small firms which are often geographically, even globally, dispersed and which provide components for the big firms:

Fordist mass production ... had fostered the growth of large integrated firms with a centralised decision-making structure and spatially dispersed production facilities. Flexibility on the other hand has promoted the emergence of smaller firms or independent divisions that intersect with each other in a complex array of supplier and purchaser relations (Graham 1992, p.395).

Sometimes this leads to the spatial concentration of big firms and small suppliers as seen in the growth of new industrial districts such as the Emilia-Romagna region, the 'Third Italy' (Harvey 1989, p.147), where small firms cluster so that they can 'collaborate on design and production and adjust quickly to changes in markets' and 'share a pool of skilled workers, equipment and services that none of them could support on their own' (Graham 1992, p.395). On the other hand, the growth of information technology as a factor in production and the expansion of labour costs in the home country can also lead to placing some aspects of the production or distribution business at a great distance from the headquarters of the major firm. These could be in territories where, for instance, working hours are longer and wages and social costs are lower, leading to new forms of the international division of labour (Castles 1990, p.6).

The film and television industry exhibits both patterns. On the one hand, in centres of production like Hollywood, or rather Los Angeles (since Hollywood is an imaginary place as much as an actual geographical location), there has been a huge growth in the number of small firms springing up to service the film and television industry, which are all located within a thirty-mile radius of the traditional centre of the industry, and which supply services like editing, location scouting, script editing, equipment hire, special effects, sound recording and post-production. On the other hand, Hollywood also looks to locate productions in overseas countries, basically for cost reasons but also in order to exploit novel locations. In the last decade, Europe, New Zealand, Australia and the UK have been used in this way. In the future it is likely to be sites in Asia that are favoured, as particular Asian economies begin to fashion themselves as specialised centres of post-production.

Christopherson and Storper (1986, p.308) see post-fordism appearing in the US film and television industry in the 1960s as a response to the threat posed by the television industry to the film industry. This led to the need for the differentiation of product characteristic of post-fordist production and consumption and to the development of new technologies that would differentiate film from television, such as Cinerama, three-dimensional films, various wide-screen forms and improved sound systems. The need to trim costs led first of all to a drive to expand exports and to the move to produce films overseas (so-called 'runaway' production, mainly in Spain, Italy and the UK) in the 1960s and 1970s. These moves had rather ambiguous benefits for the host countries, for when the nature of the industry changed again and new strategies became appropriate, Hollywood pulled out of these off-shore sites, leaving little behind. Canada is also an important site for Hollywood production; it is drawn there by the convenience of proximity combined with lower costs and advanced infrastructure. In the 1990s, Australia has also become an off-shore site for US television production, particularly in the Warner Roadshow studio on the Gold Coast in Queensland. The challenge for Australian government policy, at both the federal and state levels, is how to encourage this and gain benefits for the Australian industry in the short term, especially given the difficulty of Australia's distance from the US, while not losing out in the longer term.

In the 1970s and 1980s, Hollywood's strategies changed. Instead of moving off shore, greater disaggregation of the industry within the US began to occur along classic post-fordist lines. The major Hollywood studios began to divest themselves of studio property in order to minimise overheads (Christopherson and Storper 1986, p.310). The majority of the output had to be located within a small area and thus a large number of small independent companies grew up to service the studios. For example, in the period 1966–82, the number of editing firms in the Los Angeles area increased by 2725 per cent, lighting firms by 1050 per cent and production companies by 162 per cent (Christopherson and Storper 1986, pp.311–12).

Television production in the US has followed a model similar to that of the film industry, because the major studios were responsible for most of the television as well as the film output. Because broadcasting in the US is almost entirely private, and because of anti-monopoly regulation, the US television industry is not as vertically integrated as the film industry. This does not mean that the three, later four, major networks have not had a dominant influence in program commissioning. As cable and pay television developed during the 1980s, they too began to commission new programming for the television market.

By contrast, broadcasting in both Western and Eastern Europe, Asia, and other places such as South Africa and New Zealand, was very much a fordist industry until the changes of the 1980s. It consisted of large monolithic and vertically integrated broadcasting institutions that are nationally based, either run on a public-service model, state-controlled, or extremely heavily regulated (for example Britain's Independent Television system). The changes of the 1980s have tended to lead to a dismantling of these vertically integrated structures and their subjection to market forces. No longer are broadcasters solely responsible for transmission, program production, distribution, facilities management, engineering and technical services and training (Christopherson and Storper 1986, p.313). As often as not, these are now subjected to a price mechanism and will be outsourced to independent companies. This is in fact legislated for in the UK where there is a requirement under the Broadcasting Act that 25 per cent of programs broadcast should be produced by the independent sector, and embodied in the policy of 'producer choice' introduced at the BBC in 1991. The changes occurring in the UK have major implications for Australia, because British capital has been the main source of overseas finance for Australian television drama. This will be discussed further in Chapter 6.

Because Australia has had a rather uncommon 'mixed system' of commercial and public-service broadcasting since the inception of television in the 1950s, it has exhibited both a fordist and a post-fordist pattern. On the one hand, the ABC has had the same structure as the BBC and only began to disaggregate during the 1980s. For example, very little drama was produced outside the ABC until 1986 when the corporation began to enter into co-productions with Australian independent producers, companies that had developed during the 1970s under the stimulus of government-support policies for the film industry (Jacka 1991).

On the other hand, since the 1960s the commercial television industry has contracted out virtually all of its production, except news and current affairs, so that when the film and television industry expanded during the 1970s it did so according to a post-fordist model. In the commercial sector drama, quiz and game shows, documentary, and children's programming were produced by independent production companies. These were lean organisations which, except for the bigger scale producers, such as Grundys and Crawfords, did not maintain permanent studios, equipment or post-production facilities. This allowed a large number of small firms to grow up offering studio facilities, post-production suites, equipment hire, production and costume design, hairdressing and make-up, financial services, legal advice, insurance, research and script services. The creative personnel are also usually freelance contractors, although the technicians, musicians and actors are covered by industrial awards that include minimum rates of pay.

Like the Los Angeles case described by Christopherson and Storper, these small firms and individuals are concentrated in areas near the big players they service, in particular in Sydney and, to a lesser extent, Melbourne. Sydney's traditional dominance comes from the fact that it is the headquarters of both the television and the advertising industries – as well as being the fuel that feeds the television industry, the nexus between program production and advertising gives the production industry 'critical mass'. As a consequence of this centrality (and also of Sydney's dominance in other service industries) the regulatory body, the Australian Broadcasting Authority (ABA), and the production support bodies, the Australian Film Commission (AFC) and the Film Finance Corporation (FFC), are headquartered in Sydney. So are Film Australia, once the production arm of the government, now a government-owned but fully commercial enterprise, and the government-funded national training body, the Australian Film Television and Radio School.

Other states, especially Victoria, next in population, also encourage film and television production. Almost every state has a government-funded film and television production support body, and from 1988 onwards the Queensland government began a number of vigorous initiatives to encourage production away from New South Wales and Victoria, moves that have succeeded to some extent. The swing toward Queensland by the audiovisual industry matches a general trend in the Australian economy, a move from 'rustbelt to sunbelt' with a population shift toward the north. This is a result of a shift in the economy from a reliance on manufacturing, traditionally located in South Australia, Victoria and new South Wales, to a reliance on service industries, including tourism and entertainment.

In Chapter 3, we examine the nexus between government policy, the audiovisual industry and exports more closely. At this point, it is sufficient to establish that the post-fordist structure of the production industry in Australia fitted it well for the changes that began to occur in world television during the 1980s. The disaggregated nature of the Australian television industry provides the basis for its present flexibility and efficiency by Western-world standards. The moves toward post-fordist broadcasting models in the rest of the world increase the chances that more cost-effective production industries, like those in Australia, can move into supplying programs to a wider range of services in more diverse geographical territories. They would, of course, need to deal with any cultural screens that might exclude them.

FINANCING AND PRODUCING FOR THE
INTERNATIONAL MARKET

The pressures of globalisation described so far and the spread of post-fordist models of production have led to the phenomenon that we call 'world television'. This inter-connectedness is reinforced by the need for co-financing arrangements because of the impossibility of financing high-budget product domestically, and by the dependency of most services on some degree of television imports. As a result there is a world market for television. The main players in this market are producers, distributors and broadcasters. The subsidiary players are government agencies, financiers, packagers and sales agents. The stage on which the players appear are the international markets that are held several times a year in the US, Europe and Asia, the most important of which are MIP-TV, held in April in Cannes, MIPCOM (the International Market for Television, Video, Cable and Satellite Films and Programs), held in October in Cannes, AFM (the American Film Market), held in Los Angeles in January, Monte Carlo, and NATPE (the National Association of Television Programming Executives), held in the US in March. The other stage is the annual unveiling of the new season's programs from the major US suppliers, when eager broadcasters from the importing countries anxiously view Hollywood's wares to try to guess what will 'play' with their domestic audiences.

Some of these sales conventions are well established (the MIDEM organisation, which runs the MIP events, was founded in the 1950s), while some are just starting (MIP Asia began in December 1994 in Hong Kong). MIP-TV, the longest running of them, attracted 400 exhibitors and 9500 participants from 99 countries in 1994. MIPCOM, which began life in the early 1980s as an obscure sibling to the long-running MIP-TV grew fast to become second in size after MIP-TV by the late 1980s, and now is a huge meeting of the world's television buyers and sellers, with the established players dominant. In 1989, the number of television executives attending had grown to 6100, while MIP-TV attracted 7100 participants in the same year. The largest number of companies came from France (322) and Britain (300), followed by 266 from the US. The October 1993 MIPCOM attracted 1705 participating companies and over 8000 individual participants representing 36 countries. Xavier Roy, chief executive of the MIDEM organisation (owned by Reed International, the publishing company), said that the event could accommodate up to 15 000 participants.

In the big markets, programming is often bought or not bought sight-unseen, in job lots, based on company reputation or distributor clout. Very broad, rough-and-ready genre expectations are in play although, conversely, there is a tradition amongst some European public broadcasters of scrutinising possible foreign acquisitions extremely closely. The variety of expectation and need on the part of purchasers leads to strangely inconsistent judgements on the part of program buyers. For example, Dutch buyers praise the production values of Australian programs and the Germans disparage the very same ones as being 'poorly lit' and so on. Decisions to purchase programs not central to the schedule are made on grounds like this all the time, even though they seem highly subjective and arbitrary. In this atmosphere, the new company, the offbeat product or the unusual concept is exceptionally difficult to sell. (For its first foray as a seller into MIPCOM in 1993, the US documentary cable channel Discovery tarted up its profile by dressing its stall as a movie set and employing actors to create live-action scenarios around a Second World War theme to coincide with the use of Normandy landing documentaries as its flagship programs.)

These markets are the places where buyers can view the programs on sale from various producers, distributors and sales agents. But just as crucially it is the place where the players can circle each other at screenings and parties in the attempt to set up or consolidate partnerships, which can help to finance the next project. If one thing is true about the world television industry, it is that it works on personal contact. As AFC Director of Marketing Sue Murray points out (1994, p.19), international program trade is conducted in a very 'old-fashioned' way. The sociology of these gatekeeping forums is at present more significant than loose notions of globalisation that rest on an exclusive emphasis on new hardware and delivery platforms. Experienced distributor Bruce Gordon, head of Paramount International, has described the international television market as a club (Gordon 1993). Moving from one event to the next the same few people who wield enormous power are seen – because, of course, not all players on this stage are equal. The most powerful are the US networks, the representatives of the Hollywood studios, the major broadcasters, both commercial and public service, from the richest regions – Japan and Europe – and the emerging new pay services, like Star TV and Canal Plus, and perhaps some of the biggest television distributors, like Germany's Kirch Group, whose large holdings of library material give them considerable economic clout.

If expensive television product is to be made, by and large it will have to be financed by at least one of these major players. In this sense programs are not conceived to please audiences, they are conceived to appeal to these primary gatekeepers. The gatekeepers themselves are attempting to second guess the audiences for whom their services are designed, but program imports are designed often to be out-of-prime time filler material in the schedule, and as such the audience response is not decisive. A UK television broadcaster, interviewed in 1992, was asked how a particular Australian program had fared in a week-day 3 pm time slot. He judged it a success because it did no worse than any other program usually did in that time slot. Outside the prestige prime-time programs and the staple local programs like soap operas, which can pull a huge domestic audience, and which are crucial to a service's viability, much imported television fare does not establish a particularly strong identity with audiences. The fact that Australian soap operas such as *Neighbours* and *Home and Away* have broken through to become mainstream in the UK is rather remarkable. In Part Three we describe the way this gatekeeping function of television personnel works in various markets.

Of the various genres of television – news, current affairs, situation comedy, quiz and game shows, documentary, information programs, sport, variety, drama serials and series, mini-series and telemovies and cinema features – most are locally specific and are not heavily traded. News (except of course for international news, where most of the visual footage is imported from international news agencies), current affairs, sport (except for major international events like Grand Slam tennis, the Olympics, World Cup soccer, or Formula One Grand Prix motor racing), many information shows and much variety, are usually entirely local in character. Others are local variants of international formats, for example, quiz and game shows, which always have local participants, but which are almost all versions of a few formats mostly originated in the US (although Australian brokers such as Grundys own rights to some formats), and either sold or franchised to domestic producers. This is becoming increasingly true also for serial drama, the 'soaps'. Others – and these are the most expensive to produce – are the ones most often imported, namely documentary, children's programs and all forms of drama, especially mini-series, telemovies and some serials and series. But under the pressure of burgeoning channel capacity and commercialisation, new tradeable international formats are rapidly emerging.

The 1990s have seen the development of some new program genres that mix documentary and fiction protocols, the most spectacular of which is so-called 'reality television', productions like *Hard Copy, Cops* and *America's Most Wanted*. Programs like *America's Most Wanted* also signal the growth of interactive television, programs where viewers are encouraged to participate, presently over the phone, but increasingly it will be directly via the television system, as homes become equipped with interactive cable systems. Many of these new genres are magazine-style programs, which can easily accommodate a mixture of local and overseas content, and which have formats that are able to be easily re-versioned for local television services. The Australian company Beyond International has pioneered the popular science and technology variety of the international magazine format, while the world-wide success of the *Funniest Home Video* format or the multiplicity of dating-game shows is further evidence of this trend.

Other new genres have been prompted by new forms of delivery like pay television. A notable example in the US is the rock music channel MTV, which makes a whole 24-hour channel from the video-clip that used to be an occasional item on rock-music shows on free-to-air television. MTV is also a format that lends itself to local versioning (seen most successfully on the Hong Kong-based Star TV). Movements of production from general programming on free-to-air channels, to niche or targeted programming on specialist pay or advertiser-supported satellite or cable channels, will change both the nature of television programming – by introducing new genres or hybrids such as MTV, designed for specialist tastes – and it will change the level of demand for certain kinds of programming.

The growth of specialist sports channels will lead to the televising of sports not previously considered television fare, in order to fill the demand. The proliferation of children's channels will also create a new stimulus to production in an area traditionally difficult to finance, although the fact that a new generation of the child audience is created about every five years means that such channels can rely heavily on repeats. The growing commercialisation of television in Europe and Asia has stimulated demand for game shows and for situation comedies and serials – the cheap kind of programming that can easily be stripped in half-hour slices, and which can form the reliable backbone of a schedule. In most cases these are imported either as completed productions (the American day-time serials) or as formats.

However the most difficult area for financing, and the one where there is the most intense competition for overseas markets, is high-end (or high-budget) drama. This format is typically the most expensive per hour of production and has become almost impossible to finance by local licence fee alone. If such material is to be made, it must find an overseas market. Until the mid-1980s when public-service and/or oligopoly broadcasting was the norm, such expensive programming could be financed by local licence fee in the richer markets of Europe and the US, and overseas sales were the 'cream'. But with competition, revenues have been spread more thinly and it is now impossible to finance such production at home, even in the US (Hoskins and McFadyen 1991). Hence the growth of various forms of overseas sales like pre-sales, distribution advances, co-productions and other forms of co-ventures, which include saving costs by doing productions off-shore where costs are lower (Hoskins and McFadyen 1993).

The international co-production is a particularly favoured form of co-venture. It has the merit of locking in interests in both participating countries very tightly and of raising the maximum amount of forward commitment from broadcasters in both countries, thus ensuring that the program will receive favourable scheduling and publicity treatment. Involvement from two or more countries also assists the production to be attractive to audiences in each country, assuming that the personnel involved have a good knowledge of their own television culture.

The downside is that the need to harmonise the cultural expectations of different countries can lead to a bland homogenisation and loss of the cultural specificity likely to make the programs attractive to local audiences – the so-called 'Euro-pudding' outcome. A further difficulty is that each country involved will need to satisfy its own national regulations or other requirements in regard to raising finance, and where more than two countries are involved this can become prohibitively complex and require enormous expenditure in legal fees and international negotiation. It can also severely protract the production process. Nevertheless, co-production is becoming the norm in international financing (Acheson and Maule 1992, p.124).

For the purpose of financing and distributing television programs the world is divided into a number of territories, and what are traded are rights to exhibit the program in those territories and in various specified media. For instance, when financing a telemovie or mini-series to be made in Australia, the territories concerned would be first, Australia – where the broadcaster would pay a licence fee for first run and a number of repeats. The licence fee for a mini-series in 1993 was about A$300 000 per hour for the public broadcaster, the ABC (who paid most if not all in production facilities rather than cash), and about A$200 000 per hour for

The Barron Films comedy-adventure series, *Ship to Shore*, is a model of internationalised production for children. It is a co-production with Network Nine and Film Finance Corporation backing in Australia, and the BBC, two German networks and PBS internationally. (Advertisement in *TV World*, October 1993, p.36.)

the commercials, a sharp decline from the glory days of the 1980s, when commercial broadcasters were paying A$350 000 per hour.

Australian co-productions typically involve a UK broadcaster as the main overseas partner or less typically a European one, usually French or German. These broadcasters would also pay a licence fee that could be as high as A$500 000 or $600 000 per hour or even more on occasions (the weak Australian dollar constitutes a big advantage for exporters). For this the European broadcaster would get first and subsequent runs on their channel. In addition a European or US distributor might put up a distribution advance against certain territories, possibly the rest of Europe (that is, minus the country of the broadcaster involved) or North America in the case of a US distributor. In a big market like Europe or the US, it might be possible to sell off rights only for certain media, possibly for home video or for cable, and retain other rights in that territory. However it would be usual for the distributor to try to secure rights in all media. If a government funding organisation like Australia's Film Finance Corporation has invested in the production, its investment will be laid off against some right also, perhaps the 'rest of the world'; after Europe and North America are subtracted, few lucrative territories are left.

Developing media markets in Asia are being looked at eagerly, even greedily, to provide major new sources of revenue for television producers. At present the Asian market does not pay high prices for programs. As an indication, 1992 figures in *Variety* report the following figures for program purchase (not investment): for an episode of a one-hour series Hong Kong pays US$1000-4000, Japan US$14 000–16 000, Singapore US$700–800. This compares with US$20 000–120 000 paid in the UK, which has a population less than half of Japan's. Given the growing might of the Asian economies, and the growth of media competition, the revenues out of the region are bound to increase; however, for Western countries like Australia and the UK, there is a large cultural divide to be crossed if they are to make co-productions with Asian partners.

For Australian producers eager to supply programs to the emerging markets of Asia, the question is whether they can persuade program buyers to substitute Australian programs for those made in the US and, to a lesser extent, the UK. As a rule, the range of prices paid for Australian programs in the international market is not any lower than that paid for programs of the same kind from other sources. Therefore there would be no advantage to buyers in the Asian region in buying Australian rather than American or British. In Chapter 4 we describe how one Australian producer, Film Australia, has solved the problem of how to break into the Asian market by entering into documentary and some drama co-productions with Asian partners, while in Chapter 9 we trace the results of one of these co-productions.

We have shown that the international television market is a complex beast in a process of rapid evolution as services proliferate and serve increasingly trans-national audiences and as new ways of exploiting programs are devised. In the following chapters we shall analyse how a small country like Australia fits into this picture, both culturally and economically.

PART

2

The Domestic Optic:
Australian Industry, Culture and Production

3

The Australian Television Culture

This chapter tracks the background to the present circumstances of the Australian television culture. These circumstances are the product of a field of forces and historical factors in which Australian governments have played a crucial role. The emergence of Australia as a considerable production centre and exporter for its size has its roots in two major and long-standing sets of circumstances. The first is the nature of the television landscape – the television ecology – which has provided an environment favourable to the growth of a robust and audience-sensitive production industry. The other is the direct measures that have been in place since the early 1970s to support locally based production. But first we should consider what the results of this shaping of the Australian television culture look like from a wider comparative perspective.

THE INTERNATIONAL FACE OF AUSTRALIAN TELEVISION

It is possible to argue that '[w]hen Australia became modern, it ceased to be interesting' – interesting, that is, to an international cultural intelligentsia and anthropological audience (Miller 1994, p.206). Equally, it is arguable that the country again has attracted international attention at present, due in no small part to its audiovisual output. Australia was interesting in the nineteenth century because of the radically pre-modern cultural difference of its indigenous peoples set against a transplanted white-settler colonial culture. Now it is of interest because of its emerging profile as a post-colonial and multicultural society – a post-modern 'recombinant' culture – well suited to playing a role in global cultural exchange.

This view is put strongly by Andrew Milner, who argues that social and cultural modernity was only ever partially realised in Australia:

49

Thus Australia has been catapulted towards post-industrialism at a speed possible only in a society that had never fully industrialised; towards consumerism in a fashion barely imaginable in historically less affluent societies; towards an aesthetic populism unresisted by any indigenous experience of a seriously adversarial high culture; towards an integration into multinational late capitalism easily facilitated by longstanding pre-existing patterns of economic dependence, towards a sense of 'being after', and of being post-European, entirely apposite to a colony of European settlement suddenly set adrift, in intellectually and imaginatively uncharted Asian waters, by the precipitous decline of a distant Empire (Milner 1991, p.116).

Although it underlines reasons why Australian popular culture has a certain dynamism within globalising and post-modern cultural exchange, this view is a partial and rhetorical account. There remain strong modernist institutions and structures, of which the public broadcasting sector is a major component. There are, as well, a strong, if constantly deprecated reliance on a central state, and a ramified series of local and regional political structures that arose out of the central modernist project of nation-building. John Caughie's comments on the way post-modernist trends overlay rather than eclipse modernist traditions in British broadcasting are even more appropriate for Australia, because it has had an embedded commercial ethos for longer than Britain and the overlay process has been a less traumatic one:

> British television, and much European television, is still rooted in modernity, the concept and practice of public-service broadcasting, part of an unbroken tradition of 'good works' dating from the administration of capitalism in the latter part of the nineteenth century. While that tradition is clearly under threat from the readministration of capitalism and the redistribution of power in global markets, nevertheless the scenario of magical transformation – the marvellous vanishing act of deregulation: now you see 'quality', now you don't – in both its optimistic and its pessimistic variants seems naive (Caughie 1990, p.48).

Australia's central public broadcaster, the ABC, exemplifies this combination in its performance of its charter functions as a modernist nation-building instrument, while also enthusiastically exploiting commercial and corporate opportunities in new markets (ATV, its satellite venture in Asia), and new media (pay television). Australian historical mini-series of the 1980s (some of them exported widely) are also prime examples of this combination. Extremely popular commercial successes, screening almost exclusively on commercial networks in Australia, they were nevertheless imbued with the modernist educational public-service ethos of reconstructing popular memory about major defining moments of the nation's history.

International exposure of Australian television product and representative figures span the modernist/post-modernist spectrum. Those stellar few who enjoy mogul status in world television pre-eminently include Rupert Murdoch, since 1985 an American citizen, but whose Australian patrimony and business roots are the subject of considerable review as commentators and antagonists alike seek to chart the causes and effects of his success as 'ringmaster of the information circus' (Shawcross 1992). Supposedly Australian traditions of sharp practice and derring-do, anti-establishment commitments and brash populist beliefs are held to contribute to his interventions in British television and press, the establishment and hard-won success of BSkyB, and the continuation of that success with the takeover of Star TV in Asia and his lead in the major expansion and commercialisation of television in Asia, Eastern Europe, and India. His mastery of populist press traditions is credited with underscoring the invention of tabloid television: 'Tabloid television, as the term is generally understood, was born in the United States. But before anyone cries Yankee cultural imperialism, they should consider this: if the Americans nurtured the genre, Australians fathered it' (Lumby and O'Neil 1994, p.152).

The Australian system seems to have bred a talent for successful low-budget commercial television and, for better or worse, has attracted a reputation throughout the world for it. Australian producers, like some Latin American and Egyptian companies, have churned out a considerable body of soap-opera hours that occupy considerable space in terrestrial and satellite schedules. In many situations, this means being able to substitute for and possibly even compete with US program offers. This attracts criticism from countries that perceive themselves to be threatened by the 'Trojan horses' of US culture. In New Zealand, the view is put that 'Australian programmes are merely American programmes once-removed … as a consequence of the internationalisation of television, Australian television networks had readily adopted formats and styles "born in the USA". Such formats and styles have now been passed on to New Zealand, in the form of Australian-made programmes or as local adaptations of Grundy productions' (Lealand 1990, p.102). When a recent study showed Australia to be a significant supplier of light entertainment into Europe,

Full Name: Lisa Anne Lackey
Plays: Roxanne Miller
Born: 2nd March 1971
Height: 5´9´´
Hair: Brown
Eyes: Hazel/Brown
Favourite Colour: Blue
Favourite Food: Thai
Favourite Movie: *Wizard of Oz*
Favourite Actors: John Cleese/Harvey Keitel
Favourite Actresses: Meg Ryan/Meryl Streep
Favourite Singers: Sting/Elton John

Full Name: Dieter Kirk Brummer
Plays: Shane Parrish
Born: 5th May 1976
Height: 5´10´´
Hair: Light Brown
Eyes: Hazel
Favourite Colour: Turquoise
Favourite Food: Chicken
Favourite Movie: *Ghost*
Favourite Actor: Robin Williams
Favourite Actress: Sharon Stone
Favourite Singer: Billy Joel

Full Name: Melissa Suzanne George
Plays: Angel
Born: 6th August 1976
Height: 5´8´´
Hair: Strawberry Blonde
Eyes: Green
Favourite Colour: Earthy colours like browns, reds/oranges
Favourite Food: Caesar Salad
Favourite Movie: *Scent Of A Woman*
Favourite Actor: Al Pacino
Favourite Actresses: Jodie Foster and Nicole Kidman
Favourite Singer: Kylie Minogue

Home and Away projects an imaginary Australia – one which contains 'open plan housing, beautiful people and permanently sunny weather'. (*Shout Magazine*, 26 November–9 December 1993, p.40.)

Bay Buddies! ④

r favourite *Home And Away* stars!

Full Name: Tristan Jim Bancks
Plays: Tug O'Neil
Born: 21st December 1974
Height: 5'10"
Hair: Light Brown
Eyes: Green/Blue
Favourite Colour: Blue
Favourite Food: Lobster
Favourite Movie: *Glengarry GlenRoss*
Favourite Actor: Al Pacino
Favourite Actress: Susan Sarandon
Favourite Band: The Robertson Brothers

Full Name: Laura Veronica Vazquez
Plays: Sarah Thompson
Born: 8th October 1975
Height: 5'2"
Hair: Brown
Eyes: Brown
Favourite Colour: Red
Favourite Food: Seafood
Favourite Movie: *Beaches*
Favourite Actor: Dustin Hoffman
Favourite Actress: Shannen Doherty
Favourite Singer: Michael Jackson

this was seen as setting an unfortunate precedent for the further development of a local production industry: 'The question is whether the European programme industry has to follow the Australian recipe: imitation of American TV formulas, thus stimulating the globalization and homogenization of the international TV market' (de Bens *et al.* 1992, p.94).

At the other end of the spectrum, producers of drama in the British tradition have enjoyed a royal road to the BBC and the ITV, and have established long term co-production and co-venture arrangements with these central public services, based on the most elevated notions of quality. Australian producers can 'play at being American' – the two-edged sword of the post-colonial condition, enjoying a game of reverse imperialism, but within the rules of subordination (Caughie 1990, p.44) – without reserve. They can equally strongly eschew that path. The first model is exemplified by the advocates of increased off-shore production in Australia, or by those productions, like the 'teen' serial *Paradise Beach*, made primarily for the US market. The second finds no better exemplar than the Kennedy Miller company, whose outstanding historical mini-series of the 1980s (*The Dismissal, The Cowra Breakout, Vietnam*) were found too 'parochial' by many international buyers. These buyers expressed bewilderment that a company with a world reputation for feature film successes (such as the *Mad Max* films) should evince no interest in 'modifying' their television output for the international market. In some cases, as with the Village Roadshow/Warner Roadshow group, these two traditions can even exist under the same corporate umbrella (for example, Village Roadshow produces *Paradise Beach* and Roadshow Coote and Carroll the high-quality mini-series *Brides of Christ*).

The Australian system has neither the depth of public-service ethos and product of the UK system, nor the universalist appeal and range of talent of the US system, but its re-combination of both systems affords it certain strengths beyond those seen in similarly medium- or small-sized, peripherally placed industries. This doesn't guarantee export success, but it does suggest the variety of models available to Australia producers.

THE TELEVISION SYSTEM

Factors of an immediate industrial kind that influence the nature of a television service include size of population, gross domestic product, size of annual advertising 'spend', number of television services, competition from other media, the mix of private and public ownership of services and their audience shares, the regulation of concentration, cross-media and foreign ownership, and time spent watching television by audiences (*see* Molloy and Burgan 1993, p.16). Equally important, but of a less immediately measurable kind, are cultural and political factors, including the philosophy underlying the operation of each service; this would include, for example, the commitment to certain sorts of programming by the public broadcasters, or the values attached to an independent and high-quality news service, or the strength of particular lobby groups who have the political muscle to push for children's programming or taste and decency conventions, as well as the intersection between television and other kinds of ideologies of the state or civil society, like multiculturalism.

Even more elusive, yet pervasive, are the various practices of everyday life that influence the programming choices of Australian television stations. The centrality of sport in Australian life would be one such influence, and while Australia is not the only sports-mad country in the world, the particular sports preferred mean that there is a limit to audience satisfaction to be derived from the import of sporting programs. These factors have combined historically to produce the kind of television culture Australia has, which in turn has provided the platform on which an Australian program production industry of a particular kind has arisen.

Australia is a country of 17.6 million people; as such it must be considered a small nation in the television stakes. It compares with The Netherlands with 15 million people and Canada with 27 million, is significantly smaller than the UK (56 million), France (56 million) and united Germany (87 million), and is dwarfed by the US (256 million). This has implications for the television system; advertiser-supported television must struggle with a small population base, and therefore a small pool from which to derive revenue to provide programs; the operations of the public broadcasters (Australia has two) impose higher tax burdens per capita than many other countries. Australians spend less time watching television than in comparable countries; far less than Americans and Japanese, and slightly less than Britons and Canadians (Molloy and Burgan 1993, p.35).

In 1992–3 the three commercial networks made a profit overall of A$266.6 million before interest and tax. Revenues had climbed by 9.5 per cent to A$2035.8 million, while expenditures increased 14 per cent to A$1923.2 million, reflecting the industry's continuing recovery from the financial mismanagement and recession of the late 1980s and early 1990s (ABA 1994b). Program expenditure in 1992–3 was divided between Australian and imported programming as follows:

Table 3.1: **Program Expenditure**

	Seven Network (A$million)	Nine Network (A$million)	Ten Network (A$million)
Australian programming	204.7	158.2	78.1
Imported programming	49.8	80.6	27.5

Source: ABA 1994

In 1990, television advertising revenue was A$1738.1 million or US$1332 million (BTCE 1991, p.35). This is high in per capita terms, because Australia has a mature commercial industry compared with other much larger countries, especially in Europe, and because it allows more advertising time per hour than any other country except Canada (Molloy and Burgan 1993, p.13). In per capita terms Australia has the second highest advertising spend in the world (after the US). However it is low in absolute terms if we compare it with the US television advertising spend of US$27 970 million and with that of Japan at US$10 602 million. Canada with a bigger population spends considerably less than Australia – US$1139 million. The volume of advertising revenue places a direct limit on funds available to commission and purchase programs on commercial television. Given the differential cost of local versus imported programs, economic rationality would favour imports, even at the expense of losing audience.

Australia's particular model of a broadcasting mixed economy has begun to look increasingly attractive internationally in the 1990s. After 1963 and prior to 1980 Australia had four television networks, three commercial and one public, the ABC. In 1980, the multicultural Special Broadcasting Service (SBS) network was added; by 1994, its service reach extended to include most of the population. Until the so-called aggregation and equalisation program between 1988 and 1992 gave most of regional eastern Australia three commercial stations, commercial television networking extended only to the capitals. Even though Australia allowed a relatively high number of commercial services for such a small nation, the three networks were well insulated from competition. No new commercial services will be contemplated until a review in 1997, and the main public broadcaster, unlike in other countries such as Germany, South Africa and New Zealand, does not accept advertising. Prior to cross-media ownership rules introduced in 1987, a powerful newspaper oligopoly dominated the television industry, ensuring healthy profits.

In return for this regulatory protection, the networks were subject to a series of 'community service obligations', the most notable of which were Australian content requirements. Other obligations included requirements to broadcast regulator-approved children's programming, and to provide a so-called 'adequate and comprehensive service' (which meant a broad-based service that covered all program genres and was intended to offer programs relevant to the particular nature of the community they served). The protected environment of Australian television was further ensured by Australia's geographical distance from the major television centres in Europe and the US, so that Australia was never subject to cross-border spills of signals (though this will be an issue in the next few years as satellite services in the Asian region proliferate). It is worth commenting, however, that contrary to much alarmist hyperbole, cross-border spills of programming have usually not consituted a major threat to locally or nationally based services with the exception of those in English-speaking Canada. This issue will be taken up in subsequent chapters.

The ABC has never been subject to specific Australian content provisions but its charter, embodied in the *Australian Broadcasting Corporation Act (1973),* required it to 'provide within Australia innovative and comprehensive broadcasting and television services of a high standard', which includes 'programs ... that contribute to a sense of national identity and inform and entertain, and reflect the cultural diversity of the Australian community ...' (Section 6(1)(a)). The ABC was the first service to produce Australian-made drama and continued that tradition, despite a downturn in volume from the late 1970s to the mid-1980s. In the current period, it has aimed for and mostly attained the target of 100 hours a year of television drama (Jacka 1990, pp.28ff.). And since 1988, when the generous tax concessions for audiovisual productions (embodied in division 10BA of the tax legislation) were wound back, and the commercial networks entered a period of financial crisis, the ABC has been dominant in television drama production apart from serials.

The SBS, being a multicultural broadcaster, has rather a different charter with respect to Australian content. According to the 1991 act, its purpose is to 'provide multilingual and multicultural radio and television services that inform, educate and entertain all Australians, and in doing so, reflect Australia's multicultural society' (Section 6(1)) and in doing so to 'make use of Australia's diverse creative resources' (Section 6(2)(f)). Both its different charter and its limited budget (around A$50 million per annum for television, augmented since 1992 by advertising revenue) have not allowed the SBS to contribute significantly to Australian production.

It has none the less produced a number of innovative multicultural drama and documentary programs, which have had successful overseas sales, and the channel's world-standard subtitling services also are exported.

State Intervention

The state has intervened to ensure diversity and depth in Australian audiovisual production. Apart from significant, long-term, direct appropriations that provide the core finance for the public broadcasters, it has regulated and provided subsidy and investment funding. The most significant regulatory stimulus to the development of an Australian production industry with export potential has been the Australian quotas imposed on commercial stations by law and regulation since the early 1960s. Some commentators (Moran 1985; Papandrea 1994) have argued that they were not the most important factor in the development of indigenous drama programming; rather it was audience demand for local programming that stimulated a drama-production industry. However, regulation consistently reflected this community demand, and set benchmarks that acted as a safety net, that is, a mechanism for preventing attained levels being eroded in times of economic downturn in the industry (Molloy and Burgan 1993, p.112). It seems reasonable to say that regulation has been a necessary but not sufficient factor; this has been acknowledged by the chief executive of the Seven Network, Bob Campbell, when he noted: 'We should say thanks in part to the regulators and their foresight in forcing us to make Australian content because I think that will be the driver for our ongoing success in the new broadcast environment' (*Sydney Morning Herald,* 20 July 1994, p.41).

Australian content regulation has been of signal importance in the country's mixed economy of broadcasting, lending to that term another central meaning. The general objective that there should be overall about 50 per cent Australian content on television means that the system remains identifiably indigenous, while enjoying a structured, controlled access to a mix of American and British programs and a wide range of other material on the SBS. Compared to the direct access US television services have to most of Canada's population, Australia enjoys a screening or filtering process embodied in the programming decisions made by the Australian networks in the development of their foreign portfolios. Changes to the structure of Australian-content regulation will be driven by the growing transparency of the industry to international trends and pressures. While the aftermath of the conclusion of the General Agreement on Tariffs and Trade (GATT) Uruguay Round has seen Australia taken off the US priority watch list of countries maintaining restraints on free trade in services (as in content regulation and production subsidies), this is an uneasy truce and liable to change. The currently strong cultural rationale for an 'Australian look' on the country's television screens will have to be reconciled with the need to find overseas finance through co-production. Australia also may have to modify its regulation to accord with its Closer Economic Relations (CER) free-trade agreement with New Zealand, which would accord New Zealand programs enhanced entry into the larger market.

State subsidy and investment financing started early in the film revival period when in 1970 the government established the Australian Film Development Corporation, which became the Australian Film Commission (AFC) in 1975 (Dermody and Jacka 1987). Direct government assistance was supplemented in 1980 by the previously mentioned changes to the taxation regime that allowed generous write-offs for private-sector investment in film and higher-budget television drama and documentary (the so-called 10BA rules). These in turn were wound down in 1988, when a new state investment bank, the Film Finance Corporation (FFC), was established (Dermody and Jacka 1988b).

The AFC's brief was to provide loans and investments to films which qualified as 'Australian' under the Act (Dermody and Jacka 1987, p.137). Until the tax concessions were introduced in 1980, virtually every Australian film and high-budget television drama made was funded through the AFC. The limits to direct government funding by this route put a lid on the production potential of the industry. Until the mini-series *Water Under the Bridge* (1980) and *A Town like Alice* (1981) virtually no high-budget one-off television drama was produced by the commercial networks. This was exclusively the province of the ABC, which, sometimes in co-production arrangements with the BBC and sometimes alone, produced groundbreaking mini-series like *Rush* (1973) set in Australia's goldfields of the 1850s, *Power Without Glory* (1976) from the famous Frank Hardy novel, *Patrol Boat* (1979) an early and well-produced action drama, the anthology *Spring and Fall* (1980–1) which introduced a new realism to television and the historical dramas, *The Timeless Land* (1980) from Eleanor Dark's novel about the beginning of White Australia and the First World War saga, *1915* (1982).

It was the lack of sufficient funds to develop the industry to its full potential that led the government to introduce the generous 10BA concessions, the reasoning being that the system would thus be market- rather than bureaucrat-driven. 10BA certainly produced a boom; the number of features produced doubled within a year and the golden age of Australian television began (Dermody and Jacka 1988b; Cunningham 1988). The mini-series produced under the stimulus of 10BA are some of the finest Australian productions; they include *The Dismissal, Bodyline, Vietnam, Return to Eden, All the Rivers Run, The Dunera Boys, Anzacs, A Fortunate Life, Harp in the South* and *The Shiralee*. Almost all of these were extraordinarily well received by audiences; *Bodyline* for instance rated in the 40s, and most were also part of that important moment in Australian television culture when Australians were exposed to stories drawn from their own history.

While the 10BA mini-series boom was producing such riches, 10BA itself was coming into disrepute, in the film area rather than in television, for being a vehicle for manipulation and financial rorts (Dermody and Jacka 1988b). The AFC produced an analysis of the flaws in the 10BA scheme (AFC 1987) and the government decided to effectively replace it with a public-sector solution – the FFC – which would make investments in qualifying Australian films and television programs according to market criteria. The AFC continued to exist – its main missions now to assist script and film development, to invest in low-budget innovative features, to support new media initiatives, to undertake research and data collection, to support film cultural activities and to provide policy advice to the whole industry and to government.

Investment by the FFC effectively replaced the profligate 10BA scheme; while it has a cultural mission – funding is restricted to *Australian* films – the FFC makes decisions on a commercial basis. Its guidelines state that to receive investment from the FFC a project must have 'market attachment' as indicated by a pre-sale or other investment from a broadcaster or distributor – in practice, often a foreign entity. All three vehicles for direct government support – the AFC, the FFC and 10BA – apply only to 'one-off' projects, that is, feature films, telemovies, mini-series and documentaries. Thus this funding is not available to serials, series, or any non-drama forms other than documentaries. Nevertheless there has been a useful synergy between all sectors of production; the twin measures of broadcasting regulation and production support have worked well together to produce the efficient and highly skilled industry Australia presently has.

One area where the fit is not so good is that the two sides of the equation no longer use the same definition of 'Australian'. Until the new Television Program Standard 14 (TPS14) was introduced in 1990, the description embodied in the television standards was the same as that in the AFC Act, 10BA and the FFC Act. It is a reasonably open and flexible definition, which had worked with only occasional controversial applications since the 1970s. The group unhappiest with this was the actors' union, Actors' Equity (now part of the Media, Arts and Entertainment Alliance), because the main foreign personnel used widely in Australian films and programs were actors. Until the late 1980s there were few instances of non-Australian directors and writers being used, but foreign actors became more and more prevalent as co-production and foreign pre-sales became the normal way of financing projects (Dermody and Jacka 1988b). Actors' Equity representatives have fought back on this both through their award system, their input into immigration decisions about entertainment personnel, and also as active lobbiers in forums like tribunal hearings.

They were a strong part of the group that urged the Australian Broadcasting Tribunal (ABT) to tighten the definition of Australian during the Australian Content Inquiry of 1986–9. However the ABT needed little prompting, since it had the uncomfortable job of approving as 'Australian' a Paramount Studios re-make of its 1960s hit, *Mission Impossible*, which it chose to shoot on the Gold Coast at the Warner Roadshow studios, Although some Australian technical personnel and minor performers were used, the show was conceived, financed, written and directed by Americans and made primarily for the US market. The ABT was unable to exclude it according to the current rules, in spite of its overwhelmingly non-Australian character. The 'Mission Impossible case', as it became known, seemed to indicate that if off-shore productions became more common, as they appeared to be doing with the internationalisation of the industry, and if such programs counted as Australian in the quota to be shown on local screens, they would act as a disincentive for networks to commission 'genuinely' Australian programs; this was the reason for the new, tighter definition of 'Australian' in the 1990 TPS14.

In 1994 and 1995 the ABA reviewed the operation of the version of TPS14 introduced in 1990. Concerns had been expressed about its complexity, and the inconsistency between it and the definitions of 'Australian' embodied in the film support measures. As a result of this review the definition of 'Australian' has been simplified, while not being changed in essence, and all programs certified as 'Australian' under 10BA or official co-production arrangements will automatically qualify for full quota when shown on television (ABA 1994a).

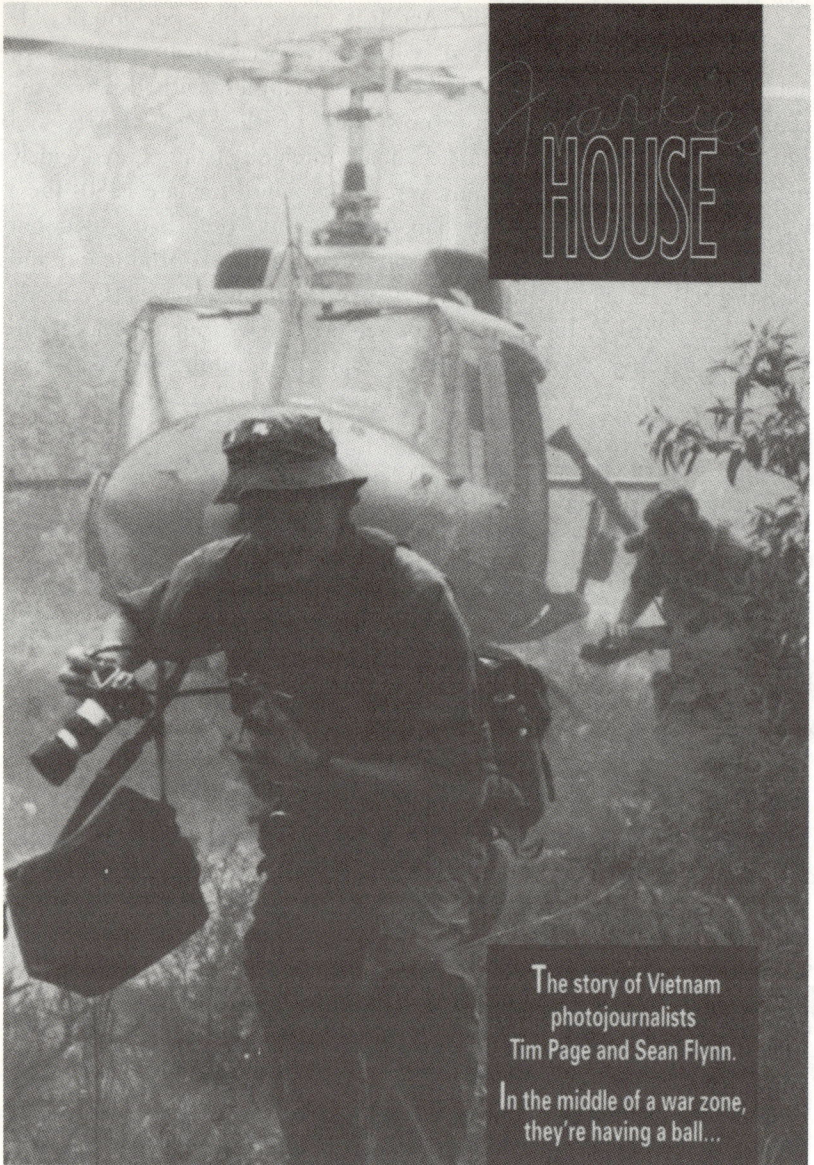

The story of Vietnam photojournalists Tim Page and Sean Flynn.

In the middle of a war zone, they're having a ball...

A co-production between Roadshow Coote and Carroll and the ABC in Australia, and Initial Films and Anglia Television in the UK, *Frankie's House* had little Australian character on-screen, but Australians controlled much of the production behind the scenes. (Roadshow Coote and Carroll publicity material.)

SHIFTS IN THE ECOLOGY OF AUSTRALIAN TELEVISION

The evolving discourse of cultural protection has enjoyed a remarkably stable history in Australia. However, strong shifts in this fundamental plank of the ecology of Australian television have begun to occur during the period we are tracing – from the late 1980s to the end of 1994. We shall track these shifts from cultural protection, under the challenge of economic rationalism and international influences, to the governing contemporary notion of 'culture industries'.

Cultural versus industry protection

The idea that the culture and society of less powerful nations should be protected from the so-called cultural might of larger ones has been as much a feature of debate in Australia as elsewhere (Appleton 1988, pp.2ff.). The anxiety is as old as the cinema itself – it was fulsomely aired during the 1927 Royal Commission into the Moving Picture Industry (Bertrand and Collins 1981, p.25ff.). The debate is perennially slippery because in it we find a coalescence of some of the most emotionally and politically loaded notions of our time. The most notable is, of course, the idea of nation and national identity. Discussion is further complicated by the systematic ambiguity about whether government intervention in the film and television industry (and cultural policy more generally) is being driven by purely cultural concerns or whether its purpose is industry development or protection of employment.

The Vincent Report of 1963 – a major government inquiry into film and television, which served as a major rallying point for the forces arguing throughout the 1960s for government intervention – articulated the dominant idea that the lack of exposure to Australian and the over-exposure to mainly American programs was harmful:

> Perhaps the greatest danger lies in (television's) effect upon the rising generation … who day after day, are not only receiving anything but the most inadequate picture of Australia, her national traditions, culture and way of life, but in its place are recipients of a highly coloured and exaggerated picture of the way of life and morals of other countries (mainly the United States of America) (quoted in Appleton 1988, p.5).

Rather paradoxically though, the Vincent Report was ahead of its time in recommending an international orientation. Its call for Australia to produce for the international market was one that was often actively opposed in later manifestos and only began to surface again as a dominant view in the late 1980s:

... there is an unanswerable case for Australia to export her best television programs in quantity overseas. A free exchange of this important cultural medium is essential in that the rest of the world should have the opportunity of appreciating and evaluating the creative artistry and culture of the Australian nation (as in other artistic and cultural enterprises, e.g. literature and painting). Likewise the Australian artist cannot give proper expression to his creative ability unless he can compete internationally. To force the Australian to create only for Australians and to be 'inward-looking' will result in an acceptance of a parochial set of values and inferior standards (Vincent Report 1962–3, p.99).

Five years later the manifesto for a new Australian film industry, the Interim Report of the Film Committee of the Australian Council for the Arts, while acknowledging the 'sociological influence of imported material', emphasised the creative lack when writers, actors and film-makers were unable to fulfil their potential here and thus Australia had difficulty in interpreting itself to the rest of the world. The 1974 report of the Interim Board of the newly created AFC emphasised the socio-pedagogical role of film and television in creating a strong sense of national identity and of citizenship. In a rhetorical innovation that was to become controversial later, a 1977 report of the newly established ABT invented the term the 'Australian look': 'an Australian television service which looks unmistakeably Australian has long been regarded as a highly desirable ideal' (ABT 1977, p.29). While protection of industry and employment was mentioned in passing, the most important consideration appeared to be the cultural value of Australian programs for audiences (ABT 1977, pp.29, 31, 33).

These early statements of the principles underlying government support for film and television are unequivocally cultural in nature. Economic arguments about the fostering of an industry, the promotion of exports or the protection of employment are secondary. The primary emphasis is on the effects on audiences; while earlier positions were anxious about the sinister effect of exposure to American culture with its vulgarity and shallow values, later ones dropped this anti-American discourse in favour of a positive one about the importance of Australian content in fostering a sense of national identity by 'showing ourselves to ourselves'. Sometimes there was a hint at the connection between cultural sovereignty and political and economic sovereignty (for example, the Tariff Board Inquiry 1973), a view which re-emerges in the current links between cultural development and republicanism.

The notion of an Australian look became a source of conflict during the 1987–9 Australian Content Inquiry conducted by the ABT. There was a sharp division of views on whether it was fostered by regulating the 'off-screen' factors of a project – the view that 'Australian programs are programs made by Australians' – or by attempting to regulate so-called 'on-screen' factors, that is to prescribe what an Australian look would mean in textual terms (Cunningham 1992, p.57). The standard that was finally introduced in January 1990 reverted to off-screen indicators to test 'Australian-ness', though it did retain the rather cryptic clause referring to 'an Australian perspective' (TPS14, 25(i) and (ii)), but the preamble to the standard made it clear that its purpose was still cultural and audience-oriented (TPS14, (1) and (2)).

The establishment of the FFC in 1988 gives an insight into the subtle differences in philosophy between that driving regulation and that which underpinned direct government assistance administered through the arts portfolio and comprising the activities of the AFC, the FFC and 10BA. Since the late 1970s, the history of this kind of support had always had a sub-theme of industry self-sufficiency. Its nature as direct subsidy had often been balanced by an 'infant industry' rhetoric, which had settled into a policy, over the life of the present FFC, of staged reduction of government support. This double nature of audiovisual support as both fostering cultural expression and supporting an infant industry is referenced in Treasurer Paul Keating's speech launching the FFC in January 1989. He reassured his production-industry audience that even though Australia is too small to recover production costs domestically, the government would continue to support the industry because this area of 'cultural expression' is important. Australia had withstood the inter-nationalising pressures introduced in 1983 when the Labor government de-regulated the financial system because Australia had by then attained a 'maturity' and a 'cultural certainty' 'in no small part supported and buttressed by the Australian film industry', which had been important in 'discovering what we are, what we're about, who we are and what our place in the world is' (Keating 1989, p.5).

Until the late 1980s then, there was general bipartisan adherence to the cultural arguments for a local film and television industry and a degree of uniformity across the two wings of this support – that administered by the communications portfolio through broadcasting legislation and that which gave direct support through agencies within the arts portfolio – which rendered their historical separation across different departments of marginal concern. However, a number of factors now began to operate that changed the ground on which film and television policy stood. These included the growing internationalisation of the Australian economy; the importance of multiculturalism in the Australian polity, which rendered traditional ideas of national culture more problematic; and the profound changes as the developed world moved from a fordist consensus to a post-fordist regime in which the certitudes of state provision were called into question.

Economic rationalism

Until the late 1980s, there was very little public discussion of the costs of television content regulation and little disturbance to agreement on the cultural benefits of a local industry. Naturally the networks continually complained about the cost imposts of the regulation, and regularly argued for the reduction or removal of the content rules, but underneath the surface theatre there was a kind of broadcasting club, a consensus between networks and interest groups, which recognised that everyone benefited from the regulation. The networks were protected from competition, and the rules lent support to the viability of the production lobby. Within the film industry there were often passionate and desperate disputes and panics about the way the measures were administered, and an ever-present anxiety about whether a sufficient number of films would perform well enough critically and financially to persuade government of the worthwhileness of the annual subsidy of over $100 million. But again, there was a kind of consensus about and bipartisan support for the merits of having a government-supported industry.

However, the winds of economic rationalism, which originated in the Thatcherite–Reaganite politics of the Northern Hemisphere, began to blow strongly in Canberra (Pusey 1991), and a new set of issues were posed for Australian content regulation. The federal economic departments like Treasury, Industry and Trade began to turn their attention to the audiovisual area and the protracted review of broadcasting regulation, which commenced in 1988, was framed within the new rationalist and pro-competition framework that was becoming so influential. In this context both Australian content regulation and the generous production subsidies were asked to justify themselves in economic terms.

There were also external pressures, primarily the move towards international free trade which was being conducted in the arena of the GATT, whose Uruguay Round included an examination of trade in services, including audiovisual services. In GATT-speak, both quotas and national production subsidies are considered potential barriers to free trade. The US government had already targeted Australia during the Australian Content Inquiry of 1987–9. The US Ambassador to Australia made a submission to the inquiry on behalf of the US trade representative, indicating the possibility of action under Section 301 of the US Trade Act whereby action can be brought by the US against countries who are engaging in 'unfair trade practices' (*The Economist*, 22–28 September 1990, p.11). The penalty is some kind of US trade retaliation, such as refusing to import goods from the offending country. This was clearly only sabre-rattling, since Europe is the main target of US wrath in the area of audiovisual industries and it had no influence on the outcome of the inquiry; however, it did, as they say, 'create an atmosphere'.

The moment of economic rationalism (the late 1980s to early 1990s) occasioned several detailed studies that attempted to undermine the credibility of state intervention in the audiovisual industries and/or canvass possible replacements for it (Jones 1991; BTCE 1991). The key questions raised in these studies are summed up in the preface to Jones' *Cut! Protection of Australia's Film and Television Industries* by well-known right-wing press commentator, P. P. McGuinness:

> Are we getting our money's worth? Why is the industry showing little evidence of commercial viability after so many years of subsidised growth and development? ... How much are Australian filmgoers and television viewers really prepared to pay for an indigenous production industry? ... For whose benefit does the industry really exist? (McGuinness, in Jones 1991, p.viii).

Jones himself then rehearses the range of economic arguments usually put forward for industry support – imperfect competition, externalities, merit goods, infant industry and income distribution. Given his polemical starting point, it is not surprising that he concludes that in each case the arguments fail. The Bureau of Transport and Communications Economics (BTCE) report is more useful in that it actually contains an attempt to estimate the cost of regulation to the industry and ultimately to the consumer. The implication is that the costs are high and that it may be possible to devise more efficient (that is, cheaper) and more 'transparent' ways of delivering the cultural benefits. It recommends the replacement of indirect assistance (through content quotas) with direct forms (production subsidies); the existing methods are 'distorting' (BTCE 1991, p.153).

These were familiar nostrums during the ascendency of neo-classical economics, with its discourses of competition, efficiency and accountability. However, as cultural-policy instruments they are blunt indeed. To anounce the cost of something and to ask 'is this too much?' is a bit like asking about the length of the proverbial piece of string. Does Australia spend too much on defence, health or foreign aid? Economics will not tell us the answer to these questions. What is generally characteristic of these analyses is the attempt to rigorously apply principles of rational economics (minimisation of government intervention, utmost transparency, consumer sovereignty) to a domain that is properly cultural and whose credibility is ultimately political. Even in sympathetic economic analyses of the bases for state intervention (for example, Molloy and Burgan 1993) it is admitted that little light can be shed on the political rationality of state support for the audiovisual industries.

A favoured notion in the neo-classical armoury is that of consumer sovereignty. This doctrine contains a fundamental misconception of the nature of subjectivity. It sees the market as the primary allocator of our broadcasting services; it addresses us as consumers able to make rational choices through the price mechanism about what we need and don't need. But we are not simply consumers. We are also citizens in a democratic nation-state with needs for reliable information and rights to cultural expression. Economists can only wring their hands in despair before consumers who are willing to support politically and materially the preservation of rain forests that they might never visit, or opera companies whose performances they might never attend, or public broadcasters they might only occasionally watch. The incommensurability between the subject constituted as consumer on the one hand and citizen on the other (*see* Miller 1991) is what the current moment of the 'culture industries' in part is designed to address.

The period of ascendency of neo-classical economics coincided almost exactly with the moment when the myths of globalisation held unchallenged sway. Although often its Australian rhetoric was designed to bring the country into line with radical applications of the doctrine elsewhere, in practice its real effects were more muted, and always overlaid with a long-running Labor government's residual commitments to social democracy and its well-honed political antennae measuring community acceptance. These effects included a slow decline in constant dollars of appropriations into the public sector, partial de-regulation (more so in telecommunications than in broadcasting) and greater accountability and performance bench-marking (*see*, for example, HRSCERA 1992).

International influences

The Australian industry became subject to a series of increasing international influences throughout the 1980s. The first came from the necessity of using overseas finance to fund Australian productions, which by the mid-1980s had become normal for film, then for high-budget television after 10BA ceased to be effective. Overseas finance was seen to bring with it the threat of overseas control. Pre-sales of any substance often involved requirements on casting and script, and any co-production arrangement was likely to bring varying degrees of intervention in the project. Sections of the industry saw these factors as threats, in particular actors, who were the occupational category hardest hit by imports, but also technicians, writers and directors, who might also have their jobs threatened by imported personnel. The producer class might also have cause for anxiety; their ability to control their own production creatively could be threatened (*see* Dermody and Jacka 1988b, Chapter 4).

By the beginning of the 1990s, these concerns were set against an emerging consensus that international relationships were to be welcomed and sought as an unavoidable source of finance, production continuity and access to major overseas markets. The success of Australian television exports began to give players a more secure sense that international partnerships might not mean being swamped by foreign influence; the ground swell of the government's 'export drive' and the increased sophistication of Australian producers in negotiating favourable overseas partnerships also made the idea of internationalism less threatening. This growing ease with the issue was in part the result of measures established during the 1980s to ensure that Australian participation in co-ventures was safeguarded. Actors Equity (later the Media Entertainment and Arts Alliance) had success in limiting the number of overseas personnel that could be used on productions receiving taxpayer funding, and secured rights for Australian actors to receive US Screen Actors Guild rates on off-shore productions.

Another element was so-called 'official' co-production treaties into which the government (through the AFC) began to enter. Beginning in 1986, the Australian government signed co-production treaties with France, the UK, Canada, New Zealand, and Italy. Since 1994, it has been negotiating with Japan, Ireland, Israel, Germany and Russia. The value of official co-productions to both parties is that once a project is approved as such, each can automatically access production subsidies in their home countries. Currently, there is a major drawback in Australia in that unlike the case for its partners, qualification as an official co-production does not also automatically qualify a project to count under the Australian content television quota. Producers argue that this uncertainty makes it difficult to secure broadcaster finance for a project when it cannot be determined in advance of the project's completion and examination by the ABA whether it will get Australian content points. This lessens the licence fee, often making it impossible to finance the program, and diminishes the attractiveness of the scheme for producers. It is an anomaly that has been rectified in the ABA's changes to the regulations due to come into effect in 1996.

Up to 1994, 14 out of a total of 23 'official' co-productions based on agreements between governments or their film agencies have been feature films. The major television projects have been *The First Kangaroos* and *The Four Minute Mile* with the UK and *Golden Fiddles* with Canada. Apart from the disincentive of regulatory anomalies, official co-productions are so formidably complex legally and logistically that there is no great incentive to use this mechanism. It is used more often for features because they are harder to finance than television. Australia is a late starter and minor player in the arena of official co-productions.

They have also been quite controversial. Feature-film projects like *Green Card, Black Robe, On My Own, The Navigator, Until the End of the World* and *Map of the Human Heart* have been accused of having no Australian 'character' at all. Some of those co-produced with Canada – *Black Robe, Map of the Human Heart, On My Own* – are Canadian in character; another – *Green Card* – is certainly American; while a couple defy national ascription – Wim Wenders' post-modern odyssey, *Until the End of the World* and the allegorical *The Navigator* which, if anything, has a slight New Zealand flavour because of the Maori presence in it.

Three of the four films nominated for best film in the 1993 Australian Film Institute (AFI) awards were non-Australian on the face of it – *Map, On My Own* and *The Piano* (the last not an 'official' co-production) – which, many argued, brought the awards into disrepute. All of them, however, qualify under the rules for co-productions, having the required levels of Australian personnel and finance. To balance the picture, other official co-productions, most of them television mini-series, have had a recognisably Australian look: *The First Kangaroos, The Four Minute Mile, Golden Fiddles, Dingo,* and *Children of the Dragon.*

Judgements such as these, however, are dubious, as there is no essential national character distinct from all others that can be read off the sur- face of a film or television program, especially when international co-productions are at issue. *The Piano*, winner of two 1994 Academy Awards and perhaps the 'runner-up' to *Schindler's List* for Best Film, illustrates the dilemma nicely. It is set in a completely recognisable New Zealand. Its white characters are all necessarily immigrants – so not New Zealanders; the Maori characters are overtly coded as a particular version of essential nativeness. The actors, when they are not American (Holly Hunter and Harvey Keitel – both very well-known Hollywood actors) are New Zealanders – the unknown Anna Paquin, and Sam Neill, whose fame derives primarily from his presence in the iconic Australian films *My Brilliant Career*, *Evil Angels/Cry in the Dark* (in which an American played an Australian) and *Death In Brunswick*. The main supporting actors, Kerry Walker and Genevieve Lemon, are Australian, each moderately well known in Australia for lovers of Sydney theatre, *Sweetie* and *Neighbours*. *The Piano* is the story of a mute Scottish woman (and her child) who comes to the colony of New Zealand to marry a man she has never seen. She then has a passionate relationship with another settler (of uncertain provenance, due to Harvey Keitel's wayward accent, but from somewhere in the British Isles). It uses well-known literary and film conventions that mix together the gothic, the romance and the woman's film, but it gives them a post-modern turn, which places the film also within a contemporary set of international cinema conventions that is somewhat self-reflexive (a kind of female version of the Coen Brothers). This last feature explains why the film has travelled so well.

The Piano is veritably a creature of a new audiovisual internationalism; it is very difficult to say sensibly what its national source is – would its French source of finance have given it a French character? Instead, in true Foucauldian fashion, we must rather ask what the function of the debate itself is. How the nationality of a film or television program is to be defined has implications for policy, for industrial conditions, for exports, for company profits, for international flows of capital, for government funding decisions. It also creates a space for cultural resonances so that audiences can recognise in their audiovisual universe signs of their environment that link with their desires, memories and sense of place. None of this is codifiable. But what rules like co-production agreements do is give a kind of anchor, which fixes some reference points in an enforceable way, so that these other more elusive spaces can be secured.

Another kind of international influence comes from off-shore productions. Just as other kinds of investment and production travel to cheaper sources of input of labour or materials, so does the audiovisual industry, so long as the aspects of the project that will attract the primary audience can be safeguarded. Australia has become a site of off-shore US, and to a much lesser extent Japanese, productions since the mid-1980s. However in spite of considerably cheaper production costs in Australia and more flexible work practices, moving productions so far from the US still incurs significant costs and remains a risky proposition. To attract US producers away from closer alternatives like Canada, Mexico or Europe, there must be a high level of inducement. Off-shore production might not have occurred at the level it has, had it not been for the very active measures taken by both the private and the government sector to attract projects to Australia.

This strategy divides opinion in the Australian film and television community. The actors oppose it because it creates little work for Australian actors. On the other hand it is favoured by some technical personnel because it does create work for them; now that these two groups of workers have amalgamated into a single union, the Media, Entertainment and Arts Alliance, there will have to be some *rapprochement* over this issue within the new union. It is also opposed by some sections of the bureaucracy and the culture lobby; they argue that history tells us that an off-shore strategy is fraught with danger. The growth of productions designed from and for somewhere else can edge out projects of a genuinely local nature (*see*, for further discussion of this highly contentious issue, Dermody and Jacka 1988b, pp.117–30).

On the other hand (as we shall see in further detail in Chapter 4), the strategy has had the strong support of some state governments and their film bodies, especially the Queensland government, for whom it is an important plank in their regional industrial development plans (Giles Consulting 1992), and from some sections of the Commonwealth government and the federal bureaucracy, not to mention the Opposition. The answer to the dilemma is not to confuse cultural-support policies with those of industry development. Pressure is being applied to the federal government to relax the definition of Australian content for free-to-air and pay television to allow this type of production to count for quota. However, as the now-defunct ABT was at pains to point out when it promulgated its standard in 1989, the regulation is not primarily intended to bring about employment or industrial outcomes. Rather its purpose is a cultural one – to encourage the expression of local stories, idioms and concerns.

Off-shore production of, say, US network series *Mission Impossible*, or features such as *Dolphin Cove* or *Escape from Absalom* in Australia will obviously not do that. On the other hand, it has indubitable industrial and multiplier benefits for the regional economy, and enhances Australia's balance of trade. If so, governments should accord it the same benefits they might give to other emergent industries – exemptions from or discounted sales tax, payroll tax, favourable loans, and the kind of government-supported initiative that is represented by the establishment of the Export Film Services Association (EFSA), a grouping of Australian producers, services providers and state funding bodies that liaises closely with overseas producers who may wish to produce in Australia. The history of the experience in countries that have had 'branch plant' film industries – for example, Spain, Canada, or the UK – tell us that acting as host to US productions may do little to foster domestic film and television production (KPMG Management Consulting 1992). Experience both here and overseas seems to indicate that what is needed is a combination of both cultural and industry development policies.

The current moment of culture industries

In Australia as in many countries (with the arguable exceptions of the old metropolitan national cultures such as France), cultural policy had been traditionally a backwater – dominated by constricting assumptions about high art and worthy subsidy; narrow in its consideration only of the arts rather than of culture more generally (an aesthetic rather than an anthropological concept of culture). In contrast, in the 1990s we have seen a dramatic coalescence around a new rhetoric of 'culture industries' and 'cultural development'. In this rhetoric we see the reverse of the notion of cultural protection limiting foreign product in order to create a zone of safety for local product; instead film and television policy is to be justified as a way of sending Australian product out into the world.

Paul Keating's accession to the prime ministership in 1991 was an ingredient; he played a leading role in giving culture a policy prominence it hadn't had before. But even before this, the federal industry department had begun to focus on the audiovisual as a possible candidate for industry development. It set up an audiovisual task force in 1991, which began a long research project into the way the industry functioned and what its export potential might be. In 1994 it emerged with an industry discussion paper that focussed particularly on the emergent area of multimedia and on the importance of the Asian region to Australia (DITARD 1994). This fitted in with the thrust of government trade and industry policy, which had begun to target Asia as a growing export market for Australia from the late 1980s.

In 1992 the Department of the Arts released a discussion paper called *The Role of the Commonwealth in Australia's Cultural Development*, which was designed as a blueprint for the next ten years of cultural policy development. It signalled both the beginnings of the cultural-industries approach at an official public policy level, and the determination of the arts portfolio not to be left out of this widening of the framework into which film and arts policy fitted. The change in perspective was reflected in the fact that the arts branch of the department re-named itself the Australian Cultural Development Office (ACDO) in 1993. Throughout the document, the term 'cultural industry' is used to cover the traditional arts and popular culture and broadcasting without discrimination.

The document attempts to undermine the perception that the arts is an 'unproductive' area of activity with no relation to the main game of industry: 'It would be wrong to see two separate worlds in the cultural industry: one subsidised and protected from the demands of the market by the intervention of government, the other operating without help in the free market.' An integration of cultural subsidy and industry-development models is appropriate for the future: 'It may be that in seeking to develop a viable cultural industry in the 1990s, the Commonwealth will be increasingly drawn away from the funding models it has used in the past and towards industry policies which emphasise self-reliance, commercial viability, employment generation, skills development and the creation of value-added products and new markets' (DASET 1992, p.25). The reconciliation of the economic and the cultural was endorsed by an extraordinary speech given by Paul Keating in 1992 to the Writers' Guild Annual Awards when he suggested that cultural industries had a role to play in Australia's economic recovery, not just because they could contribute to wealth directly but because they could help to foster a 'sense of national purpose and national cohesion' that could give Australians the spirit to overcome their economic problems (Keating 1992).

The 1993 federal election was the highest water mark for culture as a public policy and election issue since the early 1970s. There was a dramatic reassertion of the muscle of the arts lobby and an equal response from the Labor government, both of them aided to a large degree by the ineptitude of the Opposition to counter the push for greater recognition of culture as a political factor. Out of Labor's victory came a slew of cultural initiatives following on from election pledges, Cabinet-level representation of the arts for the first time since the days of the Whitlam government, and the historic joining of arts and communications in one federal government portfolio.

The moment of culture industries found its culmination in the October 1994 unveiling of the Commonwealth's cultural policy statement, *Creative Nation* (Commonwealth of Australia 1994). Its centrepiece was the injection of an additional A$250 million over four years into culture and a focus on developing new technologies, such as multimedia content creation, as platforms for improved access to the arts and for new export activity. Broadcast television production was to benefit from A$60 million over three years into a fund to increase Australian content levels and from A$13 million injected into the SBS kitty for commissioned local drama and documentary.

The policy was also the culmination of the dramatic supercession of the austere economic rationalism that had haunted the audiovisual industries in preceding years. This does not mean that issues of accountability, performance and efficiency have disappeared. What it does mean is that the historic opposition between culture and industry, between what Dermody and Jacka (1987; 1988a) call Industry I and II values, which sustained and enlivened debate throughout the 1970s and much of the 1980s, has shifted to the recognition that the opposition may actually be a reflection of needed diversity in the audiovisual landscape in Australia. A continuing slate of production for the larger producers in the country may require the opposition to be accommodated within the single corporate umbrella – this is most clearly the case, as we shall see, with the Roadshow conglomerate: Roadshow Coote and Carroll provide the culturalist material while the Warner Roadshow Movieworld Studios management strategies of attracting off-shore production to their northern production facilities provide the internationalist angle. Multiculturalism and local cultural expression are similarly recognised in changing some of the terms of the debate, while viewing the Australian audiovisual industry from the standpoint of maximising export potential and international best practice means placing these traditional oppositions within a broader framework of 'cultural and industry development' policy.

This confluence of cultural and industry development is exemplified also in the changes to content regulation that resulted from the review in 1994–5. A more commodious, 'industry-friendly' definition of Australian (through allowing all 10BA certified product to qualify under the standard) is balanced by cultural targeting of documentaries (a quota has been set for the first time) and children's programming. In Chapter 12, we shall canvass some of the limits of this confluence. At this point, however, we need to sharpen the focus of our domestic optic further in turning to profiles of the most prominent internationally-oriented Australian production companies.

4

Production Companies I

THE AUSTRALIAN BROADCASTING CORPORATION

In the context of this book, the ABC presents a paradox. As Australia's main public-service broadcaster, it is arguably the single most significant force in Australia in short-form television drama especially, in documentary, in nature programming and perhaps in children's programming, but even when these programs sell well overseas the ABC is often not actively involved in the sales and derives little financial benefit from the export trade. This is a result of the current economics of the international television industry and the necessity for co-financing and co-production. For the ABC the price of co-production is the surrender of important international rights.

The ABC has always played a leading role in local program production. It was virtually unrivalled in any category of drama until the mid-1970s. The period from 1968 until 1975 is often referred to as the golden era of the ABC, the time of popular series and mini-series *Bellbird, Contrabandits, Certain Women, Rush, Marion, Ben Hall* and *Power Without Glory*. However, as often happened, the commercials were quick to imitate once the ABC had shown the existence of an audience for a certain sort of program, and serial dramas like *The Sullivans* and *Tandarra* began to appear. The end of the 1970s brought a rush of local soap operas to commercial television (*The Restless Years, Skyways, The Young Doctors*) and in the early 1980s the bounty of 10BA produced a flood of high-quality mini-series on commercial networks.

The ABC, like other public broadcasters around the world, was completely vertically integrated until the late 1980s. That is, with the exception of a few co-productions, mostly with the BBC, all its production was initiated, financed and produced in-house. Consequently, by the early 1980s, the ABC was quite insular and rather unresponsive to the developments in the commercial sector. However, many good programs were produced in this period – the series and mini-series *Patrol Boat, 1915, Spring and Fall, Scales of Justice, Palace of Dreams* and *Sweet and Sour* broke new ground in Australian television drama. And the ABC did provide an arena for trying out new writers and attempts at formal or conceptual innovation.

In the wake of the Dix Report of 1981 (Inglis 1983, pp.425–41), which recommended sweeping reforms to the ABC, the organisation entered a protracted period of demoralisation and confusion that had a detrimental effect on drama production as on other areas of activity. By 1986, the output of drama at the ABC had fallen to an all-time low of about 38 hours per year and the costs of producing it had escalated dramatically. The new head of drama, Sandra Levy, formulated a 'drama initiative' – her aim was to increase output to at least 100 hours a year (Jacka 1991, pp.228ff.). The reforms initiated then set the pattern for ABC drama for the next seven years.

First, a decision was made to move more towards the popular end of the drama spectrum and away from what was seen as esoteric, eccentric or specialised. Second it was decided that the way to get quantity, quality and spread was by concentrating on a mixture of long-running series and mini-series and by eschewing short-form dramas, which are too expensive when related to the audience they are likely to attract. Third it was realised that the only way to increase drama hours was to enter into co-production arrangements with local producers, who could raise cash from 10BA and other government assistance schemes and from overseas pre-sales, with the ABC contributing facilities and technical staff and as little cash as possible.

This strategy was immediately successful, at least in quantity and audience terms. Close to 100 hours was achieved by 1988 and there was an immediate improvement in the ratings for mini series and series, the suburban medical soap opera *GP* was notable in the latter category. The programs also received critical acclaim; the ABC's new ascendancy in television drama was assisted in no small measure by the fact that in the period 1988–91, the quality of expensive drama on commercial television fell because of the networks' financial problems.

In the period 1988–91 a large number of prestigious mini-series were made and broadcast; all were co-produced with local and overseas partners. The involvement of an overseas partner, almost invariably a UK broadcaster, naturally meant the programs were shown on overseas television. Titles included mini-series like *Act of Betrayal* (with TVS), *A Dangerous Life* (with HBO in the US and Zenith in the UK), *Edens Lost* (with Central TV), *The Leaving of Liverpool* (with the BBC) and *The Paper Man* (with Granada). It is also the period when *GP* began to be sold to a number of overseas buyers, although it has never achieved a large success in foreign markets. And the ABC's most successful situation comedy, both domestically and overseas, *Mother and Son*, was also sold during this period. JE Productions (now Endermol) in Holland have optioned the rights to both the concept and the scripts of *Mother and Son*. It had already been sold as a series in Holland, and was broadcast with subtitles, however it did not rate well, and the broadcaster did not buy further series. (The ABC would rather sell the series than the format, because their stake in the format is quite small (Hallam 1992).)

Since 1992 the possibilities for financing programs for the British market have diminished, because of the uncertainty around the reform of the ITV system and pressures on the BBC (*see* Chapter 6). For this reason the ABC has begun to swing back towards the production of programs fully financed in-house (Harvey-Sutton 1994, pp.29ff.), partly by a special funding supplement the ABC as a whole received in 1993 and partly by small dividends from its merchandising division, ABC Enterprises. In the two years 1993–4, in-house drama production included *Phoenix I* and *Phoenix II*, *Seven Deadly Sins*, *The Damnation of Harvey McHugh*, *Heartland* and *Janus*. It is a sign of how crucial co-production is for the successful export of programs that none of these titles has sold as well in overseas markets as those produced with overseas and/or local partners. (*Heartland* was actually produced by Northway Productions, a local company, but it was more of a commission than a genuine co-production.)

The ABC is unlike all our other 'leading exporters' in that it is, of course, not only a producer but also a transmitter of programs. The financial stake of the ABC in the majority of drama programs is very small, because most of their initial investment (usually in the form of facilities rather than cash) is offset against the Australian licence fee. In order to finance the rest of the budget of expensive forms like drama, the ABC must enter into co-productions with both local and overseas partners. The investment of these partners is usually bought only at the expense of the ABC's relinquishing most significant overseas rights. Paradoxically, therefore, the ABC receives little or no financial return, although in one sense it is arguably the single most important production house in Australia, at least for drama, and a significant exporter, in that some of the most successful exports have been programs either initiated or at least co-produced by it.

A CHILLING TWO PART MINI-SERIES

THE LEAVING OF LIVERPOOL

The scandalous true story of the innocent young victims of the British child migrant programme. They were sold a dream of a better life in the New World. For many the reality was slave labour and abuse.

SUNDAY 8.35PM
CONCLUDES NEXT SUNDAY 8.35PM

ONE
New Zealand's ONE

The ABC/BBC co-production, *The Leaving of Liverpool*, is the moving story of English children who were brought out to Australia after the Second World War, and who often suffered extraordinary hardships, including physical and sexual abuse, in the institutions in which they were placed. (*The Listener*, New Zealand, 23 July 1993.)

To illustrate, recent series that are produced wholly in-house and thus available for sale by the ABC directly include the extended mini-series *Phoenix*, *Janus* and *The Damnation of Harvey McHugh*; while co-produced series that will be sold by other parties in all important territories are: *Embassy*, *GP* and *Police Rescue*. Among the mini-series (concentrated in the period 1988–91), the in-house titles are *Come in Spinner* and *True Believers*; whereas other parties hold the major rights to approximately 20 titles, including *Bodysurfer*, *Brides of Christ*, *Children of the Dragon*, *Frankie's House* and *The Leaving of Liverpool*. Most of these were co-produced with UK partners, either the BBC or an ITV company; the European rights are held by these partners and the programs are sold by the distribution arms of those broadcasters or their agents. In addition, since most had FFC backing, this body also holds some rights.

This is also the case with other program formats, including nature series, for which the ABC is internationally renowned, and children's programs. For example the successful children's comedy series *Bananas in Pyjamas* is virtually the only in-house children's program actively exported by the ABC; however, the ABC catalogue also includes children's programs broadcast but not produced by it, such as Barron Films' *Clowning Around*. The ABC is actively involved in selling nature series *Bush Tucker Man*, *Wildscreen*, and *The Nature of Australia*, which are particularly successful in overseas markets. Natural history programs sell well because they do not suffer from 'cultural resistance' (Mansoufis 1993). Although Australian vernacular in *Bush Tucker Man* was a problem in some territories, in the UK it screened on Channel 4 and received a good audience reaction. *Nature of Australia* has sold in almost every territory, and ABC International is hoping to be able to sell it again because it does not date the way other genres do (Hallam 1992).

The vehicle for overseas sales of ABC-owned product is ABC International, formed in 1990, partly under the umbrella of UK program distributor Telso, associated with ITV broadcaster TVS. At that time the volume of sales was around A$2 million a year but was expected to increase as the ABC retained more rights (*Encore* 1990, p.3). In 1992, after TVS lost its franchise, the ABC established an office in the UK whence programs are sold to Europe, the Middle East and Africa. The Sydney office services Asia and the Pacific. For North and South America, sales agents are used. Part of the justification for launching ABC International was to raise the profile of the ABC in the international market, so that it might form relationships with other broadcasters, distributors and producers and raise funds for production (Mansoufis 1993).

A recent change in the world market has led the ABC to select a more diverse range of formats. As the financing of mini-series has become harder, the ABC is no longer able to rely on that format alone, and has had to look to 13-part series to keep its production slate healthy. Although there has been a move to more in-house financed production in this way, the ABC is employing more freelance producers, directors and crews on these programs (Prisk 1994, p.4). A problem in selling to the new commercial channels in Europe is the paucity of material containing very long runs because the new channels strip programs. Programs like the comedy *Eggshells*, with only 7 or 14 episodes, is disadvantaged by this whereas *Bananas in Pyjamas* has an advantage as there are 90 five-minute episodes (Hallam 1992). The ABC has done well with children's programs. There is a big market for them because broadcasters are obliged to broadcast a certain quantity but no broadcaster wants to spend much on them. As a consequence, for example, the BBC seriously considers virtually all the ABC's available children's programming.

Thus, the ABC is a dominant force in the production of exportable television formats even though only in rare cases is it actually the exporter. Even when ABC programs are largely externally financed, and thus the ABC's copyright in them is small, the ABC exerts the major creative influence. There are very few cases in the last seven years (*Frankie's House* is arguably one, as we shall see later in this chapter) where the ABC has not kept almost total creative control (Harvey-Sutton 1994, p.35). However, there is usually a genuine creative collaboration with the local co-producer, in particular those with whom the ABC has a long association – Roadshow Coote and Carroll, Generation Films, and Southern Star. So in all categories of drama except soap opera, the ABC has played a crucial role without reaping the financial benefit.

THE GRUNDY ORGANISATION

The Grundy organisation – or Grundys as it is popularly known – has been engaged in systematic internationalising strategies for longer than probably any other Australian television production group. (As testament to this, we discuss Grundy ventures in nearly all the territory surveys in Part Three.) Strictly speaking, Grundys has not been Australian for some time, as it was headquartered in Bermuda, and in 1995 was bought by UK publishing and media conglomerate, Pearsons. However, its history is predominantly Australian and its Australian operations remain the single biggest contribution to its overall activities. Grundys was a radio game-show producer in the 1950s, and transformed into a television game-show producer for the local market during the 1960s. The 1970s brought considerable expansion into local drama production along with consolidation of its reputation as a leader in light entertainment; Moran's history of the organisation (1985) has efficiently outlined the overall shape of its internationalisation push. Reg Grundy, its founder in 1950, chairman and chief executive, retired from the Australian operations in the late 1970s to concentrate on establishing a presence in Los Angeles. He succeeded to the extent that in 1979, its low-budget serial *Prisoner* was bought for syndication (and attracted a strong, albeit limited following on the west coast), but subsequently day-time game and quiz shows have been Grundys' main packages for US television.

The dream of breaking onto the US networks still animates the Grundy organisation, with some drama concepts travelling far up the decision-making ladder, and with *Dangerous Women*, a serial concept spun off from *Prisoner*, performing reasonably in syndication when released in 1992. However, in some ways the company's fortunes in the US have gone backwards after the initial successes in the early 1980s, a situation attributed by managing director Ian Holmes to the cyclical downturn in US network preferences for day-time game shows and their replacement with talk shows since the late 1980s. While that cycle may well turn again, recent trends put Grundys' US production operations below 10 per cent of overall output (*see* Chapter 8).

While the US market remains the most difficult for Grundys, as for all foreign players, its European operations have burgeoned since the breakthrough success of *Neighbours* in Britain from the mid-1980s. While that platform was the base on which a number of Grundy and other Australian serials and series were sold into the British market, it was also the impetus to develop the key globalising formula that Reg Grundy himself dubbed 'parochial internationalism'. A strategy that has come to dominate the company's profile, this dates from the period of significant downturn in the Australian industry's fortunes from the late 1980s to the early 1990s. As Ian Holmes put it, virtually all company production has been done under the banner of parochial internationalism from the late 1980s. Program sales are still important, but there are many more company personnel and revenues involved in parochial internationalist production – it is 'much bigger than making Australian drama or [Grundys' New Zealand co-production] *Shortland Street*' (Holmes 1994).

Recognising that exporting from Australia into foreign territories is at best a hit-and-miss affair, with long-term prospects for stability of sales

dependent on others' readings of viewer preferences, a relatively accommodating regulatory and industry environment, and a preparedness to
dub material into several European languages, Grundys instead sets up
wholly-owned local production companies to do, in Reg Grundy's words,
'shows that feature local people and are made by Grundy personnel who
are nationals of the country in which the show is made' (Smith 1992;
Gerrie 1992). The strategy owes much to development by international
advertisers and agencies of the much-touted multi-domestic strategy,
which emerged from the failures of global or world brand advertising.

Well suited to cheap and transparently international formats, parochial
internationalism has been limited predominantly to game and quiz shows,
the engine room of Grundy output. The strategy has been adventurously
extended into drama, with re-versioning of their racy 1970s soap opera
The Restless Years in Holland and Germany (*see* Chapter 7), and with two
soaps *Unter Uns* ('Our Secret') and *Verbotene Liebe* ('Forbidden Love'),
loosely based on *Sons and Daughters*, in development in Germany (Lewis
1994). For Grundys, the cultural questions that might arise in adapting
program concepts to different languages and national contexts are dealt
with briskly as a matter of corporate professionalism and production ethos.

The organisation is rightly proud of its policy of employing nationals in
the countries targeted (in The Netherlands the operation employed about
70 people in 1992, of whom only one was an Australian). According to
Ian Holmes (1992), Grundys brings to Europe a 'commercial attitude to
television' as against the highly 'parental attitude' of the television culture
of the host nations. Rapid commercialisation will sweep away the cobwebs
of what are seen as sluggish and feather-bedded systems. This means
introducing assembly-line production schedules, with their emphasis on
cheapness, and replicating hitherto successful formulae, rapid-response
entrepreneurialism and insistence on controlling production when in a co
venture relationship. It is these forces that lead to change in the television
culture of countries like The Netherlands, rather than the specific content
of the programming. Moran's comment, that '[f]or Grundys the only facts
recalled about any program are its ratings and the time it ran on air'
(1985, p.95), is sharp but accurate.

By the mid-1990s, Grundys was producing about 50 hours of television
a week in Europe, the US, Australasia, east Asia and South America. It has
offices in Australia, New Zealand, the US, France, Germany, the UK,
Ireland, Italy, Spain, Portugal, Denmark, Belgium, Finland, Luxembourg,
The Netherlands and Chile. While it has interests outside television
production – music, travel, radio, restaurants, entertainment centres (it

has shareholdings in the Sydney Entertainment Centre and Darling Harbour) – it concentrates on television, with production and distribution contributing about 70 per cent of the organisation's revenues. It sells into over 70 countries world wide; its revenues in 1990–1 were A$140 million as against A$9.5 million in 1979–80 and most of the increase came from international sales and production activities. It claims to be the second largest television light-entertainment producer in the world, and one of the world's largest independent production organisations.

Before the Pearsons purchase Grundys was based in the tax haven of Bermuda, where the parent company Grundy Worldwide Ltd is registered, and where Reg Grundy is also based. Organisationally, Grundys is structured around four international divisions: Light Entertainment, Drama, International Distribution and Corporate. Within these divisions, which are based in different territories (the US, Europe and Australasia), there currently exist several dozen companies employing around 1200 people in production and administrative functions (*see* Figure 4.1). While Europe as a whole generates more production throughput, Australia remains the largest single country for production operations. The US has actually declined in importance over the last decade, for the reasons outlined previously, and the Asian operations now rival US operations in terms of revenue. These are centred mostly in the Singapore office, the node for Grundy International Distribution's presence in Asia.

Grundys' internationalising strategies differ greatly from most Australian production companies. They are virtually the opposite of those of Village Roadshow, one of the other major export-oriented companies, as the concept of parochial internationalism drives production off shore, *away* from Australia. Unlike Village Roadshow, Grundys rarely engages with regulators or state-funding support mechanisms, relying on the cheapness, popularity and international transparency of its preferred formats and genres to generate material in quantity and maintain a healthy cash flow. Moran's contrast between Grundys and many other television producers, particularly Crawfords, bears this out (1985). Indeed Grundys actively steers clear of industry controversy and follows industry trends that presage expansion, rather than staying within stagnant or recessionary situations.

Drama, particularly series and one shot, has been produced more and more outside Australia. However, the rule that commercialising industries initially open up to foreign input, and then tend to close as local production gears up to meet the increased demand, means that Grundys has been prepared to move globally in search of new market opportunities.

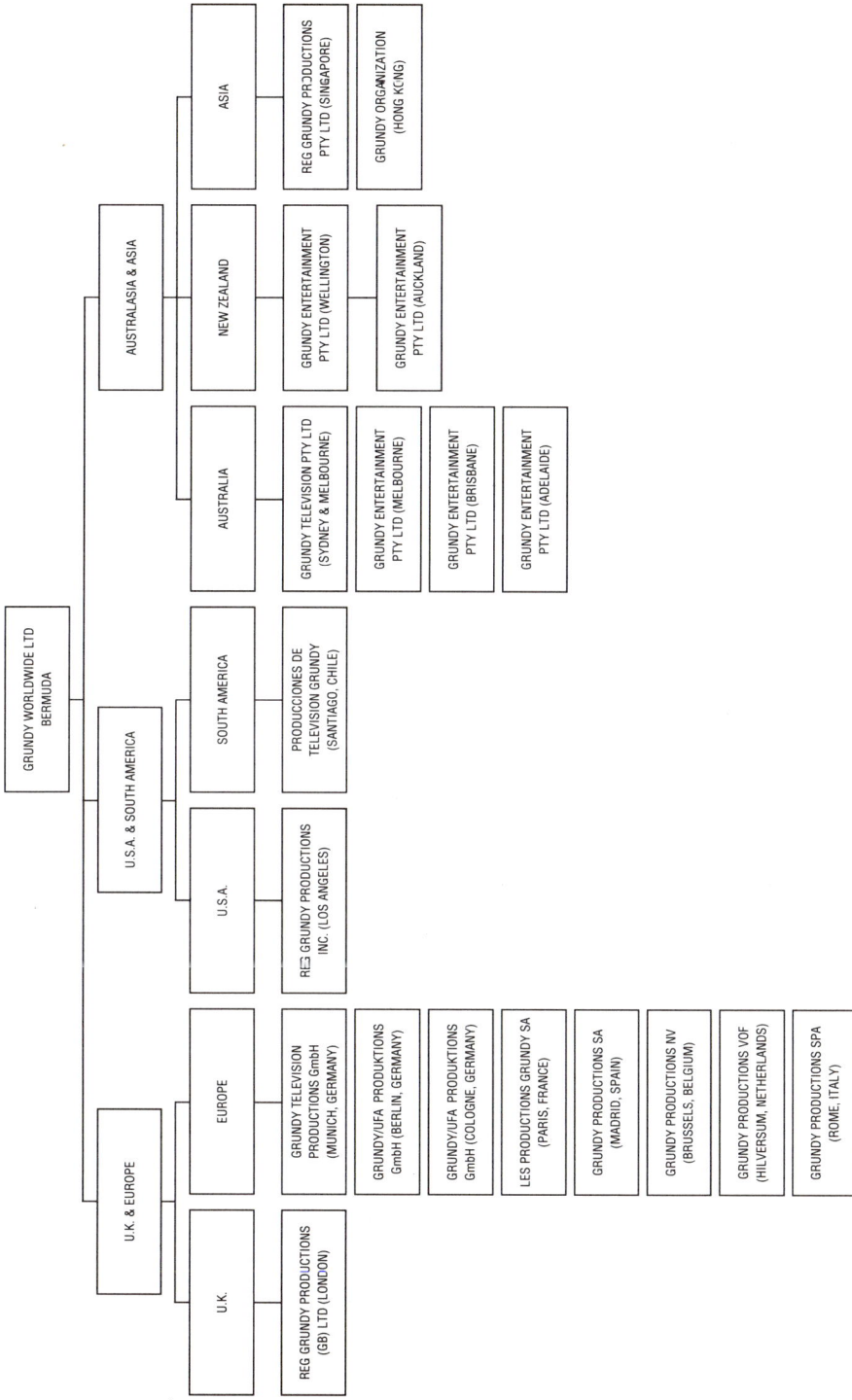

Fig. 4.1: Grundy Worldwide Limited Production Operations, 1994

Source: Grundy Worldwide Ltd.

The movement has been from Australia to the US and then Europe, where Grundys experienced its greatest growth as the continent went through its 'stripping revolution' (Holmes 1994). From that base, it has expanded into South America and Asia (while of course maintaining an active presence in previously established territories).

Among the criticisms levelled at Grundys are those that it has remained within innocuous formats (game and quiz shows) and 'safe' drama renditions, and has contributed to the homogenisation of international television through imitation of American formulas (de Bens *et al.* 1992, p.94). However, programs like *Prisoner* and *Shortland Street* were risky and innovative for their time and places of production, while a program like *Man O Man*, with its rather aggressive 'girls on top' format, represents a risky strategy in light entertainment. And the degree to which Grundys has entered European, South American and Asian countries, worked closely with local entities and employed local personnel in producing locally specific versions of their copyrighted product, would seem to indicate very different inputs and outcomes than further homogenisation. However, on the ground, Grundys' practices of localising production also are not without their critics. In Chapter 10, we look in more detail at the New Zealand experience of Grundys' parochial internationalism in this light. There, there is some evidence that Grundys' partner, South Pacific Pictures, had to resist certain conservative responses to the direction of its collaboration on *Shortland Street*. And, as we shall note in Chapter 7, Grundys' approach to re-versioning *Restless Years* for French television was sufficiently strict for the project not to eventuate (Halberstadt-Harari 1992).

By 1994, the breadth of Grundys' strategies embraced new as well as established projects. The game show *Family Feud* was sold into Indonesia, there were other game shows in France, drama (*Gute Zeite, Schlechte Zeite*) and game shows in Germany, serial drama in Holland, game shows in Spain, Belgium and Israel, game shows had been running since the early 1980s in the US and *Dangerous Women* was still playing out its 90 episodes in syndication. Spurts of new activity included a game show in Chile; a new 100 hours of serial drama and a made-for-television movie in Paraguay; and the new light entertainment, *Man O Man* (which was derived from a Spanish television format), was launched on the Seven Network in Australia. More recycled Australian soap formats are being introduced in Europe to build on *The Restless Years* re-versioning from 1990. The Australian operation is co-venturing interactive television as it believes game shows will be the first platform for direct interactivity in broadcast television. Grundys is a substantial world player in international formats, with the experience and flexibility to consolidate that role in the years ahead.

THE VILLAGE ROADSHOW GROUP

The Village Roadshow group of companies is unique in Australia. First established in the 1950s as a drive-in theatre operator, it is now the only completely integrated audiovisual entertainment company, with involvement in studio management, production of both film and television, film distribution and exhibition, television distribution, video distribution and movie theme-park management (Cunningham and Jacka 1993). The conglomerate is also moving into multimedia development and theatres in South East Asia. Its approach to internationalisation is also unique in that the main thrust of its strategy is to attract off-shore productions to its Warner Roadshow Movie World Studios at Coomera, near the Gold Coast in south-east Queensland. It has a satellite production company, Roadshow Coote and Carroll (RCC), which is an outstanding 'boutique' producer of mid-range budget television such as *GP* and *Brides of Christ*. RCC has been critically and culturally successful, both locally and in international terms, but it is not economically significant in the context of the whole conglomerate.

In 1986 the plans of American independent producer, Dino De Laurentis for a studio on the Gold Coast fell through (Dermody and Jacka 1988b, p.50), and Village Roadshow made the decision to buy the studio in a joint venture with the US-based Warner Bros. Village saw the studio as the heart of a bigger complex that would include the Movie World theme park. Faced with the prospect of a white elephant on their hands and an unpaid loan, the Queensland government continued the favourable deal it had extended to De Laurentis, and the Warner Roadshow complex on the Gold Coast was born.

The parent company, Village Roadshow Ltd, has a 50 per cent stake with Warners in the Gold Coast studios and the theme park (Warner Brothers Movie World). Warners, GU Film Distributors and Village Roadshow each own a third of the multiplex business and Village Roadshow wholly owns the two production entities, RCC and Village Roadshow Pictures. In addition, as a result of the relationship that developed between the Nine Network and Village Roadshow Pictures during the making of *Mission Impossible*, the Nine Network has a 10 per cent share in the present company and because RCC have pre-sold a number of programs to the UK ITV franchise-holder for East Anglia, Anglia Television, this company has 17 per cent.

Production Activities of Village Roadshow Pictures

The Village Roadshow organisation has two production arms, Village Roadshow Pictures and RCC. The former is more important economically, though the latter has a much higher production profile in Australia, because the huge investment in the studios depends totally on the success of Village Roadshow Pictures in attracting production to them. On the other hand, RCC is a very small organisation with very little investment and could continue quite comfortably outside the umbrella of the parent company.

The studios got underway in 1988–9, housing two off-shore television series for the Hollywood studio Paramount, *Dolphin Bay* and *Mission Impossible*. These productions were enormously controversial and provoked conflict with the unions, especially Actors' Equity and the Writers' Guild, and also a minor flurry with the Australian Broadcasting Tribunal (Cunningham and Jacka 1993, pp.22–3). *Mission Impossible* was brought to the Warner Roadshow studio by the team of Michael Lake and Nick McMahon, who had both worked previously for Crawfords in Melbourne and who had long careers in sales and production management. Their idea was to attract overseas production to Australia, taking advantage of Australia's lower pay rates and less complicated union regulations, its weak dollar, its high level of expertise and good Gold Coast locations. It is estimated that one hour of series drama can be made in Australia for about 30 per cent lower cost than in Hollywood (although there is great variability and volatility in the area of comparative costs of off-shore international production locations, with several countries including Spain, Portugal, Mexico and South Africa vying to attract the same kind of production slate).

Lake and McMahon approached Paramount and secured the *Mission Impossible* deal, which they then took to the Warner Roadshow studios. It was based on the program formula that had been so successful during the 1960s – a crack team of US troubleshooters is sent on an 'impossible' mission each episode – and the new show was entirely conceived in the US. It used mainly US principal actors, US directors and all the early episodes used US scripts. It was financed by Paramount with a pre-sale in the US to the ABC network and in Australia to the Nine Network. The Australian involvement consisted of actors in bit parts and as extras and an Australian production crew. The show was post-produced in Hollywood.

Two series were made in Australia: the first was 19, the second 16 one-hour episodes.

Since 1989 the studio has attracted part or whole production of several feature films – a mixture of Australian and overseas productions – including *The Delinquents, Blood Oath, Until the End of the World* and *Fortress*. It has also hosted a number of US series, most of which haven't been shown in Australia, including *Animal Park, Savage Sea* and a new production of *Skippy*. In 1992–3 it housed the major US series *Time Trax* which, unlike *Mission Impossible*, used a considerable number of Australian creative personnel, including directors and post-production people. It is, however, conceived, scripted in and entirely controlled from Hollywood. With 22 episodes in this series, Nick McMahon, managing director of Village Roadshow Pictures (Television), claims that A\$700 000 per episode will be spent in Australia, a total of over A\$15 million. This by itself makes a dint in the balance of audiovisual trade, and he argues that with large multiplier effects, it brings a huge benefit to Queensland and to Australia (McMahon 1992). As outlined in Chapter 3, critics of the off-shore strategy fear that it is the thin end of the wedge that will threaten the integrity of the Australian-content quota, if it leads to the widening of the definition of 'Australian' to include anything made in Australia, regardless of its cultural character.

Village Roadshow executives point out that the current restrictions mean that Australia is losing important and expensive projects to other countries. They instance the production of *The Fatal Shore*, an A\$20 million mini-series adaptation of Robert Hughes' book, which was to have been produced in Australia with mostly US finance. Because both the director and scriptwriter were to have been American, it would not qualify under TPS14, even though its cast and crew were predominantly Australian and, it was argued, would this have brought a lot of creative and financial benefits to Australia. The fact that it did not qualify under TPS14 meant that no Australian network would invest and this was enough to bring the project to a halt. This is typical, they argue, of what will happen with increasing frequency in the future as other production sites – New Zealand, South Africa, Spain and Mexico – offer better incentives, better union arrangements and a more benign regulatory environment for off-shore production.

Apart from these activities of studio and project management, concerned mainly with attracting off-shore television productions, Village Roadshow has also engaged in big-budget film investment, with problematic results. It is estimated that the FFC and Village Roadshow may have lost up to A$10 million each on two projects, *Over the Hill* and *Turtle Beach*. This experience does raise the issue of whether the pursuit of a high-budget feature-film strategy, which can only succeed if the elusive major US release is secured and is successful, is a good idea for Australia. Even a cursory examination of the FFC's recent investment history suggests that it is the modestly budgeted projects that succeed better, both aesthetically and financially.

Production Activities of Roadshow Coote and Carroll

The strategy, scale and philosophy of RCC are at the opposite end of the spectrum from its parent company. Founded in 1984, it has chalked up an impressive list of television dramas – mini-series like *True Believers, Barlow and Chambers: A Long Way From Home, The Paper Man, Brides of Christ* and *Frankie's House*, as well as the long-running ABC series *GP*. Many of its projects have been co-produced with the ABC. It is a marriage made in heaven: the expertise of RCC combined with the reputation of the facilities-rich ABC. Between 1988 and 1993 the ABC was virtually the only producer of big-budget short-form drama; the financial problems of the commercial networks dropped licence fees below the level needed to finance it, but, as we have noted, the ABC is able to pay around A$300 000 an hour in licence fees because it pays not in cash but in facilities. This sizeable licence fee, together with one from, say, a UK broadcaster, was enough to satisfy the FFC and in this way it was possible to finance high-budget drama.

With David Hill's 1988 instruction to program 100 hours of local drama a year ringing in its ears (after the much-criticised 1987 figure of about 38 hours), the ABC drama department needed to find a long-running series that would attract an audience. After the failures of the comedy series *The Last Resort* and *House Rules*, the ABC was happy to call on the services of RCC and especially of script expert Sue Masters (ex-Grundys, ex-Home Box Office) to mount an audience-pleasing series (Jacka 1991, pp.28–34, pp.91–4). *GP*, conceived by Masters, filled that gap.

Now in its sixth series, the first two series of *GP* were sold to Thames Television but did not perform very well on British television (*see* Chapter 6). *GP* is made for less than A$200 000 an hour and with a UK sale worth between £20,000 and £50,000 an hour, depending on whether it is an ITV network sale or not, the sale of *GP* in the UK market could be quite lucrative for RCC and for the ABC, who are joint copyright holders (Vecera 1992). With 200 episodes made in total, it was hoped that another

UK broadcaster would pick it up when, after losing the franchise for the London region, Thames ceased to operate in November 1992. In the event it went to the distributor Pavilion, who by mid-1994 had sold it to Spain, Holland, Scandinavia and the UK, where it appeared in half-hour blocks on The Family Channel (Vecera 1994). In both Ireland and the UK, some episodes of *GP* were considered too controversial for the afternoon slots in which they were broadcast; these dealt with themes such as incest, drug use, and transsexualism.

RCC is a small and lean organisation. In the early 1990s it had only three permanent senior personnel, producer Matt Carroll, Sue Masters (who moved to head the ABC in Melbourne in 1994) and general manager and deal-maker, Kim Vecera, together with their secretarial staff. As long as the international market for mini-series was strong, RCC aimed to make one or two prestigious projects a year as well as to continue regular production of long-running serials. The bigger-budget productions, which cost about A$1.2 million an hour, were typically financed one-quarter through Australian pre-sale (usually to the ABC), one-quarter by FFC investment, one-third through UK pre-sale, and about one-sixth by other investors (including the ABC). The UK pre-sale was held against the UK rights; extra returns typically came from markets in Europe, the US (usually to the Public Broadcasting Service or one of the arts cable channels) and Canada, New Zealand and perhaps Asia. Such returns would be modest and slow to arrive. But as long as the UK market held up and the FFC or some similar support mechanism survived, the strategy made sense, both financially and culturally. RCC projects are marked by a high level of Australian creative control and Australian cultural commitment; they are usually written and directed by Australians and the number of imported actors is kept to a minimum.

This pattern of mini-series financing characterised two contrasting, but each in its way successful, examples of international co-production entered into by Roadshow Coote and Carroll in the early 1990s: *Brides of Christ*, made in 1990 and *Frankie's House,* made in 1992. The first was originated by Penny Chapman, head of ABC drama, before her appointment to the ABC, and Australian creative control of the project was virtually total. It was produced by RCC for the ABC with a sizeable pre-sale to Channel 4 for broadcast rights in Britain and for other European rights. There was also a smaller pre-sale to RTE, Ireland, for whom the subject matter was of particular interest. While the Irish broadcaster did not insist on the casting of Irish actor Brenda Fricker, her presence in it was very attractive to them and also provided a significant selling-point for the program in Britain after the great success of the film *My Left Foot* in which she starred. The budget was A$6.2 million for six hours, of which the FFC invested nearly 50 per cent.

Brides of Christ rated 30 in Australia, which made it, in these terms, the most successful drama ever broadcast by the ABC. The repeats did almost as well (it had a third run on the Ten Network) and it sold well on video. It received uniform critical approval. It also rated extremely well on Channel 4 in the UK, gaining an audience of 6 million – high for Channel 4 which, on average, attracts a 10 per cent audience share. The UK television critics, however, had a field-day, almost to a person heaping derision upon it in the newspapers.

As argued in Chapter 6, this sort of press climate for Australian programs in Britain has less to do with either the merit of programs or their acceptance by UK audiences than with the peculiar game of Australian-bashing in which British journalists love to indulge. *Today's* critic (24 January 1992) called it 'a load of old nun-sense'; the *Daily Express* repeated the awful pun in titling its article 'Novice drama is simply nun-sense' and commenting: 'Television's first religious soap opera ... was apparently a huge critical success Down Under. With a cast of saucy ladies wearing designer habits, it perhaps titillated the jackeroos' (21 January 1992). There was much more of the same with an occasional more sober piece that praised it; for example, a commentator in *The Sunday Times* said: 'It's all done rather movingly, avoiding schmaltz and conveying a real sense of the conflict and confusion brought about by sex education' (14 February 1992). This critical reception contrasts strongly with the US where *Brides of Christ* was sold to Arts and Entertainment (A&E) (*see* Chapter 8).

Apart from Brenda Fricker (and an Irish orchestra playing the sound-track music), all other aspects of the program were Australian – writers Sue Smith and John Alsop, director Ken Cameron and all the rest of the crew and cast. The theme and mode of telling remained unambiguously Australian and the idiom and cultural feel were very local. Nevertheless, its story of moral upheavals in the Roman Catholic Church in the 1960s, set against the wider changes that were occurring, was recognisable enough in other places for it to gain wide acceptance internationally.

Frankie's House was a somewhat different story. It was a co-production between RCC, A&E and Initial Productions of the UK. RCC brought the ABC into the project and the ABC took the Australian broadcast rights; Initial Productions brought in Anglia Television, which took the UK broadcast rights. ITEL, the distribution arm of Anglia, gave a distribution advance against the territories in the rest of the world. The FFC were also equity investors. *Frankie's House* is a four-hour mini-series, based on the Vietnam War recollections of English freelance press photographer Tim Page. The drama centres around the relationship between Page and Sean Flynn, and is a tale of men testing their masculinity through risky exploits in a war zone. The Vietnamese characters are little more than background, and women have subsidiary roles.

A British writer, Andy Armitage, worked closely with Tim Page on the script, although Page was outraged at the distortions of the final product. Page was played by British actor Iain Glen; Sean Flynn by American 'brat-packer' Kevin Dillon. It was directed by Australian television action-drama director Peter Fisk (*Police Rescue*) and line-produced by an Australian, Greg Ricketson. Producer and executive producer credits were evenly split between British and Australian personnel. Shooting took place mainly in Thailand and Australia with a largely Australian crew, and post-production was in Australia.

While largely Australian-executed, *Frankie's House* was very much an English project. The Tim Page story was well known in the UK because there had been a widely watched television documentary about him in the year before *Frankie's House* appeared. Several supporting Australian characters were added to help with the FFC investment, but most of the advance publicity in the UK represented it as a British series with only an occasional mention of Australian involvement. The UK critics were less than uniformly positive about the program but the criticism was not directed to its Australian-ness but to its overly 'boy's own' character. Typical was the *Observer*, which said: 'There are scenes that convey that war is hell, and ones that portray that for some of the press, it was a hell of a lot of fun, apart from the hang-overs'. In the US, while it received the priceless promotion of a *New York Times TV Guide* front cover, featured a high-profile US actor and a theme immediately legible to US viewers, and received wide and almost uniformly positive critical reviews, *Frankie's House* was somewhat of a disappointment, probably because it traversed ground already so thoroughly tilled in US film and television, and appealed only to a male audience.

These two expensive and well-executed mini-series were set up when the European television market was still buoyant. However, in the mid-1990s the changed European environment meant that RCC began to orient itself towards cheaper 13-, 26- and 39-part series. While continuing with *GP* they also developed a country police series, *Law of the Land,* for the Nine Network. By mid-1994 it was into its third 13-part series.

With *Law of the Land* Roadshow Coote and Carroll moves away from mini-series to cater to the world demand for long-running series.
(Cover of *TV World*, March 1994.)

Within the Village Roadshow organisation we see two very different internationalisation strategies. One emphasises the modest budget and indigenous flavour and recognises the necessity of overseas financial input, while retaining a high level of local control and local specificity. The other strategy is to try to make Australia an attractive location for off-shore production, especially from the US. This range of production sits alongside the strong partnerships the organisation has forged; the stable profits generated through theatre exhibition; continuing holdings in Australian FM radio; expansion into video games, multimedia and the South East Asian multiplex business; and the export of its theme park expertise. It seems that Village Roadshow will continue to be one of Australia's dominant media businesses.

CRAWFORDS

With a track record of more than 50 years, Crawfords is one of the oldest and most respected production companies in Australia. Before moving into television in 1954, it was Australia's major producer of radio serials and the company founders, siblings Hector and Dorothy Crawford, are undoubtedly revered figures in the history of Australian television. Moran persuasively makes the case that even though it is often argued that the ABC was the nursery of Australian television drama, the claim 'is much more accurately made of Crawford Productions ... It is no exaggeration to say that, without both *Homicide* and Crawfords, neither the television industry nor the new feature-film production would have begun when it did' (Moran 1993, p.89). Certainly it seems that virtually every television-drama producer, writer and director over 40 years of age has spent at least some time doing a stint at Crawfords; it has been as important a training ground as the ABC. It was a successful family company until 1987 and it is sad to observe, as Moran does in his later book on television drama, that '[t]he fate of the company since 1987 illustrates both the financial vicissitudes of the times and the extent to which such a company has had to adapt to survive in the new economic environment' (Moran 1993, p.516).

For the first 30 years of its existence as a television production company, it occupied a central place in the industry in Australia. It pioneered police shows like the popular *Homicide*, *Division 4* and *Matlock Police* in the 1960s and early 1970s; it made an early entry into soap opera with the long-running serial, *The Box* in 1974; in 1976 it innovated again with the Second World War serial, *The Sullivans*, which ran for 520 episodes and raised long-form drama to new heights of production values and cultural authenticity; and it was one of the earliest production companies to see the potential of 10BA as a vehicle for high-quality mini-series with *All The Rivers Run* in 1982. Crawfords sailed through the early to mid-1980s on the back of productions like the glamorous *Carson's Law*, and *Cop Shop*, another successful police serial, and with further 10BA mini-series. Much of the Crawfords catalogue has great staying power; for example, both *The Sullivans* and *All the Rivers Run* continue to perform well around the world.

The company has always had its own extensive production facilities, unlike many newer production companies. In 1981 Crawfords occupied a two-hectare site at Box Hill in Victoria. In the post-fordist times of the late 1980s, the necessity to keep the facilities occupied became something of an albatross around the company's neck. Since Hector Crawford's retirement from the company in 1987, there have been a large number of ownership and management changes, which also have created some problems. By this time, Crawfords had a very valuable program library of 2600 hours of television material, which made it an attractive target for acquisition. In 1987, it was bought by the Ariadne Group, which then ran into financial difficulties; Crawfords was again sold, this time to Bruce Gordon and David Maine of Oberon Broadcasting and the Asperon Group. Ian Bradley was managing director for a period in the late 1980s – he had been instrumental in Crawfords' successful move into 10BA-financed mini-series. When he departed to head up the drama division at Grundys, he was replaced by Terry Ohlsson as managing director and Peter Herbert as head of production (Moran 1993, pp.518–9).

Ian Bradley's plan was to improve Crawfords' facilities and to aim directly at the international market (Hawker 1988, p.19). This strategy was continued under Terry Ohlsson and in 1989 the company earned approximately A$6.6 million in export revenue and was ranked as 313 in Australia's top 500 exporters (McElvogue 1989, p.1). It produced between 70 and 80 hours of product in 1989, but even at this rate the Box Hill facilities were underused and management announced plans to boost levels of production to 200 hours within the following two years. One-third of production capacity was taken up by *The Flying Doctors* but although Crawfords had the facilities and production know-how, the company needed concepts and ideas from outside (Prisk 1990, p.10).

In 1991, which was also the year Hector Crawford died, Oberon became the sole owner of Crawfords and spent A$5 million on building new studios, a decision that may have been ill-advised given the constant pressure of keeping the existing facilities occupied. This was the height of the company's prosperity in recent times; *The Flying Doctors* was making excellent overseas sales and the Crawfords catalogue had been sold to the Kirch Group (*see* Chapter 7) and in other territories. The reasoning behind the expansion was that as well as continuing with the production of series, the company would diversify into co-productions with overseas partners, game shows, sitcoms and telemovies (Maddox 1991a, p.ii).

In 1990 Crawfords and Ian McFadyen's Media Arts had formed a new group, Crawfords Media International, to develop new comedy and drama for the local market. The popular and groundbreaking multicultural sitcom, *Acropolis Now*, which was a spin-off from the hit Australian stage show, *Wogs out of Work*, was also made at this time. And Crawfords became involved with Action Time, a subsidiary of Zenith Productions of the UK, to make *Cluedo*, and other game shows, although this association did not continue. In 1992 they began development of eight telemovies to be co-produced, financed and internationally marketed as a package. In 1994 this package came to fruition as six telemovies called *The Feds*, with pre-sales to the Nine Network, TVNZ and a UK distribution guarantee.

Crawfords' main customers are the UK, Germany, Belgium, Japan, New Zealand, and The Netherlands, which is the company's best market (Ohlsson and Samulenok 1992). Countries in Latin America take programs like *The Sullivans,* because they fit into the *telenovela* mould. Packages, which may include a program like *The Flying Doctors*, are sold into markets like Latin America because it is hard to cover costs otherwise. The old Crawfords catalogue is still active with sales of programs like *The Sullivans* and *Carson's Law* to the UK, Ireland, Italy and US cable television, and children's programs such as *The Henderson Kids* and *Zoo Family* have also sold to US pay television (Bland and Cook 1992). However, Crawfords do not easily find a market in Japan, India or Hong Kong, where action-based drama is popular, rather than the largely character-based Crawfords productions.

In recent years, *The Flying Doctors* has undoubtedly been Crawfords' most successful export and has virtually kept the company afloat. Its cancellation by the Nine Network in 1992, when it was still doing well in overseas markets, was a severe blow. It has had success in most of the markets in which it has been sold, including Turkey and, for a time, the UK, where it gained an audience of 10 million viewers on the BBC on Friday nights. But the market where it has made most cultural impact is The Netherlands (*see* Chapter 7). It is also sold extensively throughout Asia. There is no special international version of *The Flying Doctors*, although the producers are influenced by various considerations when writing for the overseas market. For example, in Scandinavia the pub setting is a problem (Ohlsson and Samulenok 1992) and one episode containing a cricket match was tailored to allow for the fact that unlike the average Australian viewer, a large percentage of the eventual audience was not familiar with cricket (Maddox 1991b, p.viii).

Acropolis Now has sold to a few countries overseas including Greece (its characters are Greek), but the Crawfords managers were of the view that it is hard for audiences outside Australia to warm to the characters, and reported that in Britain they were considered too heavily drawn (Ohlsson and Samulenok 1992). The program has found more acceptance in Latin America (Bland and Cook 1992). Unlike *The Flying Doctors*, which is deficit financed, *Acropolis Now* did not depend on overseas sales for its viability, as it was fully financed by licence fee from the Seven Network. But in general the existence of the whole company does depend on export; about 40 per cent of income in 1992 came from outside Australia (Ohlsson and Samulenok 1992).

Crawfords has a close relationship with the Kirch Group in Germany, who bought the entire back catalogue. The Kirch Group is a very powerful force on the German media scene (*see* Chapter 7) and owns one of the two major private free-to-air stations as well as various cable channels. In 1991, Crawfords entered in to a co-production arrangement with one of the Kirch subsidiaries, Beta-Taurus, to produce the children's series, *Half Way Across the Galaxy and Turn Left*. This program was subsequently sold in several other territories in Europe, including Britain. The series was shown in 1994 in Britain twice a week in the 4 pm time slot and became one of the most popular children's television programs on British television.

In 1993 another management upheaval occurred at Crawfords when Terry Ohlsson resigned and was replaced by John Kearney, previously financial controller. In this year many Crawfords staff were retrenched, reflecting the impact of the cancellation of *The Flying Doctors*. It had a temporary stay of execution when Crawfords was given a chance to revamp it as *RFDS* (Royal Flying Doctor Service). The changes, though thoroughgoing, were not enough to save it.

This story reflects the weaknesses of the Crawfords' strategy in a globalised, post-fordist environment. With the huge overheads associated with keeping the studios going, the company relied very heavily on a mainstay like *The Flying Doctors*. Its cancellation and the protracted failure to find a replacement puts Crawfords' viability under a temporary cloud. The other disadvantage for the company is that traditionally it has not produced soap opera unlike, say, Grundys, and thus has no volume television to which to anchor its other activities. However, there is no doubt that Crawfords has a proud history, and even in the more uncertain years since 1987, has produced a solid and diverse portfolio of product with a good export record.

5

Production Companies II

CHILDREN'S TELEVISION PRODUCERS

The production and trade of programs made specifically for children and young people occupies a particular and growing niche in world television. The format has its own cycle of international awards for excellence (for example, Kinderfest at the Berlin Film Festival and the Prix Jeunesse), an international community of advocates and specialist executives (as evidenced in such events as the World Summit on Television and Children held in Melbourne in March 1995, hosted by the Australian Children's Television Foundation), an extensive research community and literature that canvasses the specificity of the format, and a well-established debate in television systems throughout the world concerning the needs and rights of children. Children's television is now an established international format, because it is assumed by programmers and buyers that this kind of material is more accessible and universal in its appeal, carrying with it less culturally specific elements and viewable with fewer culturally and socially specific expectations. On the other hand, it is a format that traditionally has been regarded as only marginally commercially exploitable because of the strong regulatory and ethical inhibitions against advertising to children.

Australia is a significant player in world children's television. The field is dominated by the Australian Children's Television Foundation (ACTF), but a wide range of producers is engaged, including the internationally acclaimed specialist animation from the Yoram Gross Studios. While the financial profile for producers of children's programs locally is relatively marginal, the international sales possibilities are very high. Most major children's programs made in Australia recently have enjoyed international sales success. Critical acclaim for Australian programs is a regular occurrence – the ACTF has won more than 45 national and international awards, while small producers like David Elfick/Palm Beach Pictures won Kinderfest's Best Drama production at the Berlin Film Festival in 1994.

The structure of regulation and production in Australia for children has strengths that in some respects are unmatched elsewhere in the world. Within the general liberalisation of broadcasting regulation seen in the *Broadcasting Services Act (1992)*, the only mandated regulations that continued from the old Australian Broadcasting Tribunal were those for Australian content and for children, so that in the new regime, the most detailed imposed regulations pertain to children. Advertising in so-called 'C-time' is restricted to five minutes per half-hour (compared to advertising time ceilings of 11 minutes 50 seconds per hour in general, and 12 minutes per hour in prime time), and has a variety of other qualitative contraints designed to take account of the cognitive development of children (for instance, toys must be shown with children handling them, rather than magically performing tricks without human intervention, and the hidden costs of toys, like batteries, must be included in the commercial). The Australian Broadcasting Authority's draft changes to Australian content regulation in 1994 have also strengthened children's television, with the quota for local C-time programming doubled (ABA 1994a). As in the relation between Australian content regulation and the strengths of the production industry, the relation between regulation and the flow-on effects to production for children has been clear. This regime has brought international response, with the decision in 1992 for broadcasters in the Asian region to adopt them as a model for regulatory initiatives in their countries.

It has also had strong political support. The delivery of 1993 election pledges through the Distinctly Australian funding initiatives during 1993–5 (ALP 1993) saw the federal government recognise that the 'need for television to respond more adequately and imaginatively to children's needs is supported by policy-makers, producers and broadcasters alike'. The ACTF attracted additional funding and became the 'national institution of excellence for co-operative ventures with other sectors of the film industry'. The federal government's major cultural policy statement, *Creative Nation*, extended this in 1994 to encompass multimedia initiatives for children.

The Australian Children's Television Foundation

A body established as a result of both federal and Victorian government support and incorporated in 1982, the ACTF produces, commissions and distributes children's television programming, as well as acting as a kind of think-tank and clearing house for children's television advocacy. The driving impetus behind the ACTF is Dr Patricia Edgar who, as a public lobbyist for better television for Australian children, transformed a production backwater into an international force. Edgar had had a previous career as a media academic and advocate for regulation to support children's television, and was always hard-headed about the industry forces militating against the format. While Australian networks now must fill a quota of 16 hours of first release 'quality' children's television *per annum*, Edgar says they remain unimpressed by its advertising revenue potential and therefore remain somewhat inveigled and passive investors.

Edgar countered this by drawing together a powerful board and creative participation, including industry figures such as producer Steve Vizard and writer Tony Morphett and public patrons such as Janet Holmes à Court and Hazel Hawke. It was the support of Holmes à Court's private company Heytesbury Holdings that allowed the very successful series *Lift Off* to go ahead (Moran 1993, p.509; ACTF 1992). Paul Keating personally endorsed the World Summit on Television and Children. Barbara Bush, when visiting Australia with her husband, US President George Bush, visited the ACTF (*Australian*, 4 March 1994). Bruce Gyngell, one-time Nine Network chairman and the *eminence grise* of Australian television, is also an outspoken advocate for the ACTF, saying that it will soon become 'a world children's multimedia organisation' (*Sydney Morning Herald: The Guide*, 7–13 March 1994, p.7).

In 1994, the foundation had 14 full-time staff and contract staff and consultants for specific tasks such as script editing or marketing and publicity (ACTF 1993, p.15). Its operating costs are covered by federal and state funds, while development and production funding is sought through the usual cocktail of state bodies and national and international co-productions and pre-sales.

The ACTF has experienced a distinct upswing in its production activities in the 1990s. What it has done successfully is to broker a unique link between the production industry (attracting top-quality creative personnel from mainstream drama to develop concepts and ultimately scripts in programming workshops) and social and public-policy objectives, while shaping both. As Edgar says: 'We have learned strategies for dealing with the problem of the provision of children's programming, which much of the rest of the world has not yet developed, so they are looking toward Australia as a model for what might be done' (*Australian*, 4 March 1994). This claim is certainly borne out by the figures: the ACTF has produced more than 115 hours of programming, which has been screened in more than 90 countries, and it has received many international awards (Commonwealth of Australia 1994, p.52).

Lift Off has made a considerable impact internationally. In Britain on Channel 4, for example, it consistently outrated *Teenage Mutant Ninja Turtles* (*Australian*, 4 March 1994). It has been purchased by RTP in Portugal and educational broadcasters in Canada such as Access Alberta and Knowledge Network in British Columbia. *Sky Trackers*, the movie and television series, was created when the CSIRO went to the foundation looking for a series to encourage girls into science. It has been sold into a diverse range of territories including Finland, Malaysia, Bahrain, The Netherlands, Kuwait, Denmark, Asian satellite services, Iceland, Romania, Turkey, the Czech Republic and Slovakia. *Round the Twist* and *Round the Twist 2* were two other high-profile ACTF series. The first was rated one of the two most popular children's programs in the UK, reaching an audience of 5 million in 1993 when screened on BBC 1, which also partnered the ACTF in releasing *Round the Twist* video tapes. While countries such as Germany, Austria, Italy, France (where the first series was screened three times in one year), Portugal, Ireland, Greece, Zimbabwe and Thailand have purchased the *Round the Twist* series, the accents as well as its earthy humour, according to Edgar, kept it out of the US. There is also a cultural question, particularly in Scandinavia, of whether fantasy is accepted as a premise for children's drama.

As ACTF material has found wider acceptance, it has moved to take direct responsibility for distribution. As marketing manager Jenny Buckland describes it, by establishing direct sales contacts in some territories, the ACTF was able to maximise revenue as well as target potential co-producers and sources of pre-sales. While distribution agents are still used in some territories, such as Latin America, direct involvement by the ACTF in international markets has seen an increase in co-productions – such as its partnership with the BBC in *The Genie from Down Under*, a 13-part comedy-drama series featuring an Australian genie and his British owner and their ensuing cultural clashes. In 1993, the ACTF won an award for Best Marketing Campaign by an Independent Producer for the *Lift Off* campaign at the *TV World* Marketing Awards, which recognise independent producers who sell their own product internationally (ACTF 1993, p.39).

Another aspect of marketing is the creation of an ancillary market in educational and commercial merchandising, a key strategy for programs that attract low advertising revenue. More than 650 000 publications and 65 000 videos, which articulate with classroom and daycare activities, have spun off from ACTF productions up to 1994, together with many units of commercial merchandise such as clothing, toys, music, bed linen, gift wrap and cards (Commonwealth of Australia 1994, p.52). Although merchandising returns only about 1 per cent of a typical production budget, it is an integral part of the foundation's educational mission, and Edgar sees promising links between screen exposure and merchandising sales, with real potential in those overseas consumer markets that are very much larger than Australia's (*Encore*, 18 November 1993, p.42). The ACTF may diversify into feature-film production and game shows (their first, the 13-episode *Lift Off Game Show*, screened on the ABC in 1993), and the *Creative Nation* initiatives in multimedia will see it developing in this way as well.

Other producers of children's programming

In the 1990s children's production has burgeoned. Yoram Gross Film Studios, an established specialist producer of animated children's films, has crossed successfully to television with the production and distribution of a 26-part television series based on its *Blinky Bill* films. Sandra Gross, studio director, says the company is unlikely to continue in film as the costs of development and marketing of television series are not much more than a film, and the revenue potential is higher (*Encore*, 23 May 1994). The series was cleared in 85 per cent of the US syndication market in 1994 for a start in September 1994 (that is, it is placed with American broadcasters covering 85 per cent of the population), making it, according to marketing director Tim Brooke-Hunt, 'the most profitable Australian series or mini-series sold to American television' (Bright 1994, p.11). *Blinky Bill* came into the US market at the right time, because it was opening up to non-violent, pro-social children's material as a result of Congressional intervention and Federal Communications Commission regulatory pressure.

Western Australia-based Barron Films, founded by Paul Barron, concentrates on high-quality television series for children and families, as well as social-realist films and adult television drama. It became a public company in Perth in 1986 in order to raise its capital base (Moran 1993, p.511). Before that, its first success was *Falcon Island* (1981), a children's series. The A\$3 million children's series *Clowning Around* sold to the UK, Japan, Belgium, Scandinavia, Holland and Denmark (*Sunday Herald Sun Extra*, 14 November 1993). Barron's other children's comedy-adventure series *Ship to Shore* is a model of internationalised children's production – a co-production with the Nine Network and FFC backing in Australia, and with the BBC, two German networks and the Public Broadcasting Service in the US. The second series was done with the ABC in Australia.

Jonathan Shiff/Westbridge has specialised in children's television since 1988; its biggest production was the A\$3 million adventure series *Ocean Girl*. Backing included script development from Film Queensland and production funding from Film Victoria and the FFC, Sweden's SVT and France's Teleimage, which also has distribution rights for France. *Ocean Girl* sold to Disney in the US, and to the BBC for a record sum for a children's series in the UK (*Sunday Age*, 29 May 1994). Roger Mirams/Pacific Productions, a Sydney-based producer of children's programming since the 1950s, shot the A\$8 million *Mission Top Secret* in seven countries. This high-tech adventure series features actors and storylines from each country's location. Pacific Productions' 1990 *South Pacific Adventures* had financing from Quartier Latin (France), TVNZ, Espanol TV, VARA in The Netherlands and Tyne Tees in the UK, and distribution with the European Children's Film Corporation. Media World Features, another company involved in animated features, was financed by the FFC and by pre-sales from the BBC and Connexion Film (Germany) to produce an animated mini-series based on their film *The Silver Brumby*.

The Beyond International Group produces *Deepwater Haven*, a children's drama series with a curious mix of French and New Zealand actors, in Auckland. It has pre-sales to TF1 (France), Ravensburger (Germany) and TVNZ. Millennium Productions' *Miraculous Mellops*, a fantasy-science fiction family series, has sold well overseas including to Channel 4 in the UK and RTP in Portugal and was screened in the UK in 1992. *The Adventures of Skippy* and *Animal Park,* produced by Warner Roadshow and filmed in Queensland, have done well overseas, the latter was screened in 70 countries (Moran 1993, p.62).

THE BEYOND INTERNATIONAL GROUP

A young company among leading Australian television producers, the Beyond International Group (BIG) came together first under a different name in 1984, when the ABC axed *Towards 2000,* a four-year-old popular science and technology program, because it was becoming too expensive. Its presenter, Iain Finlay, together with reporters Carmel Travers and Chris Ardill-Guinness formed a production company, CIC, joined documentary producer Phil Gerlach and sold the format to Channel 7; the licence fee didn't cover the cost of production so the company retained overseas rights. Gerlach's trip to MIPCOM in 1985 convinced him that self-distribution was the best option (*Encore*, 13–26 April 1989). In 1988, the company's name changed from CIC to Beyond International Group because of confusion with the Dutch company Cinema International Corporation. Before Gerlach became involved, he and partner Mikael Borglund had owned a management company, G&S Management, which was involved in the music industry. As BIG grew, that company was disbanded and Borglund ultimately became BIG's managing director some years later.

BIG has progressed into a highly focussed specialised production and distribution house, whose corporate portfolio also includes merchandising, music publishing, corporate video and separate media production groups in the US and New Zealand. It is a public unlisted company with approximately 200 employees, almost half of whom work on the production of *Beyond 2000*. It has an international profile by necessity as well as design. Learning from the original experience of *Towards 2000*, the company was aware of the bottleneck that occurs when three or four decision-makers at the major networks are capable of determining the fate of independent producers. BIG's principals have always maintained their strategic vision of being the *Entertainment Tonight* of popular, information-based programming (Kagan 1994). Their combination of training in solid craft skills and serious information programming with entrepreneurial ambition has allowed much of that vision to be realised.

From the mid-1980s, the group that became BIG produced programs in differing formats, participated in international co-productions and became involved in distribution domestically and internationally, but its resounding success is the *Beyond 2000* format which, since 1985, has been sold in over 90 countries and dubbed in 10 languages, has an international audience reach of 50 million, and has generated an estimated A$40 million in export revenue in 1991–2 (*Australian*, 18 July 1992). *Beyond 2000* exemplifies the rule that 'overseas material is purchased to fill holes [in the schedule]', in distribution manager Chris Gunn's words (*Encore*, 8 December 1993–19 January 1994), but that domestic success also is important, because buyers look for that to vouchsafe program viability.

In the US, its most important overseas market, the *Beyond 2000* format filled a gap in actuality programming, but it had a tortuous passage to stable acceptance (*see* Chapter 8). It could find its way into the American system only through the fledgling Fox Network in 1988 as *Beyond Tomorrow*. It ran for two series and was significant at the time as one of the few network series produced outside the US. It then built a stable base on the Discovery cable network, with additional play time on the Disney channel and the Spanish cable network Telemondo. Running parallel with the US contract were sales to Hong Kong, Latin America and Mexico. In these territories, segments of the show are recorded in home languages with indigenous presenters, and the Australian-produced stories are dubbed or subtitled. The first sale to the UK was through TVS; it was also purchased later by BSkyB. In France, *Beyond 2000* did not do well because, it seems, the French do not like presenter-led programs and re-packaging and dubbing the program proved too expensive. However, BIG did sell *Just For the Record*, an action-adventure magazine format, to the French channel Canal Plus. As well, the successful *Beyond 2000* format was cloned by the company in the production of *Fish International*, an infotainment program on fishing, which competes in an extremely crowded US market for fishing shows on the Prime cable network.

BIG has also involved itself in predominantly European co-production partnerships. In 1989, BIG and the BBC embarked upon the co-produced *Climate in Crisis*, a strong environmental documentary, and then the four-part series *Great Wall of Iron*, a documentary about the Chinese military, which was pre-sold to Network Ten in Australia, TV3 in New Zealand, Discovery in the US, the BBC, and Reitalia in Italy. BIG has also ventured into the production of drama series, mini-series and children's program-ming, with somewhat less success. The children's series *Bright Sparks* typifies the Beyond International strategy – animated robots take journeys around the world exploring science and technology. *Chances*, an adult drama series featuring nudity and outlandish storylines, was a failure and its small territory sales reflect this: Thailand, Turkey, Finland, Iceland, Cyprus and BSkyB. Its forays into local feature film-making virtually began and ceased with *The Crossing* in 1989, whose failure led the company to emphasise the more stable activity of distribution.

Beyond International established its distribution arm in 1990. It is one of two significant Australian-owned independent international dis-tributors; the other is Southern Star International. In the 1990s Beyond was sales agent for the first two FFC Film Funds, and Southern Star for the third and fourth. Between them, the two organisations handled 35 per cent of the 53 features made in 1991–2 and 1992–3 (AFC 1994a, p.68). Beyond has also handled art-house fare such as *Golden Braid*, *The Last Days of Chez Nous* and *The Story of Xinghua*, the first time an Australian film-sales company has represented world rights to a Chinese film (*Encore*, 9–22 May 1994), as well as higher profile commercial successes like *Strictly Ballroom*, *The Heartbreak Kid* and *Gross Misconduct*. Of course, a substantial part of Beyond Distribution's work is selling its own television product throughout the world, but between 30 and 40 per cent of what it sells is produced by other companies. BIG's philosophy, distribution and domestic and international production have been successfully directed to identifying niches in the complex mix of international television.

SOUTHERN STAR

Southern Star is a lean, diversified operation with an integrated approach to production and distribution through film, television and video, and merchandising. Like most front-running independents, this enables Southern Star to balance higher against lower risk ventures. In 1988, after a management buyout by Neil Balnaves of the Taft-Hardie Group (whose major shareholders included the Great American Broadcasting Co. and James Hardie Industries), Southern Star reorganised into six operating units: Southern Star Entertainment, Southern Star International, Southern Star Productions, Southern Star Home Video, Southern Star Merchandising and Southern Star Duplitek.

As we have noted in the previous section, Southern Star International and Beyond International are the only two significant Australian-owned independent international distributors, and both companies were appointed as international sales agents for FFC-funded Film Fund titles during the 1990s. Ten per cent of the Southern Star International's catalogue is the company's own product, for which it holds the world rights, accounting for approximately 20 per cent of world sales. The division represents New Line in Australia, New Zealand and South East Asia, US-based The Movie Group, Bossa Entertainment and Revcom, and the back catalogue of Qintex Entertainment, as well as titles from the Australian Children's Television Foundation. Southern Star Productions is based in Los Angeles and concentrates on animation, making programs such as *Berenstein Bears* and *Peter Pan and the Pirates* for the Fox Network.

Southern Star Duplitek concentrates on video and audio tape duplication; with Southern Star Merchandising handling BBC, Colombia Tri-Star and Paramount merchandising in South East Asia and a significant proportion of the division's business coming from Hanna-Barbera. The Hanna-Barbera catalogue (for which Southern Star holds the rights in Australia, New Zealand and Asia – with the exception of Japan) is significant not only because of the income generated by broadcast rights, but also because of the massive sell-through market (that is, video purchase rather than rental), for Hanna-Barbera videos. Southern Star maintained distribution rights in Asia, as well as the rights to home video and merchandising, after Hanna-Barbera was sold to Disney. Its programs make up about 60 per cent of the catalogue for Southern Star International. Southern Star Home Video is joint licensee for all Cinema International Corporation (CIC) sell-through product. It distributes all its in-house productions through CIC for the rental market. The Home Video operation generates 30 per cent of rentals from Southern Star titles, 35 per cent from Hanna-Barbera, and 35 per cent from independents. By 1994 the company had created Southern Star Enterprises, which handles video merchandising and film sales.

Southern Star Entertainment is a broad corporate umbrella for established independent producers: Errol Sullivan/Southern Star Sullivan, Hal McElroy/Southern Star McElroy and Sandra Levy and John Edwards/Southern Star Xanadu. The production arms run as partnerships, and Southern Star meets all running costs, producer and staff salaries, finance and administration as well as publicity. The value of this umbrella model is apparent when some of the high-budget international productions engaged in by these producers are considered. McElroy and McElroy's mini-series *Last Frontier* (1986) drew high network licence fees in both Australia and the US and a co-production deal with Zenith in the UK, and Southern Star controlled most territories for distribution. It served as a perfect model as it travelled internationally and promoted growth across the company through video release and a 22-hour series spin-off. Less successful examples illustrate the other side of the coin. The financing of Sullivan's *Ring of Scorpio* (1990) and McElroy and McElroy's *Which Way Home* during a period when licence fees had substantially decreased and when production costs were rising meant that most of the lucrative distribution territories were already committed in the financing phase, leaving few from which the deficit, let alone profits, could be secured. Even so, *Which Way Home* drew the highest ratings for a Turner Television program in 1990 (*Encore*, 30 August 1990).

A good deal of Southern Star's major co-productions have been with the ABC and the BBC, including the mini-series *Four Minute Mile* (1988), and *Children of the Dragon* (1991), and the series *Police Rescue* (1990–). The *Police Rescue* pilot was originally made for the BBC. The program is a co-production between Southern Star Xanadu and the ABC, with a pre-sale to the BBC, which retains the series rights for Britain and all markets excluding North America and some Asian territories in return for a substantial contribution to the current A$7 million budget. For their initial financial contribution to the series in 1990, the BBC maintained control over script, director and cast (*Encore*, 15–28 March 1990, p.5). The program is driven by its ongoing success in Australia, even though it is popular in the UK and is now selling well throughout Europe.

By the end of 1994 *Police Rescue* had sold in 39 territories, including France (where it is broadcast at 2.30 pm on Saturdays on TF1), Denmark, The Netherlands, Spain and South Africa. Southern Star have been particularly successful with it in the Asian market, and sold it to the Philippines (a very difficult market because of the dominance of US imports), as well as to Malaysia, Indonesia and Brunei. In these Islamic countries, where it is a very big hit, the sexual and romantic storylines apparently present no problems.

It continues to do well in the UK (it has averaged over 40 per cent share, peaking in 1994 at 47 per cent, and has been programmed since 1991 on BBC1 on Saturday nights at 8.30 pm). This high rating indicates that in the UK at least it appeals to audiences of both sexes across all age groups. The program's success has been built on a recognised format, a variation of the cop show, but with a 1990s balance between action and personal storylines, and the development of the star profile of Gary Sweet, who has become a 'household name' in Britain (Frost 1992). Consistently but quietly, it builds on the scenic and character stereotypes about Australia enjoyed so much by UK audiences by showcasing the natural and built environment of Sydney, and the unsentimental but still emotional 'action man' character of Gary Sweet.

In 1993, Southern Star was responsible for *Blue Heelers*, a new and successful long-running series produced by Southern Star/Hal McElroy for the Seven Network. The network had been looking for a replacement for its key Australian series, *A Country Practice* – a series built around a close-knit rural community – which finally was beginning to run out of steam after twelve years, and which was cancelled in 1994. In 1991 the Seven Network gave A$10 000 to six independent producers to come up with a premise and characters for a drama to fit the 7.30 time slot. Two-and-a-half years later the Hal McElroy company produced the pilot of *Blue Heelers*, a series set around a country police station in Victoria (Monaghan 1994).

The sergeant in charge of the station is played by John Wood who, some years earlier, had helped to make *Rafferty's Rules,* a series based on a small-town magistrate, a success for the Seven Network. The other characters are the younger members of the police force at the station, including an attractive young female police officer, and assorted town and country folk. The general feel of the program is very much *A Country*

Practice revisited and this seems to be succeeding with audiences all over again; in 1994 it was the highest rating Australian drama across all channels. At the 1994 MIPCOM, *Blue Heelers* sold to 30 territories in Asia and parts of Europe (George 1994), and it may be set to repeat the international success of *A Country Practice* and *The Flying Doctors*.

Southern Star's international success is based upon the synergies achieved through targeted niche marketing and vertical integration, while producing a range of program types with a sober but firmly commercial commitment to meeting the varying requirements of several markets. It has forged significant links with major distributors throughout the world, particularly in Europe and the US.

FILM AUSTRALIA

Although it has been through several profound metamorphoses over the years, Film Australia can trace its history back to 1911. Currently a government-owned enterprise that is expected to generate up to two-thirds of its own revenue, it started life as as a production unit within the federal government. In 1945, it became a government-owned film-production company modelled on the National Film Board of Canada. In 1956, it became known as the Commonwealth Film Unit (Moran 1991, p.30ff.).

Between 1945 and 1970, when the Australian feature-film industry began its revival, the Commonwealth Film Unit was virtually synonymous with film-making in Australia. It nurtured the documentary tradition, and a significant number of film-makers who went on to play important roles in the film and television industries were trained there. In 1976 the Commonwealth Film Unit became a branch of the Australian Film Commission and took on its present name, Film Australia. This change began a process of slow transformation in its philosophy, as it adjusted to a context in which there was a burgeoning film industry and where television was decisively eclipsing film as a medium for documentary.

In the ten years after 1976, it continued to produce documentaries 'in the national interest' and under contract to government departments and then, in 1987, it was made a government-owned business enterprise working under the directive to become partly self-sufficient from government. However, the mission to produce films and programs in the national interest continued, and the government continued to fund Film Australia under the so-called National Interest Program (NIP). This program is the core of Film Australia's business, and the reason why it is a government-owned company. It is still charged, as in the 1990 annual report, with producing film and television which 'illuminates significant social, cultural and environmental issues, deepening contemporary discourse in the search for self-knowledge as a nation' (George 1991a, p.20).

Since incorporation in 1988, the government has provided two three-year NIP contracts, worth a total of A$36 million over the six years. At the beginning of this period it comprised approximately two-thirds of revenue (*ibid.*). By 1994, overseas sales had assisted in reducing the government input to one-third of revenue (Moir 1994). Sixty-eight programs were made under the first NIP, of which 48 were aired on Australian television.

Until June 1991, Film Australia had an exclusive arrangement with the Commonwealth Government to produce and distribute information films and videos. Since then, the company has competed for this business with private and other public companies. In its first two years as an independent company, 25 per cent of Film Australia's gross marketing revenue came from overseas sales (George 1991b, p.23). Since 1992, according to Bruce Moir, approximately 50 per cent of gross sales revenue comes from overseas television sales; this increase is largely accounted for by an increase in the amount of drama produced, especially the *Girl From Tomorrow* series. The NIP program provides the platform from which to launch international projects, but only those that conform to the NIP philosophy are pursued this way; with other Film Australia productions NIP money is not involved. Serious documentaries like *Mini-Dragons* and *The Race to Save the Planet* used NIP money; the children's science fiction series *The Girl From Tomorrow* did not (George 1991a, p.20).

In the international market-place, Film Australia has a number of selling points. One is its reputation for well-made and family-friendly product with a social conscience. Another is its long experience, and the fact that it is the largest documentary producer and exporter in Australia. In the 1990s it has added to this a depth of expertise in producing for children. A further competitive advantage is the *gravitas* conferred by its status as a quasi-government organisation. Last, it has pioneered a form of international co-production, which it calls the 'consortium model', a convenient way of producing packages of programs with guaranteed foreign markets.

Film Australia has an extensive distribution network and can deliver product into 80 countries, in most cases directly to the end user. In more difficult markets like Japan, which has been traditionally closed to foreign programming, a local agent is used. Film Australia has an extensive back catalogue of 2500 titles, many of which, like nature documentaries, do not age significantly (George 1991b, p.23). In Europe the main markets are the UK, Holland, Scandinavia and France. From the early 1990s, Eastern European countries such as Hungary, the Czech Republic, Slovakia and Poland became more important and in 1994 Film Australia undertook Australia's first co-production with Poland – the 26-part children's series, *Spellbinder* (Barlow 1994, p.21). In Asia, the significant markets are Japan and Korea, Singapore, Malaysia and Star TV in Hong Kong. Japan is an important source of co-production for Film Australia; its semi-government status is a distinct advantage in its relationship with NHK, the main public broadcaster and program producer (Moir 1994). As a result of an increased focus on Asia, in 1992 income from that region increased by 48 per cent (Film Australia 1992, p.16). Although Europe still delivers the best financial returns, the strategy is to build networks in Asia on the grounds that it will become a more and more important audiovisual market for Australia (Moir 1994).

The Girl From Tomorrow, a fantasy science-fiction children's series, is one of Film Australia's most successful exports. The territories sold include most of Western and Eastern Europe, Canada and the US (Disney Channel), parts of Asia (China, Thailand, Malaysia, Korea, Japan) and some territories in Africa and the Middle East. It commanded the highest price paid by the BBC for an imported children's series. Many countries that bought it also took the sequel, *Tomorrow's End*. These children's series, and others like them, such as *Escape From Jupiter*, have a longer shelf life and greater chance of sales than adult drama usually has. Because the costumes are not contemporary, the series does not date easily, and the science-fiction setting allows for a range of cultures to be represented easily, and can free the series from cultural specificity (Moir 1994).

The pre-school children's series *Johnson and Friends* has sold exceptionally well, and in addition has become an international marketing phenomenon. It is an animated series, using life-size puppets, about a group of toys which wake up each night for a dose of adventure. After its notable success in Australia, Europe and Asia, Film Australia made its first venture into merchandising. New products continue to be released with the series' growing popularity and include toys, books, music, puzzles, T-shirts, shorts and cards (Film Australia 1993, p.11). The television, video and merchandising rights for *Johnson and Friends* for Japan were sold to the Fujisankei Group and it was screened on Fuji TV, the highest rating broadcaster. This led to a merchandising deal with Sony, as well as other deals involving toys, publishing and video rights. *Johnson and Friends* started as part of the NIP, filling a perceived need for quality pre-school programs, and was not specifically designed to appeal to the international

JOHNSON & FRIENDS

A TELEVISION SERIES FOR YOUNG CHILDREN

Film Australia's pre-school children's series, *Johnson and Friends*, has been sold widely overseas and has become an international marketing phenomenon with books, toys and novelties on sale in many countries.
(Film Australia publicity material.)

market through its use of Australian icons such as kangaroos and koalas. However, this turned out to be the key to its appeal to overseas audiences. By July 1994 the first three series had recouped 80 per cent of their production costs, and the US Fox Network had taken it as part of its series *Fox's Clubhouse*.

Film Australia also does well with nature programs like *Koalas – The Bare Facts*, which has had at least 24 overseas sales – mostly in Europe, but some in Asia, the US and the Middle East – and the series *Great National Parks*. Other good sales have come from documentaries with an environmental or scientific angle like *After the Warming, The Loneliest Mountain, Mini-Dragons* and *Roads to Xanadu* (Moir 1994). The company's success both with these and children's programs reflects the general point that these genres are particularly international in character with low 'cultural discount', and can be adapted very easily to local markets merely by re-voicing the commentary.

Through the 1990s, Film Australia co-produced with NHK in Japan, a number of the PBS stations in the US, and Channel 4 and several production companies in the UK on the so-called 'consortium' model. In the case of *Mini-Dragons*, for instance, Film Australia spent A$1 million producing a one-hour documentary, which they sold to the ABC in Australia, and they received the three programs of the series made by the other partners which they pre-sold to the ABC at foreign rates. They also receive 30 per cent of gross international sales. There is also the potential in this kind of co-production to gain distribution rights on behalf of all the partners; this was realised in *Teachers of the World* (Moir 1993). This program was a 1992 consortium co-production with NHK in Japan, TV Ontario, Finnish Broadcasting Company TV1, WTTW Chicago, KBS Korea and Polish Television. It was a seven-part documentary series that dealt with the life of a teacher in each of the contributing countries. As a result of the co-production, some of the partners came together again to produce a special series to celebrate the Year of the Family in 1994 (Film Australia 1993, p.5). *Family* was a documentary series that involved four Asian co-producers – NHK Japan, KBS Korea, CEC India and Radio TV Hong Kong – as well as co-production partners from North and South America and Europe, including Russia. For the cost of producing one episode, Film Australia gained the Australian rights to the ten episodes for ten years (Oliver 1993).

The consortium model has advantages and disadvantages. It creates opportunities for frequent interaction with partners, promoting cultural exchange in exploring themes and ideas that leads to further co-productions and pre-sales, but on the other hand co-productions tend to result in a more homogenised product, requiring more patience and a larger outlay in travel and development.

An example of how relationships built up in the course of documentary co-production can lead to further ventures is illustrated by the case of *Escape from Jupiter*, co-produced with NHK (*ibid.*). It began when documentary executive producer Ron Saunders was visiting NHK during the production of *Mini-Dragons*. NHK was organising a gathering of international television production companies interested in making Western-style programs for the international market. They needed a suitable children's co-production as a learning vehicle. Film Australia proposed *Escape* and it was selected for a number of reasons. As science fiction it was not culturally specific, so it could be broadcast in both Japan and Australia without looking foreign. The story contained natural potential to include children from as many co-producing countries as could be arranged, and the series structure meant more than one director could be used, thus allowing Japanese creative input.

By 1994 the volume of co-production had become self-sustaining and Film Australia's high reputation in Japan was enabling it to assist other Australian independent producers in a difficult market. Film Australia's success as an exporter stems from its history as a documentary producer and its canny adaptation to contemporary conditions. It has specialised in those program categories with the greatest international currency – nature, environmental and science documentaries, and children's programming – and it has had the foresight to focus on the burgeoning markets of Asia with product that doesn't confront too many cultural hurdles. In addition it is blessed with good facilities and the safety net of government funding.

THE SEVEN NETWORK

The Seven and Nine networks were the two original commercial broadcasters in Australia (the Ten Network began a decade later, in the mid-1960s), and until the late 1980s they enjoyed stable ownership and management, which allowed them to build up a high degree of programming expertise and audience loyalty. Albert Moran (1993, p.567) comments that 'historically, the Seven Network has been perceived to be situated midway between the Nine Network on the one hand and the ABC on the other'. One of Seven's greatest strengths has been its commitment to drama, whereas the Nine Network has been stronger in news, current affairs and sport, which are far less internationally tradeable.

More than the other two networks, Seven has often produced its programs in-house (Moran 1985, pp.68–84), and even when programs were commissioned, Seven had a very high creative input and was actively involved in selling them overseas.

With its traditional emphasis on drama, the network was well positioned to take advantage of 10BA and, during the 1980s, produced a number of high-quality mini-series with local and overseas partners. Seven forged a relationship with a British production and distribution company, Portman/Global, with whom the ABC also did business, and also entered into a co-venture with Portmans, the distribution arm, to distribute Seven-originated programs in Europe. Some of the 1980s programs that were sold that way (and that still sell today) were *Land of Hope* and the mini-series *The Fremantle Conspiracy*, *Jackaroo*, *Sword of Honour* and *Melba*. Series and serials sold by Seven both on behalf of itself and the independent producers involved include *Rafferty's Rules*, *Skirts* and *A Country Practice*.

In the early 1990s, the Portman catalogue was taken over by established distribution firm, Richard Price and Associates (RPTA), which continued to distribute the Seven catalogue. Two of the most successful programs of the early 1990s were *Home and Away* and *Hey Dad*, the first produced in-house by the Seven Network, the second produced by Gary Reilly and Associates and sold jointly by them and the Network through RPTA.

Home and Away was developed in-house as an immediate response to the success of *Neighbours* on the Ten Network. Ironically *Neighbours* had originally begun on Seven in 1985, but after indifferent ratings the channel let it go. When it achieved such success on Ten, Seven realised the potential for youth-oriented soap. The fact that the ITV network in the UK was undergoing the same realisation following the success of *Neighbours* on the BBC in Britain helped the project by giving it a sizeable UK sale. *Home and Away* has gone on to achieve great popularity both in Australia, where it outrates its rival *Neighbours*, and in the UK, where in 1994 it was achieving audiences of 12 million for ITV compared with 14 million for *Neighbours*.

Home and Away has sold in a large number of other territories, including Ireland (where it is second only to the home-grown soap, *Glenroe*), Israel, Turkey, Canada, Spain, a number of countries in Africa, and the Middle East. In the US, 520 episodes were sold to Fox Cable with options for more. Research conducted both here and in the UK indicates that as expected, the main audience for the program is teenagers up to 17, women between 18 and 24, and older women. The appeal for audiences in Britain is seen to be very much the same as for *Neighbours* – the depiction of a classless, upwardly mobile society; of ordinary people with a high standard of living; of an attractive climate; and of a supportive and close community (Monaghan 1994). The success of *Home and Away* and the economic importance of the UK and other world markets is such that even if *Home and Away* was discontinued in Australia, it would theoretically be possible to continue to produce it. It also has great potential as a format sale (Mitchell 1992).

The sitcom, *Hey Dad*, which was cancelled in Australia in 1994 after a seven-year run on Seven, was also sold in a wide variety of territories. In the UK it was acquired by BSkyB, in Germany in 1994 it was being shown on ARD four days a week at 2 pm, and it has sold to France (M6) and Spain. It is significant that the continental European countries are all territories that dub dialogue, because comedy is the most difficult genre to translate into a different cultural setting. In Germany, at least, the dialogue-track is modified considerably to make it more 'German'; nevertheless, the cross-cultural acceptance of *Hey Dad* is atypical.

By the mid-1990s, the Seven Network seemed well positioned to continue its strong record in commissioning and producing programs with strong export potential. The free-to-air service is flourishing, and Seven is exploring new markets in Asia and Eastern Europe which, while not lucrative in the short term, have great potential in the future. Seven is also exploring pay television and other broadband services and it is safe to predict that it will remain a force in the Australian entertainment industry at the turn of the millennium.

The International Optic:
Television Ecologies and Australian Programs

6

The United Kingdom and Irish Republic

For all Australia's current preoccupation with and orientation toward Asia, Britain remains of especial cultural and economic importance. It remains Australia's third largest trading partner and the second largest single source of direct foreign investment in the country. London is still the base for much of Australia's trade into Europe (although Austrade, the national trade marketing authority, bases its European office in Frankfurt, with London a branch office); this is especially true of audiovisual trade. Not surprisingly as its former colonial master, Britain is the country that takes by far the most interest in Australia's political and cultural affairs; international concern with the current debate about Australia becoming a republic, for example, is mostly restricted to the UK. Despite increasingly close links first to the US and then to Asia in the post-war period, there are ongoing structural ties with Britain in areas such as the media, sport, religion, education, and the legal, medical and military systems, which underwrite the persistence and vitality of broadly shared cultural horizons (Miller 1987). Furthermore, Britain remains the most important base from which perceptions of Australia are circulated internationally, because London remains the most important source for most English-language print-based media outside the US (Sheridan 1994, p.13).

This chapter gives an overview of the changing British television landscape, which has been a model of the macro-trends identified in Chapter 2, and outlines the implications of these changes for an Australian program presence against the background of a history of significant program exchange. A case study of *Neighbours* demonstrates the complex of industrial and cultural factors that underwrote its impact in Britain. The wide range of program types – from high quality to highly commercial soap – is exemplified as a distinctive feature of the Australian program presence in Britain, as is the dominant post-colonial critical reception, which guarantees a contested passage for such programs. There is a

121

substantial disparity between the industry's generally positive assessment of Australian programs and their producers, and the highly positive reception of these programs by audiences, compared with the critical orthodoxy of disdain. This chapter also briefly considers Ireland – another country that is culturally proximate to Australia because of high levels of emigration. This is reflected both in the general receptivity in Ireland to Australian programming and an equally receptive critical and industry environment.

THE AUSTRALIAN NEXUS WITH THE BRITISH SYSTEM

The distinctive Australian nexus with the British industry, which makes the British market clearly the most important for Australian export, is based on longstanding relationships at both the production-company and broadcaster level, some of which have progressed beyond a history of acquisition to developmental co-venturing and equity partnerships. This has resulted in Britain accepting the widest range of program formats, having the longest history of acquisition, and being the most remunerative of any market for Australian export.

Up to the late 1980s – until the consolidation of satellite broadcasting with the formation of the consolidated satellite pay-television operation BSkyB, and after the addition of Channel 4 in the early 1980s – there were four terrestrial free-to-air channels in Britain. The BBC had two channels, BBC1 and BBC2, and the independent system had two channels, ITV and Channel 4. BBC1 and ITV/Channel 3 tended to win the majority of the audience, around about 80 per cent between them, and they shared the audience roughly equally. To an outsider, BBC1 and ITV tended to be rather similar in programming styles. From an American or an Australian point of view both look like public-service schedules, because the ITV system was by and large a public-service system (due to heavy regulation in the context of its monopoly status in each regional market), even though it was privately owned and funded through advertising.

The close affinities between Australia and Britain have made cultural exchange, including television trade, albeit unequal, entirely predictable. The nature of the British television landscape and its economic structure also facilitated the connection. By Australian standards, the British television market is a rich one – the BBC television company is ninth in size in world rankings and the ITV system as a whole is among the top five (*Television Business International*, March 1994). Traditionally, the British broadcasting system has been a very generous source of money for

Australian productions. Historically, the British licence fee for high-quality drama could reach £500 000 per hour, a very attractive proposition when translated into the economies of Australian production. The British system was able to deliver that kind of money because it was carefully regulated – each ITV station, for instance, enjoyed a monopoly in its broadcast area against a background of a large television market and healthy advertising revenue. The vast majority of programming on all British channels was British, in line with a nominal 86 per cent quota – although it tended to be more like 70–75 per cent (Goodwin 1993, pp.12–13). The historical colonial relationships were also recognised in an informal Commonwealth quota within the British quota.

Australia is the biggest market for UK programming after the US, and the UK has traditionally been the most important and visible market for Australian product overseas. The ABC is, of course, modelled on the BBC, and their relationship as public-service broadcasters, sharing similar traditions, values and aesthetic preferences, has meant that each has been a natural home for the other's product. The ABC has had an output deal with the BBC for many years, worth A$10 million to the BBC in 1992, and representing 400 hours of programming. In the same year the ABC sold the BBC A$8 million worth of programs.

Prior to the changes from the late 1980s, programming followed a classical public-service model. Programs were not competitively scheduled against each other, long-running soap operas such as *Coronation Street*, *East Enders*, *Brookside* and *Emmerdale Farm* were not stripped (run at the same time every day), and there was a clear hierarchy of program quality with one-shot drama at the pinnacle. Often programming was interrupted to preserve the news slot in the middle of the evening, then recommenced after the news, a practice unheard of on commercial television. While BBC1 is a general service channel, BBC2 is a specialist channel, which services established niche audiences. Channel 4 was to be a commissioner of new and innovative material and a broadcaster of complementary programming. Ironically, in the British situation this has meant quite a high percentage of American programming; until the advent of BSkyB, Channel 4 was the main vehicle for American drama, sitcoms and football.

Children's programming is one of the public-service requirements on British television, and both BBC1 and ITV have a children's section of the schedule in the mid-afternoon. Most of the programming in this time slot is British originated, although high-quality Australian and other imported programming play a role. Early afternoon and late afternoon to early evening (the last often referred as access prime time) have been the time slots dominated by Australian soap opera. From the mid-1980s, soaps such as *Neighbours, Home and Away, A Country Practice, The Young Doctors,* and *GP* were mainstays. Late afternoon also sees quiz and game shows; Grundy Worldwide produces the majority of game shows that have been shown on British television during the early 1990s, including *Celebrity Squares, Going For Gold, Jeopardy, Keynotes, Pot of Gold,* and *The Main Event* (*TV World,* 1994, p.21).

Prime time is naturally dominated by British material, although high-quality Australian drama has been scheduled with some regularity. *Come in Spinner,* for example, the Australian mini-series made by the ABC, was programmed on two successive Sunday nights – Sunday is an especially strong drama night – at 8.30 on BBC2. The public-service ethos of British television has also meant that documentaries have retained a place in prime time. Programs made by companies like Beyond International, Film Australia and the ABC have been placed in BBC1 and BBC2 prime-time slots, including *Great Wall of Iron* and *Climate in Crisis* (Beyond International), *La Stupenda* (ABC), *Roads to Xanadu* (Film Australia), and *Medicine at the Crossroads* (ABC co-production). The ABC's Natural History Unit has a particularly high reputation with British buyers.

In the 1980s, there were two kinds of Australian dramas that were sold to the British market. The first was top-quality, high-budget mini-series, usually made as co-productions with a British partner or with a pre-sale from a British partner. Most of the 10BA mini-series – *Vietnam, Bodyline, The Dirtwater Dynasty, The Great Bookie Robbery, Ring of Scorpio* – were sold or pre-sold either to the BBC or ITV. The second kind was serials and series for stripping in non-prime time, especially Crawfords and Grundy programs.

Production-company and broadcaster relationships embrace all sectors of the British industry. From the 1970s, the output deal that had given the BBC a royal road into the ABC schedule began to be balanced somewhat by ABC sales to the BBC (it has taken most of the mini-series made by the ABC). From the mid-1980s, the BBC was also contracting with commercial producers and networks in Australia. In the period between 1988 and 1992 it acquired *The Flying Doctors, Neighbours, Come in Spinner, The Paper Man, Johnson and Friends* and *The Girl From Tomorrow.* The BBC gave pre-sales to *Ring of Scorpio,* another series of *Flying Doctors, Police Rescue, Tomorrow's End* and *Boys From the Bush.* It entered into full co-production on a number of documentaries, especially those done with Beyond International (*Great Wall of Iron* and *Climate in Crisis*) and three important ABC mini-series (*The Leaving of Liverpool, Four Minute Mile* and *Children of the Dragon*). The BBC also broadcast all the classic, nation-defining Kennedy Miller/Channel Ten mini-series including *Vietnam, Bodyline, Cowra Breakout* and *The Dirtwater Dynasty*. All of these performed particularly well except for *Cowra Breakout*, about Japanese prisoners-of-war in Australia, which Mike Frost, deputy head of program acquisition at the BBC (1992), said contained too many subtitles for the British audiences' tastes. *Police Rescue*, a big hit on the BBC, represents a departure from the established pattern: a series screened in prime time.

Channel 4 was a co-production partner in the Roadshow, Coote and Carroll/ABC production *Brides of Christ* and distributed it in Europe. Channel 4 has also acquired a number of features, mini-series and documentaries including *Act of Necessity, Malpractice* and *The Loneliest Mountain*, and the children's program *More Winners*, made by the Australian Children's Television Foundation. Its two-month 1991 Australian season of over 30 features, shorts and documentaries represents the most concentrated body of curated audiovisual work ever broadcast outside Australia. This season saw low-budget features such as *Shame*, the radical critique of small-town rape culture in Australia, garner over 3 million viewers, and represents a high point for international broadcast of the innovative, non-mainstream end of Australian audiovisual production.

Among the ITV companies, Central Independent Television, Thames Television, Granada and Anglia TV stand out in terms of established Australian connections. Anglia TV has a 15 per cent stake in Village Roadshow. Central Independent Television, the franchise holder for the Midlands, has had a long relationship with both the ABC and the Seven Network. Central took the three series of *Fields of Fire*, the mini-series set in Far North Queensland sugar cane country, which was a co-production between the Seven Network and David Elfick's company, and were very pleased with the audience results. Bill Allen, director of sales at Central Television Enterprises, sees the strength of Australian programs as their production values. The industry in Australia, in his view, is large enough to have a wide range of very highly skilled people available to make programs, and again, for the UK, this makes Australia an attractive co-production partner. Central Independent Television also co-produced the mini-series *Edens Lost* with the ABC and *Tanamera* and *The Other Side of Paradise* with Grundys.

Thames Television has had dealings with the ABC from the early 1970s and has also developed a relationship with the Seven Network. Thames gave a pre-sale agreement for *Darlings of the Gods*, the mini-series about the Australian sojourn of Laurence Olivier and Vivien Leigh made by the independent Australian production company Simpson Le Mesurier in partnership with the ABC. It had a similar agreement with the Seven Network and the Le Mesurier company on *Nancy Wake*, the mini-series about an Australian woman as World War Two hero, and with Roadshow, Coote and Carroll and Channel Nine on *The Challenge*, the mini-series dealing with the 1983 America's Cup win by Australia. In most cases these ventures were not fully fledged co-productions, as creative control remained largely with the Australian end, although the British had some say over script approval and casting. Mike Phillips, the managing director of Thames International, was of the view that *GP*'s lower-than-expected performance was not due to a lack of quality; rather it was not well positioned for the British market. It is too Australian and too melo-dramatic to be a prime-time program, but too issue-based for daytime, so it has been difficult to place in the British schedule. The Irish, however, have scheduled it on RTE1 in the early afternoon. Thames has the distribution rights for *GP* in the UK and Europe.

THE CHANGING BRITISH TELEVISION LANDSCAPE

The special nexus between Britain and Australia is being tested by the changes in the British television landscape, which have provided the paradigmatic model for the movement from a fordist to post-fordist system. Until the late 1980s, the British broadcasting system consisted of large monolithic and vertically integrated broadcasting institutions, either run on a public-service model or heavily regulated. There has been con-certed pressure to disaggregate these structures and subject them to market forces. No longer are broadcasters solely responsible for transmission, program production, distribution, facilities management, engineering and technical services and training. Most of these functions are separately costed and often outsourced to independent companies. Production out-sourcing is in fact legislated for in the Broadcasting Act 1990 and a mandated 25 per cent of production is now independent. This has had quite a traumatic effect in the UK where the changes are seen as an attack on 'quality', on revered institutions, and on values that have sustained British democracy for decades. The changes were forwarded on the basis that they would replace the 'comfortable duopoly' with a more responsive and efficient system.

In the wake of the Broadcasting Act 1990, Channel 4 began to sell its own advertising (previously it had been sold by the ITV network), a shift that has been criticised as a recipe for forcing the channel to be more conservative in programming matters. The ITV regional and breakfast licences were auctioned to the highest bidder after meeting a 'quality threshold' (Goodwin 1991). The 1991 franchise round resulted in 12 of 16 existing broadcasters retaining their franchises while four lost them (Nicholson 1991, p.vi). There were large disparities in the amount bid for licences, which put considerable pressure on those licensees who bid too much or who promised too much in the attempt to meet the quality threshold. This has led to considerable takeover activity despite the Act's restrictions on takeovers of one ITV company by another. The large companies put pressure on the government to free up the ownership rules even further, citing their fear that if the ITV system did not consolidate into large companies as a response to increased competition from cable and satellite, they would be vulnerable to takeover by powerful European interests like those of Bertelsmann and Berlusconi, which the 1990 Act did not prevent.

The workings of the ITV system also changed in the wake of the franchise round. Before 1992 it operated as a large club. There were 16 franchisees but five or six of them dominated the system because of their size (Thames, Central, Granada, London Weekend Television and, to a lesser extent, Yorkshire, Scottish and Anglia). All of these companies made programs for the network as well as for their regional schedules, but no money ever changed hands. The programs were charged out on a complicated points system that related to the size of the advertising revenue and to the audience (Allen 1992). The lack of competition in British commercial television, and the local monopolies held by these companies, meant that they were extremely wealthy, and were able to invest very large amounts of money in high-budget programming like drama. Australian producers benefited from this.

In late 1992, a network centre was set up to make decisions about scheduling and commissioning that were in the interests of the network as a whole. In 1993, action by independent producers to allow them to bring programs to the centre without having to go through a regional franchisee was successful. This decision has important implications for Australian producers, who may now enjoy access to the ITV system without having to rely entirely on broadcasters. However, because there is still an implicit, uncodified 86 per cent British content quota, and because there is also a European Community quota of 50 per cent, Australian co-producers need to find a British partner if they are to get programs commissioned in Britain. Also, unless producers have access to the funding by a broadcaster, it is unlikely that they could afford to commission a program.

From 1988, the BBC also began to downsize, disaggregate and outsource. In 1992, the controversial policy called 'Producers' Choice' was introduced. Producers were able to go outside the BBC for facilities, post-production, editing and so on, or commissioning editors could go to independent producers to make BBC productions. BBC facilities managers also were encouraged to seek outside clients. (Similar processes are evident in the ABC.) For the first time at both ITV and the BBC it was possible to budget the costs and revenues of individual programs. However, Producers' Choice was seen by a number of commentators as a threat to the quality of BBC programming. The tensions between re-affirming the BBC's mission as distinct from that of commercial broad-casting (and thus foregoing more popular styles of shows like *Neighbours*), and moving it toward a more hybrid broadcasting model, have continued through the 1990s. Government policy is set on the latter course; its 1994 White Paper renewed the BBC's charter for ten years from 1997 and retained the licence fee as the basis of funding, but also cleared the way for a further commercialisation of the BBC (Baker and Busfield 1994, p.1).

Through the early 1990s, the BBC lost audiences to the ITV system and cable and satellite began to make inroads into overall audience share. As football, cricket and movies raised subscription levels for BSkyB, it progressively added more channels to its pay television package. In 1993, for example, UK versions of the American Family Channel and Nickelodeon as well as existing cable channels such as The Discovery Channel and Bravo were added (*TV World*, 1993, p.7). In households with BSkyB, satellite and cable have made significant inroads into the audience for free-to-air television, which had dropped from 100 per cent to 67.7 per cent by May 1994. The cumulative audience share for BSkyB services of almost 20 per cent in those homes that subscribe is significant (Table 6.1).

The changes that are occurring in the UK system are especially significant for Australia because the UK continues to be the major source of overseas finance for Australian television program production. If UK finance was to contract significantly, the Australian industry would find it very difficult to lever finance for high-budget drama. The transition to a more cost-conscious and competitive system in the UK means that there is downward pressure on licence fees and thus that the UK market will be less of a cash-cow for Australian producers. On the other hand, the transition to a more post-fordist system potentially provides possibilities for the Australian production industry to act as a supplier of certain categories of programs, like serials.

The proliferation of alternative services to the BBC and ITV will increase the demand for cheaper programming. This may increase the

Table 6.1:   UK Pay Television Households May 1994

Channel	Share (per cent)	Channel	Share (per cent)
Free to air		**Other satellite channels**	
BBC1	23.3	Children's	0.6
BBC2	6.8	MTV	1.1
ITV	30.7	UK Gold	2.5
Channel4	6.8	Discovery	0.8
Total free to air	**67.6**	Bravo	0.7
		Nickelodeon	1.1
BSkyB satellite services		Family Channel	0.4
Sky One	5.25	UK Living	0.6
Sky News	1.3	TNT Cartoon	2.0
Sky Sports	3.9	Eurosport	1.0
Movie Channel	3.3	**Total other satellite channels**	**10.8**
Sky Movies	4.1		
Sky Movies Gold	0.6		
Total BSkyB satellite services	**18.45**		

Source: British Audience Research Bureau, quoted in Cox 1994, p.23.

chances for Australian program exports. On the other hand, both the EC quotas and, more importantly, the manifest audience preference for locally made programming will work in the opposite direction. The 'window' for Australian material unexpectedly to dominate in hitherto under-supplied formats such as youth-oriented drama may begin to close as the British industry stabilises after a period of major restructuring, and responds to clear audience demand. On the other hand, the unashamedly populist character of BSkyB, with its significant Australian management involvement, will continue to make it particularly receptive to Australian series and serial export. Not only has Sky One, its general entertainment channel, regularly filled its day-time slots with old Australian soap operas, it has also aggressively bid for many newer ones including *Chances*, *Paradise Beach* and *Heartbreak High* (a multicultural Australian version of *Beverly Hills 90210*).

CULTURAL *NEIGHBOURS*: THE POST-COLONIAL INTERTEXT AND THE INDUSTRY WINDOW

Given Australia's white history as a colony and dominion within the British Empire, it is hardly surprising that the metropolis' dominant discourse on Australia is in terms of its colonial/post-colonial status. This produces the structure of response already alluded to at the start of the chapter, in which soap-opera audiences especially can be highly positive about Australian programs based upon one axis of the post-colonial dynamic, namely idealistic perceptions and projections of a qualitatively better way of life enjoyed in the 'new land'. Industry responses are rather more ambivalent, but are similarly founded on pragmatic perceptions of a post-colonial nature. On the one hand, there are positive assessments of the model potentially provided by a lean Australian production industry comfortable with commercial imperatives but retaining strong notions of quality and public-service elements. On the other, there is strong resistance to perceived undercutting of the production sector in the new regulatory and service environment. The negative axis of the post-colonial dynamic is seen most clearly in a certain official critical orthodoxy of disdain for cheap and popular programming and even, at times, quality drama.

The British press trumpets instances of the upstart Australian (for example, the outrage expressed when Prime Minister Keating had the temerity to touch the Queen lightly on the back when he was shepherding her down a line of dignitaries, or the general press response to the republican debate in Australia). Similarly, at times Australian programming must penetrate a high wall of critical prejudice in Britain. There is an odd mixture of resentment at the 'poor who got away', of disavowal of the common cultural links, and of reaction-formation against the envy that is felt about the sunny plenitude in which, it is imagined, Australians live. This stance influenced the reception of *Neighbours* and also reappears in the program that serves almost as the series' perverse double – *Sylvania Waters* – a kind of '*Neighbours* from hell'.

Even an unequivocally high-quality mini-series such as *Brides of Christ* is met with this welcome from the *Daily Mail*'s critic:

> Christians may preach charity, but it's remarkable how difficult it is to be charitable whenever there's a new Australian mini-series in town. Redeeming features are scarce on the ground, and the prospect of a dozen hours or so of square-jawed heroes chewing over unutterable dialogue and regularly calling each other 'mate' is usually too much for even the sturdiest of constitutions. Even Sky One's regular output looks accomplished by comparison (Berkman 1992).

This is in spite of the fact, as we have seen, that the high-quality end of Australian dramas have had wide exposure on British screens and, because they draw to such an extent on the British drama aesthetic, have been sought out by UK-based producers and broadcasters for co-production arrangements.

But it is at the popular soap-opera end of the format range that the greatest impact has been realised. Australian soaps have been seen on British television screens for many years, including, since the late 1970s, such staples of the British out-of-prime-time schedules as *Sons and*

Daughters, *A Country Practice*, *The Sullivans*, *Richmond Hill*, and *Prisoner: Cell Block H*. On ITV *Sons and Daughters* and *A Country Practice* gained audiences of around 3 million, which is very good for day-time television. *The Flying Doctors* was originally scheduled on the BBC at 8 pm on week days, but the ratings did not justify its retention in that time slot and it was changed to 5.30 pm on Saturdays, where it gained an audience of 2.5 million. However, it does not appear to have won the large and loyal audiences seen in Holland.

The popularity of Australian soap operas on day-time British television is partly due to the fact that the heavy public-service orientation of British television has created barriers to large amounts of American programming, but it has also to do with the fact that Australian soap operas by and large are more like British soap operas in style. This does not apply across the board. *The Young Doctors*, in retrospect, looks like a humorous and high-camp version of the US serial *General Hospital*. Other Australian soap operas like *Sons and Daughters*, *The Restless Years* and *A Country Practice* are more down to earth, more socially situated, slower paced and less glamorous than American soap operas like *The Bold and The Beautiful*, and *Santa Barbara*, which are the staples of European day-time television on the private channels. *Home and Away* and *Neighbours* are in a special category of popularity, which largely can be traced to the fact that they tapped an unsatisfied demand among British youth audiences. More recent Australian soap operas in the same vein, like *E-Street* and *Heartbreak High*, seem to be continuing the success of the earlier programs.

Neighbours began on BBC1 in October 1986, stripped in the early afternoon from Monday to Friday. Its unanticipated success led to the day's episode being re-screened in the early evening, allowing it to capture a far greater proportion of young viewers and leading to its runaway popularity. By 1988, it had become the most popular program for children and young adults on British television, and it remained in the ten most-watched programs in Britain for several years. In an effort to counter it, from 1990 the ITV network similarly strip-scheduled *Home and Away* to follow *Neighbours* immediately in the early evening and it, too, became a fixture in the most-popular-program lists. These were the two major Australian serials to attract attention and popularity, but a number of other long-form drama programs appeared for several years in the schedules of the terrestrial networks and on satellite services in the late 1980s and early 1990s. By early 1989, no less than 15 hours a week of Australian soap opera was scheduled on British television, an amount far greater than the five hours of US drama, and greater even than the ten hours of local

After nine years on BBC1, *Neighbours* has become a fixture in the British soap opera universe, as this cover of popular TV magazine, *TV Times*, shows. (Cover of *TV Times*, 21–27 August 1993.)

long-form drama (Craven 1989). By 1993, there were signs that the Australian cycle had waned somewhat, with the ratings for *Neighbours* slipping and with a greater degree of industry resistance to foreign programs dominating key parts of the schedules.

Much effort has been expended by critics, academics and audience researchers to explain the factors underlying this success; this effort in itself is an index of the surprise felt that such an unprepossessing colonial export could capture the imagination of the nation. It was clear from journalistic commentary that the most public and popularised mode of explanation for the success of soaps like *Neighbours* or *Home and Away* in Britain rested on speculations about the mythological content and serial format of the programs (speculations which closely resemble Liebes and Katz's findings (1990), discussed in Chapter 1). The soaps are seen as filling a need in the public imagination once occupied by medieval morality plays and preaching, providing models of behaviour directly relevant to their particular audiences. The serial format allows the consequences of such behaviour to be followed and also allows for varying means, times and degrees of involvement and several points of association with and 'reading' of character. Stephen Crofts' detailed analyses (1993; 1995) of program form and content identify several key aspects that support and specify these journalistic speculations. These include the focus in *Neighbours* on the everyday, the domestic and the suburban, its portrayal of women as doers, teenage sex appeal and unrebellious youth, its 'feel-good' characters and wholesome neighbourliness. Social tension and values conflict are always resolved, dissolved or repressed, and the overall ideological tone is of de-politicised middle-class citizenship.

A viewer survey (Wober and Fazal 1994) also provided interesting conclusions relevant to the question of consumption of non-domestic material, which underline the importance of what we have identified as cultural proximity. There was some evidence to bear out one of the *East of Dallas* team's dictums (Silj 1988) that a moderate foreign-ness (or what one British critic called the soaps' 'slight foreign-ness' (Marin 1989, quoted in Wober and Fazal 1994) engendered more involvement and enjoyment among some viewers. This idea is expanded by Marin in these terms: 'characters outside our class system ... can speak to us more freely than any well-defined character in an English soap, whose very definition would risk provoking all the class antagonisms which are so easily aroused here'. The 'morality tale' element put forward by critics for the appeal of soaps, which parallels so closely Liebes and Katz's findings, needs to be framed within this sense of slight foreign-ness. The exotic or foreign elements –

that 'Australians get into each other's lives and homes more than British people do', that there is a pleasing degree of 'old-fashioned' verbal cliche in the scripting, that overall the most widely noticed characteristic is an inference about life in Australia (that social interaction is more fluid) – carry with them a sense of attractive difference, which is read in the act of viewing as a commentary on British life. Again, this correlates well with a critic who points to 'a complete alternative universe, one ruled by goodwill, common sense and a faith in the power of hard work. It is … sunny, decent, fair, not preachy, not guilty … nobody is rich but everyone has a nice big kitchen. When one job falls through there is always another … with *Neighbours* that dream is of ordinary people in a land of opportunity … it is optimism with a bright shiny package' (Gillian Reynolds, *Daily Telegraph*, 14 December 1988, p.15).

Marie Gillespie's ethnographic study (1991) of west London Punjabi communities' reactions to *Neighbours* is the most in-depth audience-use study yet conducted of Australian soaps in Britain. Gillespie studied groups of teenagers' use of *Neighbours* in negotiating the relations between parental and peer cultures in an environment where much of their knowledge of white Anglo society perforce comes from television. Whereas the key cultural studies audience research of the 1980s examined variables of class along with gender, Gillespie focuses on ethnicity, age and gender. With regard especially to her focus on a youth demographic, Gillespie's research performs a particularly useful function in illuminating that age group that has allowed *Neighbours* to perform so strongly in Britain.

The Australian-ness of the serial is reported to be of little importance compared to its being about a white society (Gillespie 1991, p.29). But this should not be taken at face value. Several indications in the research lead to the conclusion that the degree of interaction and association with *Neighbours* could not be readily substituted for any other serial at the same slot in the schedule. *Neighbours* by far outranked all other soaps among Gillespie's cohort in terms of popularity, with the other major Australian serial *Home and Away* second – so there is strong circumstantial evidence that it is something about Australian serials particularly that provokes interest. The 'social text' created around *Neighbours*, with its stars Kylie Minogue, Jason Donovan and Craig McLachlan enjoying considerable extra-televisual exposure in British youth culture, cemented the specific attractions of the serial.

The character networks of *Neighbours* are based on a set of extended families in a single locale, Ramsey Street. This is a fictional space which corresponds at times quite literally to the living conditions of Gillespie's

Southall cohort, where gossip and rumour have the potential to conflict strongly with both the sense of family honour and the aspirations to peer acceptance of the teenagers studied. Given that the 1990 Social Trends analysis (quoted in Gillespie 1991, p.35) states that 82 per cent of the surveyed British population claim they would never have moved into their home had they known who their neighbours were, there are obvious attractions in an imaginary location, in which scenarios for dealing with 'far from ideal' neighbourly relations are routinely played out. One of Gillespie's key findings is that her teenage cohort constructs associations between their social world and the fictional world of the serial, creatively 'misreading' the fiction by folding it into the realities of high-density, urban extended family and community life. It also suggests the possibility that as in Eric Michaels' observation (1991) that indigenous Australians living in remote communities associate more with African-Americans in US television than with white Australian characters, these British-Indian teenagers have constructed a 'shared' social space with another displaced ideal world.

This is the point at which perceptions of a distinctly 'Australian' social space, intertwined with aspects of the format of *Neighbours*, might come into play. The fluidity of the (fictional) social life portrayed, that 'Australians get into each other's lives and homes more than British people do', facilitates perceptions of the serial's usefulness for the Punjabi teenagers in participation in and negotiation of gossip and rumour. Moreover, the format, including the production values, of the serial (low cost, cheap sets, naturalistic camerawork), which differs markedly from popular US soaps like *Dallas* and *Dynasty*, places an emphasis on dialogue, on the verbal over the visual. This observation allows Gillespie to make a series of connections between her cohort's social reality and a fiction based to a larger degree than in most soaps on young people and a narration of 'proximity, intimacy and intensity' dealing with the central themes of family and kinship, romance and community relations.

Textual and audience-reception studies of the success of Australian television in Britain are valuable but partial explanations. What they miss is a sense of the 'sharp end' of the social intertext created around Australian soaps, and any ideological evaluation of their impact in the industrial circumstances of British television in the late 1980s. A case can be made (*see* Copley 1991) for *Neighbours*, and at least some of the other high-rating Australian drama, fitting all too well into the dual trajectories of de-regulation and re-regulation of British television in the late 1980s. On the one hand, it was cheaply and readily available soap opera that answered

Edited by Marianne Jones

★★★ Excellent ★★ Good ★ OK

FILMS

A girl who wants to murder her mum, but doesn't know how, is the chilling theme of **DEADLY ADVICE** (15). It sounds dreadful. In fact, it's a superior, British-made black comedy, with an impressive cast that includes Jane Horrocks, Imelda Staunton and Edward Woodward. Brenda Fricker plays the mother from hell and it's all wonderful stuff. ★★★

MOTHER'S BOYS (15) stars Jamie Lee Curtis as another difficult mum—this time one who'll stop at nothing to win back the family she once abandoned. It's an exciting thriller, spoilt just occasionally by a wild storyline. ★★

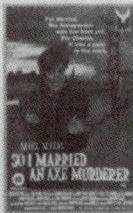

VIDEOS

Not much around this week worth recommending. The best of the bunch is the underrated, but not very friendly, **SO I MARRIED AN AXE MURDERER** (15). Don't be put off by the title—this is actually an enjoyable comedy about a man (Mike Myers from Wayne's World) who fears his fiancée is the killer in question. Busy actress Brenda Fricker stars in this one too. ★★

PAPER BACKS

Jilly Cooper fans weren't disappointed when **THE MAN WHO MADE HUSBANDS JEALOUS** was first published. The man is Lysander Hawkley, who's handsome, broke...and irresistible to women. It's that weapon he decides to employ to make money (and you can guess what else besides!). All superior tosh—just the sort of book you want to take on holiday (Corgi, £5.99).

ON THE BOX

On the face of it, the new 10-part drama series **LIFEBOAT** (BBC1, from Thursday) seems promising enough. The fact that it's been written by Lynda La Plante is another bonus. Life, death, heroism, tragedy...all these play their part in what will surely be dubbed Casualty-on-Sea. One to watch out for.

NEIGHBOURS SPECIAL

The war paint and Wonderbras are on. Eyelashes are fluttering, lips are pouting and pulses are racing. It can only mean one thing...a new man is about to arrive in Ramsay Street. And both Annalise and Gaby are determined to make him theirs.

It's going to be a tug of war in which Mark Gottlieb (played by Bruce Samazan—an actor who has cornered the market in bewildered expressions) finds himself pulled in every direction.

'Mark's kind of the meat in the sandwich between these two women who basically want to chew him up and spit him out in little pieces,' says Bruce.

'It's a tough job playing someone that two beautiful women want to go to bed with. But obviously someone has to do it.'

Bruce isn't joking. To be honest, he'd hate to be in Mark's position. 'I'd find it embarrassing if two girls started squabbling about me in public as Gaby and Annalise do.

'Perhaps I'm old-fashioned, but I like to do a little bit of the chasing myself. I don't like things offered on a plate.'

Apart from this, he adds that even on a plate with all the trimmings, neither Gaby nor Annalise would be to his taste.

'I wouldn't touch either of them with a barge pole. If I met them in real life, I'd run a mile.

'I mean, Gaby's so uptight and into her career that you could never have any fun.

'Annalise is worse. She's totally ruled by material

If I met Gaby or Annalise in real life, I'd run a mile

things and the [w]... looks. She's just [a] doll with a hear[t]... could never be a[...] to someone like t[...]

For all that, in[...] bours anyway, it['s] lise who finally win[s] heart—and everyth[...] that comes with [...] his personal life, [...] committed to a ver[...] ent kind of girl.

'My girlfriend i[s] lutely the opposite [...] lise. She isn't vai[n]... material possessio[ns]...

...fe... yo... a n... ar... on... the... do...

neither of us is t[...] up about vanity [...] Obviously I ha[ve]... to care about [...] the way I look [...] because my [...] job depends [...] on it. But to [...] me there's [...] something [...] ugly about a [...] person who [...] thinks they [...] can make it [...] just on looks.'

He got his acting break when he ac[...] companied a girlfriend to an audition for E Street—an Aussie soap shown on Sky.

'I was sitting in the car and the casting direc[...] tor spotted me an[d]... asked if I'd come[...] and try out for a p[...] says Bruce.

'In the end I wa[s]... fered a role in [the]... show—and my g[irl]... friend wasn't. Pe[r]... haps because o[f]...

The introduction of ex *E-Street* star, Bruce Samazan, gives *Neighbours* a boost. 'So who wins *Neighbours'* newest hunk?', asks the cover of a leading British women's magazine, *Woman*, incorrectly referring to the actor as 'Mark' Samazan. (Cover of *Woman*, 2 May 1994.)

NCE PUT 25 GIRLS OSPITAL!

Mark Samazan is ready to set pulses racing in Ramsay Street as Annalise and Gaby get down to a tug of war for his affections...

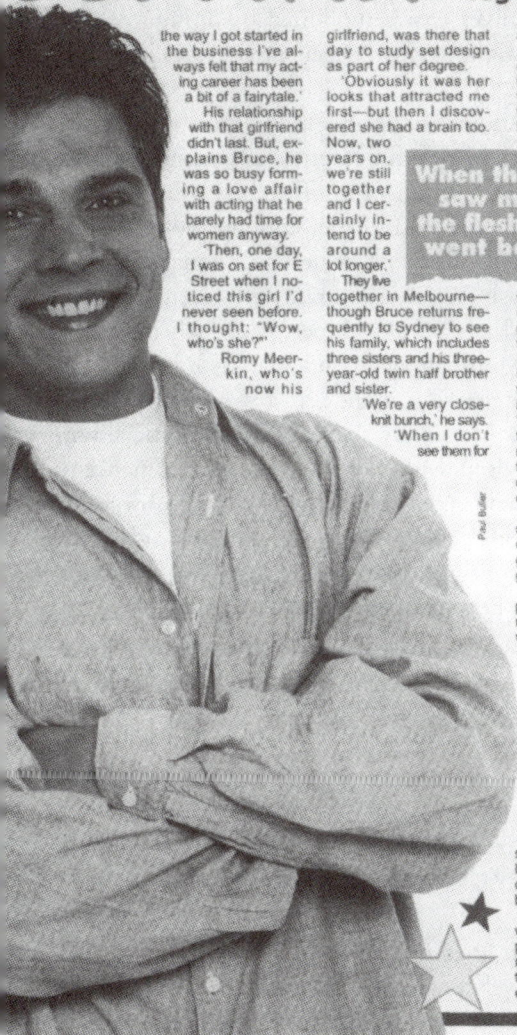

the way I got started in the business I've always felt that my acting career has been a bit of a fairytale.'

His relationship with that girlfriend didn't last. But, explains Bruce, he was so busy forming a love affair with acting that he barely had time for women anyway.

'Then, one day, I was on set for E Street when I noticed this girl I'd never seen before. I thought: "Wow, who's she?"'

Romy Meerkin, who's now his girlfriend, was there that day to study set design as part of her degree.

'Obviously it was her looks that attracted me first—but then I discovered she had a brain too. Now, two years on, we're still together and I certainly intend to be around a lot longer.'

They live together in Melbourne—though Bruce returns frequently to Sydney to see his family, which includes three sisters and his three-year-old twin half brother and sister.

'We're a very close-knit bunch,' he says. 'When I don't see them for a while I miss them badly.'

At 24, Bruce is the eldest of the brood. He was born in Madagascar, but the family moved to Australia when he was four. His British mother re-married five years ago after divorcing Bruce's dad, who's French.

Bruce admits that he has always been his mum's blue-eyed boy. Even now he regards her as 'his best friend in the world'.

'If it hadn't been for her I'd probably still be working on a building site,' he says. 'But she always had this amazing belief in me and gave me confidence to believe I could do something else with my life.

'If I'm feeling down, she's the first person I call because no one gives a pep talk as good as my mother.'

When he landed his part on E Street, Bruce's mum was overjoyed. She went out and bought a mountain of blank videos to record all his performances. She also keeps every press clipping relating to her son.

In the nine months since his first appearance in Neighbours, it must have amounted to a small forest of newspaper.

'Even she thinks it's a bit excessive at times,' says Bruce. 'But what I've learnt is that you can't be on TV and then expect to be anonymous.

'Being nice to people who come up to you is all part of the job. If you're not prepared to do that, there are plenty of others who are. In Australia,

Attack of the man-eaters: 'Annalise is a Barbie doll with a heartbeat and Gaby is uptight about her career'

98 per cent of actors are out of work.'

There are times though, when Bruce finds the attention overbearing.

'I was making a public appearance in front of a crowd of 1,000 and when the fans saw me in the flesh they went beserk.

'Thirteen ambulances had to be called because girls were fainting and getting bones broken in the crush. Twenty-five of the girls ended up in hospital that day. 'I found it pretty scary.'

Oh well, it was all good practice for Neighbours. It isn't just the female fans who get all hormonal around Bruce. Just ask Annalise and Gaby.

■ DAPHNE LOCKYER

> When the fans saw me in the flesh, they went beserk

Paul Butler

19

a need for the BBC to respond, in an increasingly constrained financial environment, to attacks on its elitism and the challenges of the new commercialism. On the other, it was clean, morally unproblematic soap, well suited to the moral re-regulation that proceeded apace with structural de-regulation and the skew toward commercialism. This argument is bolstered by evidence that what *Neighbours* could be construed as representing in terms of a moral universe, was mobilised by opinion leaders like the tabloid press in campaigns against 'degenerate' values in British television.

Fuelled by a history of US dominance in cinema and other popular arts and a strong, if aggrieved, sense of rightful cultural leadership, there has long been an entrenched anti-Americanism in official British culture of both the left and the right. The drive to further commercialise and de-regulate British television in the 1980s therefore needed alternative models of media culture. In the bullish 1980s, the brash entrepreneurship of Australian or Australian-linked figures like Rupert Murdoch in ringing changes in the British press, Murdoch again and Alan Bond in satellite television and the morning television franchise TV-AM boss Bruce Gyngell attracted the admiration of many scions of British officialdom, not least Margaret Thatcher. Indeed, Murdoch had a marked influence on the British Prime Minister's policies of 'blowing away the cobwebs' of public-service broadcasting (Shawcross 1992) and he was aided and abetted by Thatcher in his drive to outmanoeuvre his erstwhile satellite rival, BSB. Gyngell was sent a personal prime-ministerial apology when the Thatcher-inspired ITV auction in 1991 led to TV-AM losing its morning television franchise. The *Radio Times* in 1989 summed up the confluence with this flourish:

> Overnight it seems, the Aussies have come out of the outback, armed to the teeth with television soaps, cinema block-busters, newspaper magnates, City financiers, victorious America's Cup yachtsmen, lager kings … suddenly the sky's the limit Down Under (quoted in Craven 1989, p.1).

It is in this general context that the BBC was, by the mid-1980s, desperate for popular but relatively low-cost serial drama that would begin to recapture some of the audience lost to both Channel 4 and the ITV network. *Eastenders* was launched in 1985, the first continuing serial the BBC had produced since 1969 (Buckingham 1987, p.2). About the same time, the popularity in Britain of US soaps such as *Dallas* and *Dynasty* had begun to wane considerably. Finding substitutes for US programming, paralleling the need for alternative commercial media models, became a priority. Buckingham (*ibid.*, p.10) argues that *Eastenders'* ratings success was financially and politically crucial to the BBC. But the program's high production costs meant that it was only a partial solution. The BBC reputedly needed to pay only £27 000 for a week's *Neighbours* (five episodes stripped twice a day, amounting to ten hours of high-rating programming), as against £40 000 production costs for half an hour of *Eastenders* (Kingsley 1988, p.363).

Buckingham's study of the first two years of *Eastenders* notes prominent themes of unemployment, urban deprivation, nervous breakdowns, infidelity and divorce, prostitution, illiteracy, drugs and acoholism, and conflict between the generations leading to breakdowns of the extended family. *Eastenders* was the first English soap to feature Afro-Caribbean, Asian, Greek and gay and lesbian characters; it attempted to show the multicultural composition of the inner-city community and to examine racial and sexual stereotyping. Elements of the press that mobilised against the soap argued that its 'bleak realism' was 'squeezing out' moral standards.

Often, the press rated the appeal of *Neighbours* against the 'bad' models of soap: 'not high life like *Dallas*, not low life like *Eastenders*, just everyday life' (*Trader*, 6 April 1987). Hilary Kingsley (*Daily Mirror*, 7 July 1987) said that 'one of the reasons for *Neighbours'* success is people have tired of the low-life, working-class themes of *Eastenders*'. *Eastenders* was written up as threatening, polemic, difficult; *Neighbours* was cosy, unopinionated, ordinary. Germaine Greer's withering commentary in the *Radio Times* highlighted the values the tabloids saw fit to lionise: 'There are no Asian characters in *Neighbours*, the only Southern Europeans are ridiculous stereotypes. There is not even a Jew, let alone a Muslim or a Buddhist. Religion is never discussed, sexual orientation is always heterosexual ... If a group of Aborigines were to camp on the manicured lawns the good neighbourliness would evaporate immediately' (Greer 1989).

The 'moral crusade' that some newspapers mounted around their constructed opposition between *Neighbours* and *Eastenders* demonstrates the degree to which Silj's 'sedimentation of other social practices' (1988, p.40) peculiar to a host country can dramatically affect the reception of popular imported television material. The press's stance (and the brief flurry in May 1991, when British Junior Education Minister Michael Fallon and his Labour shadow Jack Straw both attacked *Neighbours* for 'dulling the senses' of schoolchildren and being 'pretty trashy') reveals more of the deep cultural and moral elitism that can be mobilised in the British polity than it does about audience uses of the soap opera. Instead, the most intriguing aspects of audience response to *Neighbours* may lie in the fantasy projections the program fortuitously generates in a particular host society with historically close ties to Australia. Copley (1991, p.39–40), in a small survey of opinions about *Neighbours* among mothers at a south-east London play centre, found that Australia can be introjected as an alternative utopia of exotic holiday brochure and cinema images creatively pitted against that which is seen as inferior in the British life-style: 'They do work, but the pace of life is slower, like when you're abroad and people slow down because of the climate and spend less time worrying'. Regardless of whether viewers believe the fantasies or not, this form of engagement evidently provides much pleasure and defies any simple correlation between the moral cause espoused at a public level, and viewer reception.

These aspects of *Neighbours* are complemented by program scheduling and marketing. Kate Bowles (in Taylor 1993, p.13), argues against the 'common mythology' that 'open-plan housing, beautiful people and hot weather' in *Neighbours* and *Home and Away* are the key ingredients. It was the programs' placement in the schedules – stripped in the late afternoons as well as, with *Neighbours*, the early afternoons – that laid the basis for their idealised Australian-ness to become a featured factor. Indeed, it was supremely good timing that *Neighbours* became the first such program to be stripped across the week days in Britain; the leading edge of a scheduling revolution within the commercialisation that both BBC and ITV have pursued strongly since the mid-1980s (the second program to be similarly stripped was *Home and Away*). Another strategy that worked as an influence external to program content was the marketing to young audiences. This strategy set both these series apart from the majority of established soap operas, such as *Coronation Street*, which featured mostly middle-aged and older characters and themes appropriate to them. This is borne out in the BARB Appreciation Index measurement of reasons for viewers watching the Australian material, which shows a very strong youth preference (BBC 1989; 1990; 1991). Importantly, this audience is not likely to be influenced by critical discourses of disdain for colonial television products.

This review of the success of *Neighbours* demonstrates that a middle-range approach – which focusses on the mediating role of gatekeepers and the industry windows of opportunity that fortuitously open – is necessary to explain the careers of export countries' product (especially peripheral ones). The exercise shows, as well, that Leibes and Katz's primordiality and seriality (1990) – the structure of the content and the form of the drama – cannot operate as a fully generalisable mode of explanation. And it underlines the specificity of Britain's unique position in the post-colonial intertext created by cultural proximity overlaid with a history of colonial subordination.

Sylvania Waters is an intriguing case of translation of this post-colonial intertext into television production. *Sylvania Waters* is a BBC production (in association with the ABC), produced by Paul Watson and screened as a 13-part prime-time series in 1993 both in Australia and Britain. It is particularly relevant to our consideration of the cultural conjuncture within which Australian television has circulated in Britain. Indeed, the project was probably inconceivable without the growth of UK–Australia audiovisual relations and the cultural impact of the soap operas. A *cinéma vérité*-style documentary from a senior BBC producer who has made several international portraitures of family life (including *The Family* in 1974), *Sylvania Waters* profiles the life of a *nouveau riche* middle-class family headed by Noeline Donaher and Laurie Baker and is set in their suburb of Sylvania Waters in Sydney. The choice of a 'prototypical' family always would have been a tendentious one – the producer is reputed to have rejected an alternative family who represented all that was multi-cultural, educated and refined about contemporary Australian life. The ultimate choice of the Baker-Donahers typifies the colonial/post-colonial British projection of the Australian as crass, unrefined and brash, but who enjoys an ostentatiously upwardly mobile life-style in nirvana-like surroundings.

As more than one commentator (*see* Rowe 1994; Stratton and Ang 1994) has pointed out, it is against the conjunctural background of a particular time – of the decline of British quality of life and the eclipse of the last vestiges of empire – that *Sylvania Waters* should be seen. Idealised projections of Australian life-style were powerful factors in the unprecedented success of some soap operas. As a documentary portraiture, *Sylvania Waters* sets out to correct these projections, while inevitably affirming many of them: '*Sylvania Waters* can be viewed as the symbolic rebuttal of the proposition that *Neighbours* and *Home and Away* represent desirable designs for living. This task was achieved not, as is often prescribed, by highlighting the existence of poverty, diversity and structural conflict in Australia … Instead, it operated by rendering as excessive the logic of materialism and the aesthetics of Australian suburbia which made the programmes attractive in the first place' (Rowe 1994, p.19).

Stratton and Ang, in seeking to analyse the reception of the program in Britain, focus on the split between 'an old European nation-state where the tenets of modernity are much more entrenched than in the settler societies of either the USA or Australia' (1994, p.14). As a consequence, representing the crisis of family life in a post-modern era shifts outside the home country, to a site – Australia – which can be viewed as prototypically post-modernist. However, this will always be an ambivalent project, as the reception of *Sylvania Waters* in Britain demonstrated. The critical discourse operated to reconfirm perceptions of mindless hedonism in a sunny Down Under, highlighting the fissures in the facade of material success enjoyed by the Baker-Donahers.

THE IRISH REPUBLIC (EIRE)

If the English heritage in Australia makes Britain an obvious market for Australian television product, then so does Australia's Irish history smooth the path for Australian programs in Ireland. The long history of Irish immigration to Australia means that there is a high level of awareness of and attachment to the country amongst Irish viewers. Other themes in Australian culture – the role of Roman Catholicism and the mythical traditions of rebellion, egalitarianism and championing the underdog – mean that much of Australian cultural product finds a ready affinity with the Irish. As a very small market, Ireland can never be significant for Australia in economic terms but its cultural proximity makes it a special case.

In the Republic of Ireland there is only one broadcaster, RTE (Radio Telefis Eireann), which operates two channels, RTE1 and RTE2 or Network 2 (an attempt in 1991 to establish a commercial service foundered on regulatory and financial difficulties). However, in most of the country other channels are available. Ireland's population of 3 million makes it a very small television market, with high levels of imported content, low prices for program acquisition, and rare ventures into co-production since it is unable to provide significant sources of finance.

Ireland has three different television communities. The first is in the west, the 'Gaeltach', which for geographic reasons has access only to RTE1 and Network 2. The second is in the east, where viewers can receive the two RTE channels and also the UK (including the Welsh) terrestrial channels through signal 'spillover' (the east coast is close enough to receive British signals). All this is free to air and delivered by standard VHF transmission or by microwave – Ireland has the most extensive use of microwave transmission in Europe, possibly the world. The third group, about one-third of the population, are those that are cabled. They are mainly in the urban areas, especially Dublin and Cork (the latter's system is modern fibre optic). This group has access not only to all the terrestrial channels but also to satellite channels from the rest of Europe through cable re-transmission.

During the 1990s, the two national channels evolved differing styles. There has always been some Irish-language programming on Network 2, including a daily half-hour of news and current affairs in Gaelic. RTE2 is also now programming more arts and sport than RTE1. In spite of the availability of arguably 'superior' programming from the UK channels, the Irish channels have by far the biggest audience: *Television Business International Yearbook 1991* reports 1990 figures as 43.4 per cent for RTE1, 20 per cent for RTE2, 16 per cent for BBC1, 12 per cent for ITV and the rest shared between all other sources. Of course these figures are distorted by variable availability of channels in different parts of the country.

Predictably most imported programming in Ireland comes from the major English-speaking sources, mostly the US. There is difficulty in getting UK first-run material because, with the UK channels available in Ireland and vice versa, UK suppliers do not wish to see their audience affected by spillover to the UK. As one of the two other major sources of English-language programming – Canada is the other – this would seem to give Australia some advantage. Bill Harpur, head of acquisitions at RTE, reported a heavy reliance on both Australian and Canadian sources as alternatives to the US and the UK. Australia, however, is the biggest source of imports after the US; Canadian programming is 'excellent but there is not the volume'. This bears out again that the depth of Australia's production industry in the area of long-running serials and series is a strength in the export market. Not surprisingly however, locally made programs are preferred to imported; the highest rating drama program on Irish television is the soap opera *Glenroe*. In the early 1990s, *A Country Practice* was stripped every day at 5.30 pm on RTE1, and *Home and Away* at 6.30 pm on RTE2. This is in spite of the fact that *Home and Away* was also available on UTV (the Ulster ITV channel) at 5.10 every day. *Neighbours*, of course, was available on BBC 1.

The historic links between Australia and Ireland made Australia a natural source of programming from the earliest days of television; an awareness of Australia as a film-making and television-exporting nation has existed since the early 1970s. Australia is seen as having particular strengths in 'family programming', which is code for programs that do not offend what is still a very conservative official morality. Australian programs were compared favourably with those from the US in this respect. The gatekeeping function of executives in charge of acquisition, like Bill Harpur, is exerted with particular vigour in the area of morality. *Home and Away* was appreciated because it 'avoided controversial issues'. US series are seen to be 'obsessed' with broken families and problems like AIDS and drugs. Australian programs deal with such issues more gently, if at all. An episode of *A Country Practice* about a footballer with AIDS was broadcast after much deliberation; this was seen to be quite a courageous decision. *Beverly Hills 90210* was an ongoing problem because of its emphasis on pre- and extra-marital sex.

Australian programs were also compared favourably with those from the US in terms of production values and storytelling skills. As in other European markets the US is seen to be supreme in action genres, but the Irish gatekeepers saw programs that reflect Australian culture and history as of much more relevance to the audience than similar programs from the US, not least because a significant number of exportable Australian programs feature Irish-Australian characters and plotlines (*Against the Wind, Eureka Stockade*). A program like *The Shiralee* was mentioned by Bill Harpur as a prototypical sure seller in Ireland.

Brides of Christ, the prestigious mini-series that charted a history of changing values in the Roman Catholic Church from the point of view of an Australian convent of nuns living through the period of Vatican 2, was of enormous interest because of the theme, but also tested the limits of acceptability. RTE entered into this co-production only because there was also a UK partner, Channel 4; on the whole, according to Bill Harpur, RTE is wary about entering into co-productions with Australia since they appear to operate too much in Australia's favour, as Ireland has no local-content requirements. The focus on issues like abortion and the sexuality of nuns and priests made this a more contemporary intervention than in Australia or in the US (*see* Chapter 8), where it had a more nostalgic appeal for viewers for whom these issues are now settled. The selling-point for both Ireland and Channel 4 was the casting of Irish actor Brenda Fricker as a nun unable to adjust to the rapidity of the changes in the church.

Ireland is clearly a ready market for social issues-oriented programs, which are not too confronting. Programs which promote a sense of community and community morality find ready acceptance. *A Country Practice, The Flying Doctors* and *GP*, all of which are popular in Ireland, fall into this category, although there have been episodes of *A Country Practice* and *GP* that have been held back because they dealt too problematically with difficult social issues. Bill Harpur saw *The Flying*

Doctors as a 'well-turned drama with likeable characters and good medical situations'. It has 'family values, no bad language, no sex or violence'. He compared it with recent US series in which 'the nuclear family is no longer valued; it appears less and less; now it is all broken homes and single mothers'. Australian children's programs, including *Round the Twist, Lift Off,* and *Half Way Across the Galaxy and Turn Left,* are also acquired in the context of the prevailing moral parameters.

Home and Away is the most successful Australian program in Ireland. In 1992 it was attracting 580 000 viewers on RTE 2: an extremely good figure for the size of the population. In multi-channel cable homes (34 per cent of the total population) *Home and Away* is the second-highest rating program in its time slot. Tony Fahey, head of audience research at RTE, reported that Australian programs are perceived positively as distinct in content and style compared to US or UK material, and successfully youth-oriented.

7

Europe

In this chapter we use the term 'European' to designate continental Western Europe, where the largest and richest television markets are France, Germany, Italy and Spain. The next is The Netherlands. Of these the most important for Australia are France, Germany and The Netherlands and we shall concentrate on analysing these three. These countries buy the most Australian product and enter into the largest number of co-productions with Australia. This largely reflects the size of the markets and their ability to originate expensive categories of programming, like drama, rather than any particular affinity with Australia. In fact, other markets in Europe, notably the Scandinavian countries, buy as many or even more Australian programs than the larger markets but their small size means that they are less economically significant and that they do not have the financial strength to provide up-front funding or to enter into co-productions. More significantly, Australian programs do not make a significant cultural impact in these countries. Until the early 1990s, the Scandinavian television cultures were very heavily weighted towards the public-service model and thus the programs imported from Australia tended to be documentary and children's material.

In the smaller countries of Europe subtitling is used on imported programs rather than dubbing because it is up to ten times cheaper (Kilborn 1993, p.646). There is a fair correlation between good English speakers in Europe and small countries that use subtitling rather than dubbing. The number of English speakers in The Netherlands, Denmark, Norway – subtitling countries – is much higher than in dubbing countries like France, Germany and Italy (Tracey 1987, p.80). This, coupled with their greater openness to imports generally, is one of the factors that makes them more ready to accept Australian programming than the bigger markets. The history of acceptance of British programming in countries like The Netherlands and Denmark and Sweden also predisposes them to accept Australian programming as a substitute.

In no European country do Australian programs have the prominence they enjoy in the UK and Ireland. However in The Netherlands at least one Australian program, *The Flying Doctors*, enjoyed huge popularity for several years and in 1992 the Dutch people voted it their favourite imported program. Both France and Germany have had a long history of buying and scheduling Australian programs and of co-producing programs with Australian producers and broadcasters. In addition, Grundys has successfully sold formats to the Dutch, the Germans and France. In the other two large markets, Italy and Spain, Australian programs have hardly appeared and as yet there is virtually no history of co-production. The reasons for this probably have to do with the particular history of television in those countries. The radical de-regulation of Italian television that took place in the early 1980s produced a headlong rush towards importing American programs in the desperate struggle for ratings, leaving little room for imports from other places (Silj 1992, p.39). And the fact that Spain has only recently introduced private ownership of television stations (Ostergaard 1992, p.199) and that if they were to import from anywhere other than the US it would be from Latin America because of common culture and language, means that few if any Australian programs make it on to Spanish screens.

It is still necessary to treat European countries as separate entities for the purposes of this discussion. There is simply no pan-European market for television (Silj 1992, p.39), although the European regulators continue to put in place arrangements designed to foster one. Silj considers that the politics of regulation designed to promote a 'European identity' as a bulwark against American cultural invasion are misguided. Audience preference for national programming, if sufficient volume can be produced, will ensure that the so-called US invasion is limited. The history of the various national television cultures since 1990 bears this out. In every country where new private systems have attained a degree of maturity (Italy, Germany, France, increasingly The Netherlands), the trend is towards indigenous production within the economic limits of the system. Most successful satellite and cable stations, whether pay services or advertiser-supported, are also nationally based. Pan-European satellite television has been spectacularly unsuccessful.

The fact that there is no pan-European market, let alone a 'European identity', means that Australia has to sell programs on a territory-by-territory basis, an arduous and economically unrewarding process since the returns from most markets are so small. Outside the UK, genuine co-ventures and co-productions between Australia and the countries of Europe are still few and far between. Most broadcasters buy programs 'off the shelf' at the markets, which is the cheapest method of acquisition. Therefore, Australian producers must depend very heavily on well-placed European distributors, who have sizeable volumes of product and who can thus afford to give reasonable distribution advances, which can be used to finance the program.

EUROPEAN TELEVISION SYSTEMS

Until the developments in Asian television in the early 1990s, Europe was the area of the world experiencing the biggest changes in its television systems. Despite the European Union, and the use of the term 'European public-service television', there is actually a great degree of variation among Western European television systems. The three we are looking at in detail are different from each other, and different again from systems like the British and the American. The Netherlands in particular has a television system quite unlike any other in the world. What they all have in common is that up to the 1980s their systems consisted entirely of some version of public-service broadcasting, though, unlike Australia and the UK, this was funded partly by advertising, and that from the beginning of the 1980s each of them has begun to introduce, mostly unwillingly, competition from private interests.

In all cases the adjustment to the late entry of private broadcasting and the concomitant increase in the number of channels has had a traumatic impact on the public broadcasters, as they struggle with dramatic loss of audiences, consequent falls in revenue and, in their attempts to respond to these changes by becoming more entrepreneurial themselves, a confusion of purpose and direction. Since they are funded partly from licence fee, as their audiences diminish the argument that they are entitled to receive all the income from licence fees gets weaker, thus threatening their revenue further. In addition, many of them are over-staffed compared with the lean private broadcasters and they are subject to often heavy cultural and regional obligations, which add to their running costs. In some cases they also have limitations on the amount of advertising revenue they can earn, which further disadvantages them in comparison to their competitors (although obviously access to the licence fee is the *quid pro quo*).

The faltering of the public broadcasters in Europe has important implications for the Australian production industry. Traditionally, it has been the monopoly-rich public broadcasters who have had the revenue strength to buy high-budget drama without a great deal of anxiety about cost, and to enter into co-productions and pre-sales to help finance it. In addition, their public-service charter has made them open to the import of high-quality drama from other countries, regardless of whether such drama had maximum audience-pulling power – they could act as a kind of art cinema of the airwaves. Their cultural mandate also meant that they would import categories like documentary and children's programming, all staples of the Australian production scene.

When revenues fall and competition becomes keener, these luxuries can't be afforded unless they guarantee big audiences. Many public broad-casters have had to reduce costs to compete with the private stations. This means cheaper formats like quiz, game and chat shows, variety, soap operas and reality programs – none of which travels well across borders. This then creates less space for imports of program formats like drama and docu-mentary. This should not be exaggerated; the transformation is not total. The public broadcasters still command very large audiences and revenues, especially in the bigger countries, and they retain a commitment to a distinctive public-service charter – but the trends we have described can only become more marked as more channels are added to the mediascape.

For the purposes of considering European television as a destination for Australian programs, we can divide the television services in most of Western Europe into four categories. In the first are the public broadcasters which are under siege, but which still command at least 50 per cent of the audience in all countries and which are still (at least by Australian standards) quite rich. Theirs is general programming – meaning that they program across virtually every genre and for all sections of the society (though not necessarily all at the same time). Their programming also tends to have a high proportion of national content – about 80 per cent – and to emphasise programs for minority audiences, for example regionally specific programming in Germany, or programs for children. It also tends to be highbrow, cultural, or educational programming. Thus there is a higher proportion of serious documentary, serious news and current affairs, discussion programs and high-quality drama.

In France, this roughly describes France 2 (FR2) and France 3 (FR3), although in France there is less difference between public and private television than in other countries. In Italy it describes RAI1, RAI2 and RAI3 but, with three main public channels, it is possible to allow the first network to compete head to head with the private channels, while keeping the second and third for a purer public-service mission. Germany's ARD and ZDF both conform to the public-service model (although this picture will change if ZDF is privatised), as do the three Nederland channels in Holland.

In the second category are the major private channels which have developed in all main countries. In Germany this includes RTL, RTL2 and Sat 1, in France TF1 and Canal Plus, in The Netherlands RTL4 and RTL5 and in Italy Canale 5 and Italia 1. Between them, the major private and the public networks command around 80 or 90 per cent of the national audience with the other 10–20 per cent being shared between all the other channels. France is a special case. Because there is virtually no advertiser-supported satellite or cable and only one big private channel, TF1 (although M6 is increasing in significance), the pay service Canal Plus has won a bigger slice of the audience than comparable services in other European countries and is very significant in economic terms in the French market.

The major private channels initially had a very different programming philosophy to their public counterparts. When they started they relied heavily on US imports and emphasised the populist programming avoided by the public broadcasters. They tapped an unsatisfied audience demand for this kind of programming and for US programs with their glamour, pace and novelty. An interesting exception is the new Greek private broadcaster, New Channel, the backbone of whose original schedule was Australian series – 500 hours of *A Country Practice* and 65 hours of *Rafferty's Rules* – thus demonstrating the value of bulk libraries (*TV World*, June 1992, p.4). But as these channels matured, gaining a foothold in the market, they turned away from heavy reliance on US and other imported programming and towards local programming. This new local production concentrated on lowbrow genres like game and quiz shows and variety, which these new services had made popular.

The third kind of service includes the other private channels, whether they be advertiser- or subscription-based and irrespective of their technical means of delivery; these have not won a mass audience. In most cases they are not genuine niche channels; they are more like channels for 'left-overs'. In Germany, Pro7 and Kabelkanal are cheaply run channels on which the Kirch Group, the big media conglomerate, can unload the programs it has bought in a package, usually from US distributors, for which they can win small but sufficient audiences to support their margins. In Italy, Berlusconi's smaller channels, especially Retequattro, fall into this category. These channels are still nationally based but marginal; they have a very high level of imported content, mainly very old and mainly

American except in the case of Retequattro, which is almost wall-to-wall Latin American *telenovelas*. They do not commission any original programming.

In the fourth category are the various pan-European satellite and cable services – MTV, Superchannel, Eurosport – which have very small audiences in any country but which across the whole of Europe gain sufficient audience to remain viable. These are more genuinely niche channels, meeting specialist tastes for sport and music video, for example. They do not originate program production either, but simply buy program rights. Discovery Europe, which started in 1991 and was bought by the US Discovery Channel in 1992, has used Australian documentary material as a backbone of its fledgling schedule. It was estimated that 24 per cent of the channel offering in 1993 was Australian-originated, with *Beyond 2000* enjoying great popularity (Carrington 1993).

From the point of view of a small-to-medium-size producer like Australia selling to the markets of Europe, there is no financial windfall from services in the third and fourth categories. Even where Australian soaps were purchased for a channel such as Retequattro or Kabelkanal, the prices paid would be so low that Australian producers would not be able to finance programs on the strength of them. It is not likely as things now stand that these channels would buy first-run programs. They would be more likely to acquire German rights from one of the bigger broadcasters who had already shown the program several times.

AUSTRALIAN PROGRAMS IN FRANCE AND GERMANY

Interrelated industrial and cultural factors influence France's openness to Australian programs. In prime time the schedule is divided into 90-minute slots rather than one hour slots as in US or Australian models. After 8.30 pm there are two 90-minute time slots, which take the schedule through until approximately 11.45 pm. They are usually filled by two telemovies, or two magazine programs or two films one after the other. The reason the 90-minute time slot can accommodate a film is because of restrictions on advertising. These 90-minute slots were spoken about by almost everyone we interviewed as if they were immutable, even though they make much more complicated co-producing with partners with a different time frame to their schedule. We can conjecture that such a time slot may be related to the extreme cinephilia of the French audience and to the fact that before the days of the blockbuster, cinema films were traditionally 90 minutes long. This three-hour period of prime time after the news is extremely important in the French schedule. It is called the *rendez-vous* and is listed separately in the TV guide. It is a time when, if access prime-time programming has worked to win its attention, the audience can settle back with its TV channel and feel part of its temporary community.

Another feature of the schedule is the prominence of game shows, usually from imported formats, the element of cabaret or variety in *Le Chanson* and the prominence given to French films and telemovies in the movie slot. In the week of 24 June 1991, only two non-French films were shown on France 2 (FR2) and only one was American. This reflects the regulatory requirement to broadcast a certain amount of EOF (*expression originale Française*) programs. EOF generally means a work shot entirely in French, or one primarily shot in French with the script and dialogue originally written in French (Jezequel and Pineau 1992, p.505–06). In addition, to qualify for production support it is necessary to produce EOF programs. This complicates co-production with the French.

French television is thus quite resistant to imported television from outside the US. In 1989 just 1.1 per cent of the amount of fiction shown on French television was Australian; 36 per cent was French and 41 per cent was from the US (ibid., 1992, p.463). The combination of regulation, the nature of the schedule, French tastes for local variety programming, the fondness for categories of programming like game shows and magazine shows, which are inherently national, means that there is little room for programs from new sources. Canal Plus has a large proportion of imported programming, so does M6 to a lesser extent. So far the latter shows a definite preference for American programming. However the space in the schedule for series on M6 indicates that this is a place where Australian programming might fit. On the main channels – TF1, FR2 and FR3 – there seems less room unless marked changes in taste or scheduling strategy occur.

For Simone Halberstadt-Harari, managing director of Tele-Images, the largest independent French production company, and who is known as 'the queen of soap', a problem for the entry of Australian programs into the French market is that broadcasters buy programs in large packages and in order to get desirable programming from the US, a lot of less desirable programming is also acquired. This fills the off-peak times, leaving little room or money for programs from elsewhere. She was, however, fulsome in her praise of Australian programs and production methods. For her the question was whether France could match Australia in terms of program innovation and efficiency. This accords with a view that is general among French producers: in their view Australia is actually a better and more advanced producer of television programs than France. It has larger independent production companies with more continuous production. They were impressed by the level of professionalism and efficiency with which Australia turns out programs across a wide number of genres, and reported that they thought Australian costs were up to two-thirds cheaper than French (Belet 1992).

Tele-Images is a rather exceptional company for France as it operates, and has always operated, at the extreme end of popular television, making the successful sitcom, *Maguy*, based on the American sitcom, *Maude*, which is in its eighth year on FR2, and a large number of other sitcoms, series, and telemovies. Tele-Images has an ongoing relationship with Grundys and, in 1992, was negotiating to produce a French version of *The Restless Years*. This failed to eventuate because of 'creative differences'. It also has Australian programs in its distribution portfolio, including *A Country Practice*, and pre-bought *The New Adventures of Skippy*.

One area in which Australia can make and has made inroads in France is in the area of children's programming. French regulation requires a large quantity of programs for young viewers (TF1's commitment is for 800 hours a year of programs for 'youth') and in France, as elsewhere, financing them is difficult since they do not attract high advertising revenues. The production company Quartier Latin has continued to look to Australia as a natural co-producer in this area and in 1992 was involved in a French/Australian/European co-production with Grundys called *Mission Top Secret*. The program synopsis describes it as 'an adventure series in which children of the International Centauri Network link up via satellite and computers to defend the world treasures from criminal attack' (*Encore*, 10 (3), p.44). With a budget of FF33 million for 12 hours, *Mission Top Secret* was a complicated co-production with location shooting in France, Germany, Japan, and Australia. Pre-sales were obtained in all those territories because of its multi-national character, and because its science-fiction theme makes it the sort of program likely to sell in a large number of markets over several years.

Australian children's programs such as the Australian Children's Television Foundation (ACTF) production *Round the Twist* enjoy a high reputation in France. The first series was sold to FR2, was shown a number of times in repeats, and was very popular. Partly on French initiative, FR2 and the ACTF commenced a second series in 1992. Other co-productions in the children's area include *Deep Water Haven* (*Port Cook* in France) made by France's F Productions with Beyond International and TVNZ's production arm, Pacific Pictures. Soap operas are not prevalent on French television because, compared with other European countries, especially Germany and Italy, there are not many commercial channels. Only two, TF1 and M6, are sizeable and there isn't the same hunger for soap opera to fill the hours (Halberstadt-Harari 1992). At the same time Tele-Images was attracted to the idea of a clone of *The Restless Years* because it was about young people, and since 1992 in France there has been a race to attract a younger audience.

Apart from cinema features, Australia has sold a small number of programs to France. They include: *Neighbours*, originally sold to La Cinq and then to FR2, which failed; *A Country Practice*, but there is no evidence that it has been broadcast; *Johnson and Friends*, a Film Australia program sold to TF1; *The Leaving of Liverpool*, sold to FR2; *Police Rescue*; *Skippy*, acquired by Tele-Images; three or four documentaries made by Film Australia and sold to TF1; and the children's programs already mentioned.

Neighbours is an interesting case as it has been such a success in Britain but a failure almost everywhere else that it has been shown in Europe. (The exception is in Germany, where it has been showing for two years in an 8.30 am time slot on Sat 1.) Stephen Crofts has analysed the reception of *Neighbours* in France. Dubbed as *Les Voisins* it was launched by Antenne 2 (now FR2) in August 1989 (Crofts 1995, p.115). At first it was screened twice daily at 1.30 am and 5.45 pm. It secured ratings of 24 per cent, which was roughly FR2's average for that year. However, for reasons FR2 was unwilling to disclose, the evening screening was shifted to 6.30 after only ten episodes. This put it against stronger competition from the other channels and its ratings dropped to below 16 per cent. After a further schedule change it was taken off the air after a total of only seven months' screening. Of 185 episodes originally purchased, only 169 were shown (ibid.).

The French agent had bought *Neighbours* on the basis of its great success in Britain. Kylie Minogue's fame was also a factor; by 1989 this had spread from the UK to France. Other potentially appealing features were the images of sunshine and the good life, its acceptable exoticism – both familiar and different enough to appeal; its lack of racial difference, a sensitive topic in France because of latent racism; and its lack of disturbing social issues and concentration on banal and everyday issues. In other words, many of the same factors that are alleged to account for its appeal to the British. Nevertheless it was scheduled in a way that indicated a lack of faith in the program, and especially a resistance to series not from the US.

The French love of *Americanité* makes it difficult for serial fiction from other countries to make an impact. Stephen Crofts' research (1993; 1995) indicated that the French media commentators did not know how to judge *Neighbours*. It puzzled them, partly because it was not American. They are predisposed to look for narrative drive and polish, at the same time they denigrate the spectacular and superficial nature of American soap opera. Perhaps *Neighbours* was puzzling because it was not spectacular, or pacy like US shows, but neither did it fit in with the high-culture expectations of French audiences. And the French do not have a soap-opera tradition, which is of course in marked contrast to the UK. In their local versions of series each episode is semi-complete, for example the *Maigret* series, so again, *Neighbours* was puzzling to them because of its serial nature. At the same time the history of Australian programs in France of any kind is not very wide. Series like *Young Doctors* and *A Country Practice* had very short runs. Apart from cinema features, Australian television material is known only through some of the classier mini-series such as *All the Rivers Run* and *Return to Eden*.

By contrast, Germany is rather more open to Australian programs. There are several factors at work here; one is a closer cultural proximity between British and German sensibilities than between British and French, and the shared cultural traditions of Australia and Britain give Australia a greater natural affinity with Germany (and Holland) than with the Latin countries. The second reason, which perhaps flows from this, is that there is a more substantial history of Australian programs on German public-service television and further, the styles of programs and scheduling practices in Germany harmonise rather better with Australian ones. In particular the Germans do not have the passion of the French and Italians for variety and quiz and game shows. There is really no longer any counterpart to the European variety show on Australian or British television and, in any case, programs like quiz and game shows are very local in character, both in the sense of incorporating local codes of presentation and in involving performers who are very well known within national boundaries but not outside them.

Another factor in France are the local-content regulations, which make co-production and even acquisition harder. Germany has no specific local-content quotas, although the general cultural obligations imposed on the public broadcasters would make a certain amount of German programming essential even if audience demand did not already dictate it. Germany is the most likely European destination for Australian programs outside Britain. The size of its market and its economic strength give it the capacity to finance co-productions, and the expansion of services and of the advertising market as well as the eventual development of former East Germany give it good prospects for the future. When these economic factors are added to the cultural ones mentioned earlier, it seems a market worth pursuing for Australia.

RTL, the most popular private station in Germany, has acquired a number of Australian programs including: *Bellamy, Da Lacht das Krokodil* (re-cut Paul Hogan shows), *Dirtwater Dynasty, Elly and Jools,* and *Let the Blood Run Free*, as well as over 50 movies including most of the *Dot and the Kangaroo* series, *The Big Steal, High Tide* and *Midnite Spares*. RTL also broadcasts *Gute Zeiten, Schlechte Zeiten* ('Good Times, Bad Times'), the German version of the Grundy serial *The Restless Years*. It commenced in 1992 and is stripped at 7.40 pm every day. It is produced in Berlin by Grundy Worldwide in collaboration with UFA studios, owned by the Bertelsmann empire, which is a part owner of RTL.

The setting-up of production in 1992 was overseen by Michael Murphy, Grundy vice-president responsible for serial drama in Europe. At that time there were only two non-Germans involved in the production (Wroe 1992, p.15). The cost is DM80 000 (about A$68 000) per half-hour episode, which compares very favourably with Australian soap-production prices. In 1992 it was rating about 11, which a Grundys European publicity executive called 'not great but OK'. It has done well enough for RTL for them to renew it and its production was still continuing in 1994. The initial rewriting of re-versioned Grundy serials is done by Grundy writers. It has been necessary to update *The Restless Years* (which originally began in 1977) in some obvious ways like substituting Ecstasy for LSD in a story about drugs, and the storyline is made simpler and more 'universal' by not referring to any contemporary social or political issues. *Gute Zeiten, Schlecte Zeiten* is made within walking distance of the site of the Berlin Wall, but never so much as a whisper in the program alludes to what it represents (Wroe 1992, p.15).

Gute Zeiten is the first daily soap to be made in Germany, but it is unlikely to be the last. German production, as in the rest of continental Europe, was previously tied to high-budget long-form drama, made in the style of rather ponderous art cinema. Writers, directors, actors and technicians were accustomed to this way of working. The factory system of daily soap production, which Grundys has perfected since the 1970s, was alien. As private television continues to make inroads on the public system, and as revenues are spread thinner, the demand for serial drama must grow. Soap opera combines familiar locations, which are preferred by audiences, with cheapness and abundance. Grundys is passing on its skills and methods by re-versioning successful Australian soap, but it is doubtful that this stage can be protracted indefinitely. Sooner or later European producers will learn the skills required and will be able to dispense with the Grundy services. By 1992, the advent of private television in Germany had in fact produced a burst in the local production industry; in October 1992 there were 18 drama programs in various stages of production. Some of these, like *Der Bergdoktor* (DM75 000 per episode) have since become very popular with audiences.

Regional public-service broadcaster ARD – the first German channel – has acquired a smattering of ABC and commercial mini-series and documentaries over the years. In 1994 the Australian sitcom *Hey Dad* joined the ARD line-up. It was stripped in an afternoon time slot; this scheduling was a major concession in the face of commercial competition, but its ratings performance was disappointing. As would be expected, the translation of humour presents a particular problem. Manfred Schutze, head of acquisitions at ZDF, said that English humour is very difficult to translate. For that reason dubbing is less translation than rewriting – making the jokes more 'German'. This is a problem even for the much better-recognised American humour in the US program *Cheers*, which was considerably rewritten.

ZDF, the second public-service channel in Germany, has a long history of Australian program-buying. Recent acquisitions include *Bony*, *The Flying Doctors* and *The Adventures of Black Beauty*. ZDF reported that *The Flying Doctors* was 'quite successful'. At the end of 1992 had bought 220 episodes which, at the rate of one a week, 'lasts a long time' (Schutze 1992). The program's appeal for German audiences is seen to lie in the mixture of its exotic location the 'big land' – and its familiarity – 'the same thing happens there as could happen in Europe'. Germans have a good knowledge of and interest in Australia, partly because it is a popular German holiday destination but, according to Schutze, *The Flying Doctors* was 'made into a German thing by the dubbing', indicating that Australian idiom, slang and culturally specific references were removed. However Schutze also praised the production values, the good stories and cast.

This opinion of the aesthetics of Australian television is in direct contrast to that offered by Michael Schmidel of Taurus Film, part of the Kirch Group, which distributes *The Flying Doctors* in Germany and whose series department does the dubbing for it. He voiced a view often made by the gatekeepers: Australian programs are hard to sell because they have no stars, and when they are of the action genre they are not as fast or as polished as a US program of the same kind. He thought also that there were problems with the technical quality; programs shot on 16 mm and post-produced on video had poor-quality colour compared to German productions, which were shot on 35 mm. Shooting on video for him was beyond the pale because of the flat uniform lighting it required (Schmidel 1992). These opinions are part of the 'folklore' of many of the European buyers, but they are hard to square with observations of popular German *Krimis* (crime series) like *Derrick* and *The Investigator*, which don't appear to be of very high quality technically or even aesthetically. Schutze gave a similar opinion about the Australian soap, *E-Street*. For him, it was 'too slow', although he was unable to articulate more clearly what he meant by this and it is a surprising view given that in terms of plot moves the early episodes of *E-Street* burnt up storylines at a cracking pace.

In the analysis offered by another gatekeeper, Gottfried Langenstein, deputy director of ZDF, US programs do better in Germany because US cities and manners are understood by the audiences through their exposure to them in cinema and television since the end of the Second World War. 'They know what happens in Washington. They know that in San Francisco you're always driving up and down hills. But it would be very "far out" for a German to know Woollahra or North Queensland' (Langenstein 1992). He also talked of the difference in dramaturgy between Australian and US programs. American films are faster and have much shorter shots than the European or Australian style. However he praised Australia as 'one of the best television producers in the world'. In his view, when Germany was looking for co-production partners they would look to the US, the large European countries and to Australia; Japan would be considered only for certain categories of program, namely, documentaries and cartoons. The advantages that would be gained by producing with Australia include the low cost, variety in locations and expertise in certain categories of programming, such as children's.

Sat 1, owned by the powerful Kirch Group, and the private channel next in popularity after RTL, has acquired *Return to Eden* and *Neighbours* (*Nachbarn*). The latter commenced its run on Sat 1 in 1992, initially stripped twice a day at 8.30 am and repeated at 2.30 pm. By 1994 it was on only once a day at 2.00 pm. *Return to Eden* was broadcast in 1991 and rated well. The dubbing job done for *Neighbours* is not nearly as polished as that for *The Flying Doctors*. The daily schedule of the program makes the time and costs involved in high-quality dubbing prohibitive, so the dialogue is closer to a straight transliteration without rewriting or adding new sound effects (ibid.).

The Kirch Group is the biggest production concern in Germany and one of the biggest in Europe. It has more than ten subsidiary or associated production companies, including the flagship Beta-Taurus in Munich. The Kirch Group has been producing for ARD and ZDF for a long time and, with its move into broadcasting, is now producing also for its own channels. It has a working relationship with Grundys, with which it co-produced *Bony*, putting up two-thirds of the money (Holmes 1992), and with Crawfords, with which it co-produced the children's series *Half Way Across the Galaxy and Turn Left*.

Beta-Taurus were keen on the *Bony* project because the earlier series made in the 1970s was a success in Germany. The program was controversial in Australia because a white actor, Cameron Daddo, was cast as the central Aboriginal character. The Beta-Taurus producers would have preferred an Aboriginal actor because they wanted something 'very Australian' (Schmidel 1992) but Grundys in Australia made the judgement that the Australian audience (the non-Aboriginal part of it presumably) would not accept an Aboriginal actor (Holmes 1992) and alleged that there were no suitable actors available – a claim that even in 1991 would have been difficult to sustain. Thus the Bony character was changed from an Aboriginal to a white who had been brought up by Aborigines (Holmes 1992). Beta-Taurus also wanted something that met European perceptions of Aboriginal belief systems, perhaps like the 1977 Peter Weir film, *The Last Wave*, which is very popular in Europe because of its perceived 'mysticism'. Grundys, perhaps wisely in view of local Australian readings that see such elements as phony, if not also racist, resisted this pressure (Schmidel 1992). Beta-Taurus also insisted on a well-known German actor to play one of the main roles in *Bony* with the aim of increasing the program's appeal to a German audience. The German broadcaster ZDF clearly had reservations about the result and there was some delay in scheduling it (Holmes 1992). It finally went to air in February 1993, on week days at 5.30 pm; the rating results were reasonable for the time slot. A second series had been considered by the Germans before it went to air, but this has not eventuated (Schmidel 1992).

Half Way Across the Galaxy and Turn Left was a co-production between Beta-Taurus and Crawfords. It was made as two series of 26 half-hour episodes and was adapted from the popular book by Australian children's author Robin Klein. The overseas component, both the level of investment and creative control, was much higher than it is for a program like *The Flying Doctors,* which in Australia can be made almost for its licence fee. The return in Australia for C (children's) drama is so small that any program such as this, with high production values, including special effects, requires a high overseas involvement. The German financial element was a pre-sale to ZDF, which we estimate to be two-thirds of the budget; the German creative involvement was control over casting, crew and scripts. The production was carried out using all Australian writers, directors, cast and crew, except that the leading female character was played by a popular young German actor, Sylvia Seidel, and illustrates the way in which children's programming tends to cross borders more easily than that for adults. Michael Schmidel of Beta-Taurus talked of its 'universal theme – a fish out of water', and how it was not too locally specific in its references and idiom.

While Australian programs have had, and will continue to have, a constant presence on French and German screens, as well as in various other sites within the European television system, they have not made a large cultural impact. They have not entered the 'social imaginary', as it were, and are not reflected in other artefacts of popular culture like rock music and fan magazines, nor do they have a prominent tabloid identity as they have in Britain. But in one country in Europe there is an Australian program – *The Flying Doctors* – which has achieved this level of recognition and audience loyalty. A number of factors in the television ecology of The Netherlands combine to account for the extraordinary success of this Australian series, but perhaps the most important is the unique nature of Holland's public-service tradition and the way in which *The Flying Doctors* harmonises with it.

SOCIAL VALUES IN A SERIOUS CULTURE: *THE FLYING DOCTORS* IN THE NETHERLANDS

The Netherlands had an exclusively public-service television system until the advent of private broadcaster RTL4 in 1989. However its model of public service is quite unlike any other in the world, being based not on 'internal diversity' as in the BBC model but on 'external diversity' (Nieuwenhuis 1992, p.204). This comes about because the bodies responsible for broadcasting are not the actual broadcasters (transmitters of programs) but organisations which are offshoots of the so-called 'pillars' of Dutch social institutions. Each pillar has its own broadcasting organisation and is given air time on the state-run channel in proportion to the size of its membership. The traditional broadcasting organisations are VARA (socialist), KRO (catholic), NCRV (protestant), VPRO (liberal protestant) and AVRO. The idea is that diversity is ensured by virtue of each of these organisations choosing programming material that reflects their various ideological positions.

Even though the system has never been controlled centrally as in comparable countries, a Reithian philosophy, the traditional public-service rationale based on broadcasting's role in nation-building and education, associated with the past director-general of the BBC, does to a considerable extent permeate all the broadcasting organisations. This notably is the case with VARA, the socialist grouping, where a philosophy has developed that attempts to wed popularity and progressiveness (Ang 1991, p.130). VARA is the main purchaser of Australian material in The Netherlands and this broadcasting philosophy animates the taste regime through which its acquisitions staff choose programs. VARA's head of acquisitions regards the BBC as the quality benchmark, and prefers, for instance, *Law and Order* over *LA Law* among US programming 'because it has more of a documentary flavour' (van Essen 1992). *The Flying Doctors* fulfilled the conditions of being both sufficiently progressive, in VARA's sense of the term (this can be read as with pro-social and pro-communal values, but without the elitism often attributed to classical Reithianism), and popular in the sense that it has a very large and very devoted following among audiences. When first runs of *The Flying Doctors* finished in 1993 because of the program's cancellation in Australia, VARA replaced it with *Police Rescue*, which also evidently conformed to the 'progressive and popular' ethos of the network.

The Netherlands has been moving toward a mixed system of broadcasting since the mid-1980s and even more than in other European countries the journey has been a painful one. When private channel RTL4 commenced in 1989 it had an instant and destabilising effect on the broadcasting scene. With its early diet of wall-to-wall American series it quickly won a third of the audience away from the public broadcasters, who were forced for the first time to behave in a more commercial manner and to co-operate, more especially in the matter of program acquisition and scheduling. By the end of 1992 audience shares had settled down into a pattern in which RTL4 gained a regular 30–35 per cent and the public service stations together gained 50–55 per cent, with the rest distributed across all the other stations available to Dutch audiences. In 1992 the public stations dominated only at the weekends and this was aided in no small measure by *The Flying Doctors*, which was programmed at 8 pm on Saturday nights and easily won the audience for the time slot.

The Netherlands is one of the most densely cabled countries in the world with 85 per cent of Dutch homes connected. This gives Dutch audiences access to more than 30 channels that include, as well as Ned1, Ned2 and Ned3 and RTL4 and RTL5, the national broadcasters of adjoining nations such as the UK, France, Germany, Belgium and Italy and all the pan-European satellite services and national satellite services of countries like Germany. Thus the Netherlands is a perfect prototype of the multi-channel environment. The five national channels are watched for about 90 per cent of the time and all the others have to share the remainder. Unlike Germany and France, which have sizeable migrant or guest-worker populations, and unlike Italy and Spain, which are internally divided by regional and linguistic variations, Holland is an unusually ethnically and linguistically uniform (and of course geographically small) country. This may partly account for the attachment of audiences to the national channels, which have a particularly Dutch character.

As well as the longstanding commercial relationship between VARA and Australian producers, JE Productions, the biggest production company in The Netherlands, also has an Australian connection. At the end of 1993 it amalgamated with another independent production company, John De Mol Productions, to form Endermol Entertainment. This merged company is now the biggest independent production house in Europe, outstripping its UK and German rivals. It specialises in soap opera, game shows and variety and produces 2500 hours a year (Fuller 1993, p.46). Dutch soap opera production has been highly influenced by the Grundy model. The first soap opera format sale that Grundys made was the 1977 production *The Restless Years*, which it sold to JE Productions. This company made the program as *Goede Tijden, Slechte Tijden* (*Good Times, Bad Times*). It is stripped daily on RTL4 at 8 pm, where it rates very well. By 1994 it had been running two years. Its success in Holland led to the use of the same model in Germany.

The transformation of *The Restless Years* into *Good Times, Bad Times* illustrates the process by which soap formats are traded. JE Productions bought the Australian scripts for *The Restless Years* and translated them into Dutch. The plots and situations were kept the same, the dialogue was kept more or less the same but certain adjustments were made to make it appropriate for a Dutch situation. As time went on, certain characters who had not been popular in the Australian version became popular in Holland and vice versa and so the plots started to diverge from the Australian originals. By 1992, the Dutch scripts had become entirely independent from the originals, but the format was still used.

Hedy von Bochove, production executive at JE, reported that the motivation for buying the format was the popularity of *The Restless Years* in Australia, but also that JE was very eager to get a new soap opera going and by buying existing scripts the company saved development time and expense (von Bochove 1992). There was also no tradition of making soap opera in Holland – no factory production of stripped serial drama. Expertise was needed very quickly, so the Grundy scripts and know-how were important elements in Dutch television. Reg Watson adapted the scripts and they were separately translated. Together with Michael Murphy, at Grundy International, he set up the production process at JE Productions; this whole process took eight to nine months. *Good Times, Bad Times* was the first stripped soap opera to be shown on Dutch television.

As in Germany, JE Productions reported that what appealed to the company in *The Restless Years* was the focus on teenage characters and problems. Like much European television, Dutch broadcasting was very much focussed on an older age group. With the addition of private stations there was a desire to reach the younger viewer, and *The Restless Years* was a good vehicle for this. The teenage problems were retained but other social issues, like problems of the environment, were added. The kind of audience that likes to watch *Good Times, Bad Times* is also the audience that watched *Beverly Hills 90210* and, as Hedy von Bochove said, it was important to win back the audience aged between 14 and 20. In October 1992, *Good Times, Bad Times* had a market share of 35, which means that 35 per cent of sets in use were tuned to it.

But without any doubt it is *The Flying Doctors* that has made the biggest impact in The Netherlands. Australian productions generally have a high level of acceptability in Holland – a subtitling country – because the Dutch are very used to seeing programs in English and programs from the United Kingdom; Dutch audiences speak English in very large numbers, and they are used to British styles of comedy and drama. Being a small to medium-sized country, Holland has a somewhat higher level of imported programs, including British productions, than the bigger European countries. So, there is a propensity to be open to British programming, and to the extent that Australian and British drama styles are similar, and more to each other than to American styles, then there is a particular preparedness in Dutch audiences for Australian drama.

However, the 'exoticism' of the Australian outback in *The Flying Doctors* also appeals, as in other countries where the program has done well. It is also a relatively safe program concept. Whatever progressiveness there is in the program is found in the warmth of its portrayal of social solidarity and communitarian values of helping people in crisis. This contrasts with US programming which, according to a senior Dutch public-service executive, dwells on racial and social conflict that 'wouldn't wash with the Dutch audience' (Tolen-Worth 1992). Hedy von Bochove accounted for *The Flying Doctors*' popularity in the following terms: 'It's about helping people. We love hospital series. But there is also something Australian about *The Flying Doctors* that appeals. It is very down to earth – that basic earthiness. It shows good people, a healthy people, and an attractive Australian way of life' (von Bochove 1992).

VARA began programming *The Flying Doctors* in 1987. For the six years until 1993 when the program was cancelled in Australia, it formed the backbone of the public channel's Saturday-night schedule, where it regularly won the 8 pm or 8.30 pm time slot. Because of its huge popularity with Dutch audiences, in 1994 VARA began repeats of the program from its beginning at 6.30 pm.

There is a devoted *Flying Doctors* fan club, located in the small town of Nijmegen. It has only 700 members but they are fanatical and club membership is an intensely involving business. The club publishes a regular photostatted magazine, which contains episode summaries, photos of personalities and places from the show, *Flying Doctor* quizzes and even copies of letters between Dutch fans and the actual Royal Flying Doctor Service operating out of Broken Hill to which fans send donations of money. In 1992 a club day was held in Nijmegen, attended by 400 fans. The major stars of the show were flown in and the *VARA TV Guide* contained extensive pictorial coverage of ecstatic fans meeting Robert Grubb (Dr Geoff Standish) and Lenore Smith (Sister Kate Standish) who are by far the most popular characters. The Dutch fan club has spawned another in Germany where, as we have noted, the program is shown on ZDF, and there is also one in the UK.

The show has also led to a series of novelisations of *Flying Doctor* episodes, which are jointly published by Crawfords, the Australian producers, and VARA, and which appear at popular magazine outlets. Five such books have been published with the first three selling very well. Like the extensive television guide and newspaper coverage that the program enjoyed over the six years of its run, the novelisations embody the traditional preoccupations of soap opera fans everywhere. There is a particular attachment to Dr Geoff and Sister Kate, whose perfect marriage topped off with the perfect baby represent a romantic fantasy for the mostly young (teenage) and mostly female membership of the fan club.

However, not all the fans are young women. A young male viewer reported in the fan club magazine that he liked the series because all the characters help one another irrespective of rank. In the Dutch context this is rather unusual. In a contemporary and very popular Dutch medical series, *Medical Centre West*, doctors are more important than nurses, with the former usually male and the latter female.

The media coverage of the program repeatedly accounts for its popularity by citing the pleasure that viewers take in the sense of community and belonging at Cooper's Crossing, and in what they see as the devotion to duty in the face of danger and hardship that is part of the image of the Flying Doctor Service. As one television commentator expressed it, the attraction is that the program depicts 'people of real flesh and blood, living in the heat, the drought and the isolation of the outback, and coping with it with a combination of willpower and humour' (Mars 1992). It is seen as less depressing than *Medical Centre West*. One young female fan said that whereas in the Dutch series you can have four people with cancer, or two with AIDS, in *The Flying Doctors*, whatever ails people can be cured. This is reminiscent of the British discourse comparing *Neighbours* to *Eastenders*.

The gender equality exhibited on the program also draws favourable mention from commentators and fans. A July 1991 article in *Psychologie*, a popular magazine about psychology, points to an episode in which the female doctor in the program, Dr Chris Randall (Liz Burch) can fly, while the male doctor, Dr Tom Callaghan (Andrew McFarlane) can't, and when his pilot becomes ill he has to fly the plane with her help. The article approvingly observes that 'Tom is very scared while Chris is completely calm and in charge of the situation. This challenges traditional role models.' It comments that male and female viewers have equal opportunities for identification. Dr Geoff is continually cited approvingly by female viewers as masculine but gentle and understanding. One interview with Robert Grubb (whose photograph is ubiquitous) called him a 'heart-throb' – a man of understanding who is interesting, charming and unthreatening. He is conscious of his shortcomings, but doesn't boast about his strong points. He is witty but not a 'smart-arse', serious but 'with a wink'. In short, he is the ideal man.

It would be easy to draw the conclusion that *The Flying Doctors* represents wish-fulfilment about values lost in modern urban living but this alone does not account for why it has done better in The Netherlands than in any other export market. The answer may well lie in the way qualities of the program – a sense of community, lack of competitiveness,

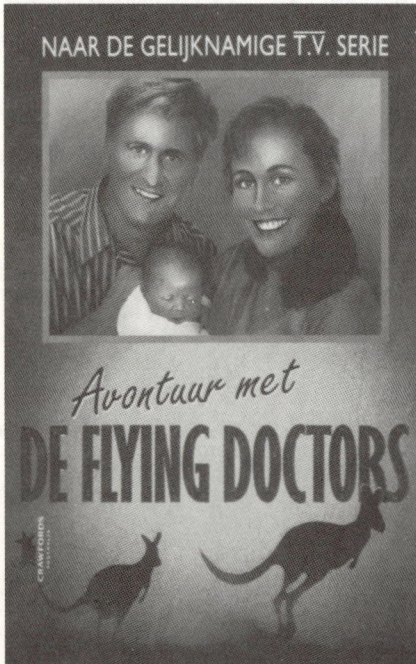

The popularity of *The Flying Doctors* in The Netherlands is reflected in a series of books about the characters in the series published in Holland. The themes of these stories are romance, community and the exotic character of the Australian outback, and the focus is heavily on the 'ideal man', Dr Geoff.
(VARA Television and Crawfords Media International. Illustrations by Francien van Westering.)

gender equality, the absence of violence, tragedy or threatening models of masculinity – are a perfect fit with the social democratic values that have been the foundation of VARA's broadcasting philosophy, and which clearly also resonate with the Dutch viewing public.

8

The United States and Canada

Let us consider a week of television in the US and the screening of Australian and Australian-related material. We chose the week of 13–20 March 1994 relatively randomly, and based the survey on the general program guides for New York, one of the largest multi-channel regions. Feature films included *Green Card*, *The Lighthorsemen*, *The Road Warrior*, *Crocodile Dundee II* and *Dead Calm*; some of these were repeated several times, as they were playing on cable channels, as was the mini-series *Angel at My Table*. *Beyond 2000* was stripped on the basic cable channel Discovery from 7 to 8 pm, with repeats in the early morning and on Saturday afternoon. The Indy Car Grand Prix from Surfers Paradise screened on a network sports program on Sunday afternoon. Australian actors Nicole Kidman (in *Far and Away*) and Jack Thompson (in *A Woman Called Golda*) appeared also, while a nature documentary *Penguin Island: Australia's Little Penguins and Phillip Island*, was screened on public television.

This is not an inconsiderable offering by any comparative estimate of Australian program presence on foreign screens. However, it is minute when seen in the context of the total amount of television routinely available. In the largest markets, such as New York, Los Angeles, Chicago, or Boston, there are typically at least four network-affiliated stations, several independents or syndication stations, up to three public stations, specialty broadcasters (such as Spanish language), then usually half a dozen premium or pay (individual payment per channel) cable channels, about fifteen major basic (advertiser-supported) cable channels, and a varying number of basic cable local-access stations. Non-American material is rarely seen in quantity, and then usually on cable networks, which receive ratings in the 0–2 per cent range. Any non-American material, including Australian, will tend to be lost in the flood of images and sound in the most developed multi-channel environment in the world.

While the US market is by far the biggest in the world, it is also the most resistant to foreign programming, particularly in the commercial broadcasting sector. The broad reason for this outstanding mono-culturalism is not hard to fathom. Because the US market has traditionally been large enough to finance its own productions, and because the creative and services infrastructure has generally been large enough to supply sufficient product, there has not been the imperative felt in most other countries to look outside for co-financing or to complete schedules. Thus generations of US viewers have grown up with an overwhelmingly home-grown diet of television. Such historical taste-formation is extremely difficult to modify, even if there was a need to contemplate doing so – which, from the American point of view, there isn't, except in the area of servicing non-English-speaking communities. Australian programming sits on a second tier of import sources into the US behind Canada, Mexico, other Latin American countries and Britain.

The main changes in foreign sourcing are occurring outside the main-stream networks. Varis' international flows studies (1974; 1984) showed that of total broadcast hours, the US imported 3 per cent in 1973 and 2 per cent in 1983. Of the latter, about half came from the Mexican conglomerate Televisa's supplies to its Spanish International Network (SIN), and largely British imports by the PBS. The bulk of the other half came from a range of other Latin American and European countries. There has been some overall shift upward in this minute amount in the decade since 1983, with some figures putting the cumulative (not ratings-based) audience per week for foreign programs in the US in 1993 at 20 per cent (Weinstock 1994, p.13). All the significant part of this growth occurred on cable, two-thirds of these shows were Spanish, and a quarter came from Britain. But the fastest growing area is in Cantonese, Arabic and Indian programs.

US programmers, schedulers and purchasers offer some standard reasons for the inappropriateness of foreign material, including Australian, on commercial broadcast television. These are unfamiliar accents and language use, slow pacing of narrative-based programs, and low pro-duction values. These reasons don't necessarily indicate a special level of US ethnocentrism or narrowness – the same explanations are sometimes voiced by gatekeepers in other countries. But the fact that there is relatively little incentive to find foreign material for US commercial broadcast television usually means that such reasons are the end of the story; whereas that is not the case for purchasers in other markets.

We shall examine gatekeeper perceptions of Australian program values at various points in this chapter. It is useful to mention here, however, that the mention of accent is usually a shorthand means of indicating cultural differences that are often difficult to conceptualise within industry discourse. There is already a hegemonic US accent – the flat mid-Atlantic coast accent – which excludes much US speech from mainstream television, or at least seeks to modify it. Even an immensely popular sitcom like *Cheers*, although set in Boston, had only one main character speaking with a Boston–New England accent – the rest had mid-Atlantic accents. In television executive James McNamara's opinion, no mainstream drama could succeed with a complete fidelity to regional accent (McNamara *et al.* 1994). There are also major differences between genres in the significance accorded English-accent variation, with talk-dominated soap opera being the most accent-sensitive. That *Neighbours*, for instance, had a 'wrap-around accent problem' – one of the reasons offered by Carol Martz (1994) for its failure in the US – should be seen in this context.

While the US market constitutes a significant proportion of overall Australian television export – with figures in the 25–30 per cent range during the late 1980s and early 1990s – it is typically one-shot features, children's drama and nature-documentary magazine segments, much of it carefully contextualised to minimise its foreign-ness. It thus does not build potential audience expectation for more Australian product or create a platform for significant cross-cultural exchange; the biggest absence is series and serial drama which, more than other television genres, build audiences over time. We shall consider how some producers have tried alternative strategies to the traditional export of completed product to the US in an attempt to break into the long-form drama market (for example, Grundys produced *Dangerous Women* in the US and Village Roadshow made *Paradise Beach* directly for the US syndication market, while it also qualified as local drama on Australian television).

As we have seen in Chapter 4, there has also been a substantial amount of US off-shore production in Australia, estimated to have amounted to about A$300 million spent in Australia during 1988–93. In some cases, like the first series of the revamped *Mission Impossible*, this kind of production qualified, controversially, as Australian for regulatory purposes. Others, like the second series of *Mission Impossible* and *Dolphin Cove*, did not. However, the extent to which programming (either sold into the US market or otherwise directed at it) must be tailored to fit the most culturally non-specific notions of commercial television underlines the

The Beyond International adult drama serial, *Chances*, was not an international success in spite of, or perhaps because of, its groundbreaking sexual frankness and outlandish storylines.
(Cover of *Television Business International*, June 1992.)

difficulties in attempting to deal with the most lucrative but most resistant market in the world.

We shall approach the issue of Australian program placement through the four US industry sectors: broadcast network, broadcast syndication, non-commercial broadcast, and cable. These sectoral divisions are not hermetic, either in their structure or in terms of program placement. Fox's fourth national network under Rupert Murdoch's ownership has drawn many stations out of the syndication sector as well as from their affiliation with other networks. The syndication sector has also seen a trend toward building mini-networks. And players within different sectors routinely compete for programs. The case of *Beyond 2000/Beyond Tomorrow* illustrates this; it was imported originally for non-commercial broadcast, it went both to the fledgling Fox broadcast network and then to cable with Discovery. Interspersed within these sectoral analyses are program case studies of *Paradise Beach*, *Beyond 2000*, and *Brides of Christ*. These embrace a range of program formats (low-budget long-form serial drama, the infotainment sci-tech magazine format, and high-budget high-quality mini-series drama), and illustrate the degrees of success and failure possible in the different sectors of US television.

BROADCAST NETWORK

The four national networks, CBS, NBC, ABC and Fox – the main three with about 200 affiliate stations each – constitute the vast heartland of US television. The rare Australian program screened on a US network tends to be either culturally indistinguishable in origin (the documentary *Nostradamus* in 1990), or a hard-action genre flick (*Grievous Bodily Harm* in 1990), or characterised by some definite US angle through co-production, character or narrative content, and the presence of US actors (the *Crocodile Dundee* films, *Mad Max Beyond Thunderdome*, and mini-series such as *The Last Frontier*, *The Thorn Birds*, *The Far Country* and *The Barlow and Chambers Story*). Grundys had its licensed game shows *Sale of the Century*, *Scattergories* and *Scrabble* on day-time network for periods in the 1980s, but very few slots in network schedules are left after the dominant players in light entertainment in the US, such as Kingworld (producer/distributors of *Jeopardy*, *Wheel of Fortune*, *Oprah Winfrey*, *Inside Edition*), have tied up most opportunities.

BROADCAST SYNDICATION

The broadcast syndication market is made up of those free-to-air stations unaffiliated to networks as well as network affiliates during so-called 'off-network' times such as after school (4–6 pm) and late night (11 pm–7 am). It involves distributors selling directly to individual stations or small groups of stations at significantly lower prices than the networks pay. The market is led by the distributors or syndicators, who set a cost price for a particular program, and syndication stations or groups bid with this floor price in mind, usually with the highest bid winning. The key difference between network and syndication is that many of the latter's programs are off-network re-runs, though increasingly syndication groups are making successful bids for first-run programming. Also, the syndication market typically will seek to use a program in a far greater variety of schedule slots than contemplated on network, and can be open to the possibility of non-US material.

This 'back-door' route to US broadcast television has been attempted with some success by Australian program makers. Drama series sold into syndication include *Against the Wind* (1979), the first major Australian production to be broadcast in the US, *Woobinda – Animal Doctor* (1978), *Prisoner: Cell Block H* (1980), *The Sullivans* (1980), *Eureka Stockade* (1984) and *Sword of Honour* (1990). *Return to Eden* (1983) was 'hugely successful' because it resembled US prime-time soaps and mini-series, with its far-fetched plot of a glamorous and vengeful woman (Martz 1994).

Grundys, perhaps the Australian company that has attempted over the longest period to break into US broadcast television, has had an uneven run: *Prisoner: Cell Block H* during 1979–81, which was described as 'cutting edge and ambitious for the time' (Martz 1994) and which was re-versioned in 1980 as *Willow B: Women in Prison* in a pilot that was not taken up to series; the series *Embassy*, the mini-series *Tanamera* and the game show *It's a Knockout* in the 1990s. Timing was a significant factor in the sale of *Embassy*, with its problematic orientalism a hook right at the start of the Gulf War.

Concerted attempts to build Grundys' international hit serial *Neighbours* into the schedule, however, ultimately failed (*see* Crofts 1994). KCOP Los Angeles and WPIX New York both tested the program, scheduling it in a good late-afternoon slot in summer, and marketing it to a youth demographic, but it failed to gain an audience (Crofts 1994). An additional problem, from the perspective of more than one industry source, was that it didn't get adequate distribution support (Kagan 1994). Certainly for the LA station that trialled it there was no shortage of precedents for adventurous experiments with foreign product. *Threads, Shaka Zulu, Jewel in the Crown, Brideshead Revisited* and *Edge of Darkness* had been used as 'impact' material in limited runs, marketed as 'upscale theatre' to attract new advertisers to independent stations in the 1970s and 1980s. Australian mini-series taken on this basis were disappointing – they included *Alice to Nowhere* and *Shout*! And while Kylie Minogue promised wide appeal at the time, un-reconstructed suburban Australian accents presented a real barrier. Complaints about accents were logged at the station: 'LA might be multicultural but that doesn't mean Australian'. When it was taken off, there wasn't a 'whisper' from viewers (Martz 1994).

Playing at being American: *Paradise Beach*

Paradise Beach, a relatively short-lived serial screened between May 1993 and July 1994 on the Australian Nine Network, and in several international markets, represents a contemporary example of 'playing at being American', in Caughie's two-edged sense of the term (1990). The production and marketing strategy for *Paradise Beach* was, in contemporary Australian long-form *serial* television, a unique one. While unequivocally an Australian production (both for regulatory purposes and for maximising opportunities for local success), it was aimed primarily at the US and other major ancillary markets. It was presold to BSkyB in Britain, South America and European territories mostly sight unseen, a testament to the distribution profile of its co-venture partners (Shoebridge 1993, p.10).

It appeared to bring together an exceptionally strong production, distribution and exhibition alliance. *Paradise Beach* was co-produced by Village Roadshow, which offered complete production facilities at its studio complex at the Gold Coast; the Nine Network, the strongest rating network and an equity partner in the studios; and New World International/Genesis, a large US distribution company specialising in mostly US soap opera (*Baywatch, Santa Barbara, The Bold and the Beautiful*) for the US syndication and international markets. Village had studio space to fill and a commitment to internationalise local production and facilities, and the Nine Network needed successful local drama. For their part, New World and its subsidiary Genesis, in co-venturing on *Paradise Beach*, were responding to a contracting US market for soap opera by capitalising on overseas sources of finance and lower cost structures, thus in effect turning the US into a secondary market and diminishing the importance of network sales (Lowry 1993).

Paradise Beach was virtually simultaneously launched in Australia and the US, and soon after in other territories. It was heavily promoted in Australia, initially filling an early-evening slot directly before the nightly news, then was shifted back half an hour (to insulate its poor performance from the powerful news and current affairs rating period). Ratings for the program indicated that it received its highest exposure at première (18), a promising figure for its place in the schedule, dropping quickly to 11 at the end of its first week, and falling into single figures when it was moved back to 5 pm. Production ceased in May 1994, with some states running episodes until July 1994.

In the US, it was cleared by Genesis/New World for 85 per cent (or 150 stations) of the independent syndication market, an unprecedented exposure for a foreign-made serial. This compares markedly with the 1980s campaign for *Neighbours*, which was not handled by a major distributor. The US strategy was to test *Paradise Beach* during the 1993 northern summer, and then re-launch it in January 1994 if it showed promise. Paralleling the theme of the program ('It's where teenagers from everywhere converge to cut loose, find the perfect wave, and fall hopelessly in love'), it was aimed at its target teen audience at the end of the school year. There was also a deliberate strategy to cover all possible schedule slots in major markets, so that its best performing times could be determined for the re-launch (McNamara *et al.* 1994). It was disastrously placed in the 'black hole' of 3–4 pm against Oprah Winfrey on KCBS Los Angeles and so didn't stand a chance in one of the most important US markets. It did not survive the summer, and was pulled from US schedules before it had run the length of its test campaign.

Why did *Paradise Beach* fail? There are several answers, underscoring the inadequacy of any single industrial, cultural or textual explanation. From a purely financial perspective, it was structured to avoid significant risk. The experienced partners knew the program was an experiment and had determined to make it cost-efficient, so that it was virtually certain of returning modest profits even if it failed to secure ongoing screen time. Produced at a rock bottom A$150 000 an hour, it certainly would have returned reasonable profits to its backers, especially as costs were split three ways. Even a 3 per cent rating (which it reached in only a few markets) would return $US18 000 for a 30-second commercial in US syndication (McMahon, in Shoebridge 1993, p.10). And, of course, there were additional residuals from other markets – it was still running on RTL5 in Holland in May 1994.

However, as a strategy that could be built on by further Australian serial production aiming at long-term acceptance in international markets, it was a signal failure. This may be due in part to the very factor that guaranteed its bottom-line security – its extreme low-budget instrumental production protocols. This approach to production (actors with very limited experience or models with no acting experience) and similar limitations in the script and technical departments (partly because of the need to meet regional expectations for Queensland personnel involvement, and to fulfil requirements under the state's Revolving Film Fund) virtually guaranteed a fulsomely negative critical reception in Australia, as well as elsewhere (for a derisively dismissive New Zealand account, *see* Wichtel 1993, p.71). This cannot be discounted as a factor in the fate of the program, especially when serial programming needs to build audience by word of mouth and peer influence.

Such protocols irresistibly attracted the wrath of critics. Dubbing it 'Stupidity Beach', 'Paradise Lost', 'Suffering Paradise' and similar sobriquets, some critics, like Robin Oliver in the *Sydney Morning Herald* (1993a, p.15s; 1993b, p.15s), adopted something of a personal crusade against it. Those few defences mounted for it centred on the development opportunities it offered for the fledgling Queensland industry, and on the cost efficiencies for which it set new benchmarks. Adrien Stewart (1994, p.6) allows that the 'virtues of *Paradise Beach* are mostly industrial'. The rate of completion – five episodes a week – made the production the fastest in the country, while it also gave many learning opportunities to aspiring Queenslanders. One of the program's assistant producers, Jo Porter (quoted in Stewart 1994, p.7), also argued that the technical ineptitude of the first series was largely overcome in the second, a point not pursued by the critical establishment.

In some ways, the unprecedentedly hostile critical reaction was misplaced, as the cost structure and schedule slots (both locally and overseas) for *Paradise Beach* suggest the pertinent comparisons should be with day-time soap opera, as Peter Schembri and Jackie Malone (1993, p.32) have argued. However, such a reaction was to some extent invited by the high expectations raised by Village Roadshow for the product: it was to be a cross between *Baywatch*, *Beverly Hills 90210* and local products like *Neighbours* (all of them prime-time, higher-budget and/or established long-term successes). Given the traditions of high-quality prime-time serial drama produced in Australia and the lack of day-time and access prime-time traditions of soap opera, together with these invited comparisons, *Paradise Beach* was an easy, if probably misplaced, target.

Other middle-range factors intervened against the serial. The US market for pre-prime-time soaps has declined considerably. There hasn't been a successful launch of a new soap opera at this time in many years in the US – since *The Bold and the Beautiful*, and even this program (along with *Santa Barbara*) has fared better in Australia and Europe than in the US. It seems that the fragmented nature of the market-place and the shortened attention span fostered by multi-channel viewing works against building a traditional soap opera following. In 1994, there was no stripped soap opera in the US that ran after 3 pm. As well, a crucial ancillary marketing outlet, the soap-opera press (*Soap Opera Weekly*, *Soap Opera Digest*, *Soap Opera* are the three main magazines) did not promote the program. Decisions on what the industry calls the 'rightness', or the cultural relevance of *Paradise Beach* probably defeated the expectation that the specialist press would jump at the opportunity to get behind one of the very few new soap operas in the market in several years.

There was a similar absence of promotion in teen magazines like *Sixteen*, *Tiger Beat*, and *Sassy*, which points to its uncertain address to its primary audience. By positioning itself so close to successful teenage prime-time soaps, the program was under pressure especially to capture ephemeral teenage argot and fashion. The serial was considered un-necessarily chaste – even kissing was rare; plot scenarios were too 'square', 'cheesy', and old-fashioned; characters can be noticed wearing the same clothes in different episodes, which would never be permitted in US drama (McNamara *et al.* 1994). The only way the program's US distributors saw such difficulties could have been overcome would be for US scriptwriters to have been imported to oversee and generate storylining and dialogue. Such importation, of course, would have defeated the objective of qualifying *Paradise Beach* for the Australian drama quota.

Accent certainly could not be discounted as an obstacle. The more significant question, however, was of non-translatable slang or argot. Although experienced executive producer Nick McMahon personally oversaw the removal of specific Australianisms from the script, it still contained examples like 'go to uni/university' instead of 'college' or 'school'. More significantly (with voice coaches on set to enhance articu-lation), the effort to speak for international audiences meant that actors spoke slowly and this contributed to the stageyness and frontality of performance.

The distribution principals' comments on writing and technical style also went to fundamental issues of televisual culture (McNamara *et al.* 1994). On the one hand, the writers tended to 'burn through story' much more quickly than in US soaps. Events and emotional reactions that could be milked far more are tossed off, in off-camera asides, for example. Like much Australian audiovisual culture, the program consistently de-dramatised action. Dramatic angles and opportunities occur off camera for cultural reasons as much as to avoid expensive effects or complicated set-ups. Therefore, narrative pacing was unfamiliar – the storylining was too fast (the slowness of US soaps is so that audience can miss episodes and not miss story); but the emotional temperature was too low.

Clearly, the program's 'look', its background texture and *mise-en-scene*, was designed to compensate for eviscerated storyline and wooden performance. This led to the emphasis on what's referred to as the 'MTV moment' (Shohet 1993, p.5) – the lyrical set-piece, slow-motion and/or panorama sequences of sleek bodies set against the 'unique combinations' of beach, rainforest or high-rise skylines. *Paradise Beach* set 'a new high water mark' for location use in low-budget soaps. It achieved 20 per cent exteriors per episode, a proportion unmatched in the world. The cost of stripped soap in Los Angeles, according to McNamara (1994), is seven times that of *Paradise Beach*, without the locations. The program continues a long tradition of location exploitation in attempting to position Australian audiovisual product internationally; the Gold Coast tourist mecca backdrop was central to its marketing concept. (It was interesting to note the similarity between the shooting styles of *Paradise Beach* and the Indy Car Grand Prix from Surfers Paradise screened in the US in March 1994. We might also note that, when Victoria hosts a race in the Formula One Grand Prix from 1996, it will be staged in Melbourne city streets rather than on Phillip Island, to provide the requisite cityscape backdrops.)

The failure of *Paradise Beach* suggests that, at least in terms of acceptance of foreign long-form drama by US broadcast television, the English language is not necessarily an advantage – Spanish-language soaps have more success in cable. This is because the point of comparison will always be with US broadcast television – in the soap format, it seems, an absolute benchmark for audience acceptance. The Australian long-form successes in the US have not been live-action adult or teen drama. Rather, they have been sci-tech (*Beyond 2000*) and children's animation (*Blinky Bill*); the first, a format Beyond International built up as an exploitable international format, the other a tried and tested children's formula from a highly credentialled Yoram Gross Studios. Soap opera, more than any other format, must be allowed to build an audience through stable scheduling and committed marketing, for their 'dispersed narrative structure and incremental characterisation make of them an acquired taste' (Crofts 1995, p.98), all the more when they are foreign.

NON-COMMERCIAL BROADCAST

Non-commercial broadcast television is dominated by the Public Broadcasting Service (PBS). This was designed in the idealistic late 1960s as an attempt to create an alternative to the commercially dominated television environment. The charter of the PBS is 'Jeffersonian in its conception but the reality is different' (Ashley 1994). It has grown to include over 350 stations in a complex network that spans the country, but it continues to rely on an unstable mix of government and corporate sponsorship and public subscription. The cable boom of the 1980s saw strategic moves to colonise the niches that the PBS had filled: Nickelodeon and Disney aimed at children; FNN and CNBC at business; A&E and Bravo at culture; CNN and C-SPAN at public affairs; and the Discovery Channel and the Learning Channel programmed documentaries. The non-commercial nature of public television was challenged by the commercial narrowcasting of the cable channels and the explosion of market-driven niche programming.

Why doesn't the PBS take more Australian product, when it takes so much from the UK? The PBS is positioned between two contending constraints. On the one hand, its funding sources and capital base mean that it must continue to look outside the country for program material to a greater extent than even the cable companies, now that they are beginning to trend toward home-based acquisition, production and commissioning. On the other, there is extreme sensitivity to the perception that PBS could stand for 'Pommie Broadcasting Service' (the PBS has always had output deals with the BBC). The network is almost as sensitive to the perceived lack of audience acceptance of foreign programming as are the commercial channels. This has meant that the commissioning and scheduling culture of the PBS is dramatically affected by the highly commercial climate within which it works; that it is beholden to sponsorship sources for a large proportion of its revenue; and that it doesn't have the flexibility or market presence of other public broadcasters.

Whole program totals show that only 14 per cent of total programming for 1991–2 is foreign-sourced, but that 'is a subtly misleading figure'. Many more segments of programs are foreign-made but skilfully and expensively re-versioned for the PBS. It is estimated that about one-third of public television's national programming is financed in part from overseas (Task Force 1993, p.138). Historically, the PBS has looked east rather than west for program-sharing and co-production relationships; any reverse of that is relatively recent and tends to be directed at Japan, and even then the PBS encounters a 'completely differing sensibility' for television production protocols of pacing and packaging information within entertainment (Ashley 1994).

Whereas the PBS's most direct competitors, the up-market cable channels, work to a well-defined demographic segment, the PBS continues to schedule like a full-service broadcaster, but with only 2.2 per cent of the total audience. It tries to maintain a reputation for quality and its scheduling revolves around established series-slots that have long-term viewer following. This rigidity resembles the BBC or ABC of more than a decade ago, with the crucial difference that the PBS' revenue stream is utterly unlike that of the BBC or the ABC. Unless a foreign program fits into an already established series-slot which has, crucially, attracted a sponsor, the PBS system will not be able to compete for programming because it cannot fund it highly enough. Only a few million dollars a year are available from the network for direct program acquisition, and sponsorship has declined in the 1990s. Key series-slots that have major corporate backing include 'Masterpiece Theater' (drama, with only 22 hours per year available), 'Nova' (science) or 'Nature' (natural history). The PBS' notion of quality may well have disqualified it from contemplating such populist fare as *Neighbours*, in contrast to the BBC, which had the flexibility to take a risk on it.

But the question can also be redirected toward the lack of volume and strategy in Australian programming, according to Nelsa Gidney, head of acquisitions at the PBS until 1981 and later for the American Program Service. Australia is relatively inexperienced in the international co-production arena; the ABC is a small producer by major market standards; high-quality drama producers like Kennedy Miller have shown a distaste for the US market; and most Australian documentaries lack the production values of the PBS 'Nature' series, she suggested (1994).

There is no clear pattern in the acceptance of Australian programs on the PBS. A 1993 success story was the award-winning *Encounters with Whales*, independently produced by Jenny Cornish, which fed the 'insatiable appetite' for nature documentary on US television (Gidney 1994). The PBS has taken some children's material, documentaries and features, including 'safe bets' like *Breaker Morant*, *My Brilliant Career* and *The Shiralee*. A recent example of the PBS's ongoing co-production slate, which has included the ABC (and the BBC and Television Espanola SA), is *Medicine at the Crossroads* (1993). This program looks at the long-term future of medicine and at its intractable problems and, typically for these kinds of co-productions, sequences were shot in the countries of each of the participating broadcasters. *The Nature of Australia*, an outstanding BBC–ABC co-production, was 'a huge hit and had appropriate production values' (Gidney 1994). But it was re-tracked with American voices to tie it into the 'Nature' series.

CABLE

Cable television services are a mature industry in the US. They reach almost every municipality. In 1993, 60 per cent of households were passed by cable, 62 per cent of US homes passed were subscribers, and nearly 80 per cent of these subscribed to at least one premium channel as well as the basic cable service. More than 60 satellite-delivered channels were downlinked by cable companies for retransmission; these included about 50 basic cable networks, seven superstations, and premium networks. Cable channels show greater receptivity to foreign programs, including significant amounts of Australian material. With a greater propensity to target niche audiences, they escape the imperative to program always for broadest appeal.

Many are also backed by powerful media and communications conglomerates; these invested in cable as a loss-leader in the early-to-mid-1980s in order to position themselves for an era of convergence. This meant that the cable companies were able to survive inevitable financial losses as the sector established itself, and by the 1990s to flourish, with healthy advertising revenues for the major basic cable operations because they are able to reach targeted demographic niches. For example, in 1990 Disney, Discovery, A&E and CNN were together spending US$358 million on programming, compared to the PBS' $261 million (Task Force 1993, p.141). Cable, while being addressed to niche audiences, is nevertheless a thoroughly commercial and intensely competitive system. The most successful Australian programming on US cable has been children's and documentaries, and the most receptive systems have been A&E, the Disney channel, the Discovery Channel, Showtime and Nickelodeon. Beyond International has been the most successful seller. Many one-shot dramas, especially features and mini-series with high production values, have been screened on HBO, the movie channel.

Pioneering in international magazine formats: *Beyond 2000*
Beyond 2000, and associated programming (such as *Beyond Tomorrow*), from the Beyond International Group, is one of the most successful Australian-based program concepts world wide. It is into its tenth series in

1994, with over 320 episodes produced without hiatus since 1985. Currently screening on the Ten Network in Australia (it was first seen on the ABC then, prior to its current placement, on the Seven Network), it has been distributed in over 80 territories, and has had substantial exposure in some of the most difficult, such as the US. This extensive distribution indicates a greater achievement than many short-form programs sold into multiple territories, because in most cases *Beyond 2000* continues in the schedule over several years. With its continued acceptance in many territories, the program has internationalised its stories considerably. During the 1990s, Sydney-based reporters have spent about five months a year overseas, and have reported from over 50 countries, by 1994 generating over 230 magazine-style segments and 80 studio stories, as well as several documentary specials (*Beyond Distribution Catalogue*, April 1994).

Beyond 2000 has been a world leader in popular science and technology ('sci-tech') programming, it has both provided a platform and ridden itself on the emergence of the format as an international genre with strong transferability across television cultures and systems. Most industry observers agree that a feature of *Beyond 2000*'s success is its personalisation and narrativisation of sci-tech stories (in the words of Beyond's catalogue, 'The key to the program's effectiveness is that the reporters experience their stories, conveying not only the facts but also a sense of adventure to viewers'). The narrator–reporter participates in unfolding the story of the discovery; re-enactments are common; goods are handled and trialled; and services are tested. Each breakthrough or new device is customer friendly, and brought as far as possible to the level of everyday experience (or at least the experience of medium-to-high income, technologically literate, consumption-oriented viewers). Complex science and unresolved mystery are either avoided or represented through potential breakthroughs.

Typical of magazine-style programs, *Beyond 2000* is a highly modular format. Further customisation of the program involves different lead presenters, producing in different languages (for its Discovery Europe program), and often noticeably different thematic concerns. Customisation for these varying markets can produce some dramatic tensions in the format. Australian reporters regularly feature stories on developing nations' problems of access to technology, while a recurring theme in the more recent series of the Australian version of the program, and of the Australian-produced segments which are used in the US version, is environmentalism. Stories concerning recycling, 'green' consumer products, low-energy transportation and emission control are now regularly produced. However, these contrast quite noticeably with the typical US-produced story, which tends to boost devices and processes for greater control and mastery over nature.

The program began in the US on the PBS network. A short-lived, re-versioned series – *Beyond Tomorrow* – was produced for the fledgling Fox Network in 1988–9; at that time it was one of the only network series produced outside the US. *Beyond 2000* went to the basic cable Discovery Channel in 1990. There, re-versioning is an indication of its importance to Discovery as one of that channel's 'signature' programs (Crystal 1994). The television 'syntax' for overcoming perceived accent difficulties includes replacing the Australian lead presenter with an American, re-versioned sets and graphics, and American-produced segments, which tend to be in more of a narrator-based, traditional talking-head documentary style. The success of re-versioning lies in the program not necessarily being perceived as Australian at all (Ashley 1994).

US-produced segments include strongly militaristic themes, and are all focussed on US stories. The episode screened on 19 March 1994 on Discovery included an Australian-produced segment on the archaeological reconstruction of the ancient harbour at Caesarea in Palestine. The storyline dealt with the highly sophisticated way in which first-century-BC engineers had built sea walls that worked in harmony with tidal currents to naturally re-direct silt away from the harbour. In the lead-out from the segment, the US compère radically rewrote the 'working with nature' theme to trumpet instead our contemporary mastery over nature:

> Since the time of King Herod, harbour building has gotten a lot bigger and a lot better. For example, in Hong Kong, they are levelling the entire island of Chep Lap Kok to construct a new harbour. It's optimistically set to open in 1997 and the finished product will be one of the few man-made objects that is so huge it will be seen from space with the naked eye and, actually, it's the airport that is getting the most attention. To build it they will almost double the size of the island by constructing a nine-mile seawall that will reclaim 2500 acres. It's expected that 87 million passengers will pass through its gates in the years beyond 2000.

It is important to ask why sci-tech has emerged to join children's animation, nature documentary and game and quiz shows as one of the most globalised of television's international formats. Part of the answer seems to be that it addresses a cultural need to assuage anxiety about technological progress and indeed fits the condition of modernity, that 'media representations of science privilege technical control as a value and

pre-suppose the extension of control techniques to all aspects of society'
(Bell and Boehringer 1989, p.118). From an industry standpoint, it is a
particularly significant genre in that it delivers a difficult demographic:
working-age males, usually technically literate and having valuable dis-
posable income (Crystal 1994).

The Australian success can be attributed to being a market leader in
an emerging international format, which in turn can be attributed to
Beyond's principals being products of the distinctive mix the Australian
audiovisual environment nurtures. According to one of their US consultants (Kagan 1994), they are highly media-literate, were trained in solid
craft skills and serious informational thematics at the ABC, but are highly
aware of international best practice in terms of extremely flexible management and the creative and technical inputs necessary to overcome the
tyranny of distance. They have a clear strategic vision of wanting to create
the *Entertainment Tonight* of sci-tech – that is, a long-running stripped
infotainment series with wide popular international appeal. The program's
international acceptance depends on it being extremely modular, capable
of attracting differing demographics, and able to be customised quite
radically. Where there are cultural screens inhibiting acceptance (for
example, accent, particularly that of a lead presenter or host, or too great
local specificity in stories or environmentalist themes), these can be readily
edited away through customisation. The Australian production team,
however, has built in such a high degree of internationalisation that it
could be said that customisation is a structural feature of the original, as
well as of the various re-versioned *Beyond 2000*s.

The quality zone: *Brides of Christ*

Since 1984 Arts & Entertainment (A&E) has successfully occupied a
niche as one of the only cable services dedicated to up-market arts-related
entertainment targeting affluent and older AB demographic segments. By
1994, it was carried on cable systems reaching about 60 million homes in
the US and Canada. It sits in the middle of the three tiers of basic cable in
terms of audience reach, which means that it generally rates in the
1–1.5 per cent range. A&E specialises in four genres: comedy, documentary, performing arts and drama. Typically for cable channels in the
US (and new services elsewhere), it first relied heavily on imports – usually
from the BBC – and on US re-runs. As it became financially viable, it
dramatically increased its domestic purchases. Senior Vice President
Brooke Bailey Johnson gave us the following figures for the 28 hours a
week of prime time (8–12 pm), comparing the first half of the decade

since it started with the second half: documentaries have shifted from 60 per cent international and 40 per cent domestic re-runs to 80 per cent domestic (new and re-run) and 20 per cent international. Drama remains international, so has performing arts (80–90 per cent international). Comedy is mostly domestic, any imported component is usually British. It still buys off-network re-runs for non-prime time.

A&E is one of the few zones in the US mediascape for high-quality foreign drama. Recent Australian programs include *Breaker Morant, The Lighthorsemen, The Paper Man, Frankie's House* and *Brides of Christ*. Co-producing *Frankie's House* with Roadshow Coote and Carroll was a big investment for A&E. Normally however, it enters into co-production only with UK companies (*Pride and Prejudice, Year in Provence* and *King Tut* are examples) – 'Australia is just too far away, and Discovery can lock in *Beyond 2000* because they specialise in documentaries' (Bailey Johnson 1994). Most Australian material has been bought through British brokers.

Brides of Christ represents the best outcome for an Australian program for A&E. It premiered to a gross average audience of 1.76 million households in June 1993. This represented a 3.12 rating, a record for A&E for an original television movie, and averaged 2.73 for all episodes. It was nominated for an international Emmy and won 15 other major awards, including a Gold Medal at the New York Film and TV Festival. According to Brooke Johnson, '*Brides of Christ* is the best thing to come out of Australia and, with Kennedy-Miller not in the game any more, Roadshow Coote and Carroll is the best quality producer'. There was 'great coverage', with the program featuring on the cover of the *New York Times* television guide (*Frankie's House* also featured, the first and second A&E programs to achieve this). The advertising campaign for *Brides of Christ* focussed on Mother Ambrose (Sandy Gore) with the teaser 'Not every woman who takes the vows of Poverty, Chastity and Obedience can keep them'. The advertisement doesn't work accurately, Bailey Johnson said; it should have focussed on Brenda Fricker (since an Oscar winner for *My Left Foot*) as she was the only known performer in the US. The campaign at no stage indicated the source of the program (Bailey Johnson 1994).

Critical response is crucial for a high-quality cable channel in terms of its target demographic – literate readers. Leading up to the première, *Brides of Christ* received substantial newspaper reviews in the *New York Times, New York Daily News, USA Today* and the Gannett Suburban Newspapers chain. *TV Guide*'s 'Best of the Summer Season' listed it top of the top ten movies and mini-series and positioned it as the perfect program for the A&E audience: a mildly feminist mini-series, which was driven by

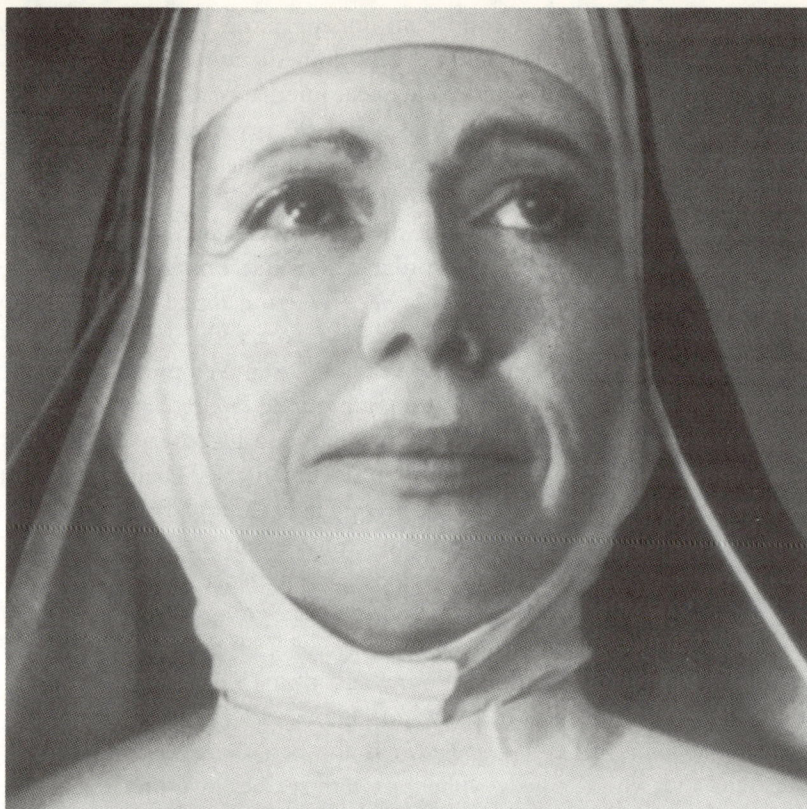

Not Every Woman Who Takes The Vows Of Poverty, Chastity And Obedience Can Keep Them.

Academy Award-winner Brenda Fricker stars in the premiere of **"Brides of Christ,"** *the story of women struggling between the sacred and the secular. A 3-part Special Movie Presentation beginning* **tonight at 8:00.**

Sponsored in part by MCI Communications.

A&E
Time Well Spent.

To order cable, call 1-800-OK-CABLE

The US critics seemed surprised by *Brides of Christ*. One said: 'What's truly amazing about *Brides of Christ* is that it is an Australian production of quality; we're used to some awful drivel from Down Under.'
(Publicity Material. Courtesy of A&E Television Networks,
© Arts & Entertainment Network, Hearst/ABC/NBC. All rights reserved.)

character rather than action or situation, contained enough historical flavour, and was alternately sharp and nostalgic. It was received as a welcome relief from US television's diet of gruel. 'Why can't American television be this good?' (Martin 1993); 'Those who have kicked the TV habit will be inspired to renew their tube vows if they watch *Brides of Christ*' (Gardella 1993). A Christian publication comments that it is:

> 'sure to stir memories in older viewers of the old days (good or bad). It should also stimulate debates over some of the issues raised in the show: authority versus conscience, change versus status quo, the connection of Church and state, and the teachings of the Church on divorce and birth control. Imagine an American TV program even raising such topics, much less presenting them in a creative package and in an even-handed way' (Breig 1993).

It was also considered a shift from standard Australian fare: 'What's truly amazing about *Brides of Christ* is that it is an Australian production of quality; we're used to some awful drivel from Down Under. Not once in this excellent series do we hear anyone utter the word "mate"' (Gardella 1993). In one case, *Paradise Beach* is offered as a corrective to *Brides*, 'just in case you thought ... that Australian television is better than the domestic brand' (John Leonard 1993).

The unthreatening universalist humanism of the series is emphasised. Audiences can revel in character that even at its most rigid (Brenda Fricker's Sister Agnes), 'avoids stereotype' (Roush 1993). The universal message of the series can be summed up as 'sisters are people, too' (Mann 1993). 'It restores one's belief in the power and the glory of serious-minded, enthralling TV drama. Because it takes seriously the intellectual aspect of religious belief, *Brides of Christ* is a feast for the mind as well as the heart. Its characters are thrillingly real' (Keller 1993).

Questions about accent or relevance to the US audience are hardly ever raised, underlining the different audience for A&E, compared to syndication and commercial broadcast. The universality of the story is easily emphasised: 'The in-a-land-and-time-far-far-away sense will help touchy or overly conservative Catholics swallow some of the more bitter moments ... Issues relevant only to the Australian church in the 1960s are not addressed' (Golphin 1993). The school's headmistress and mother superior (Sandy Gore) 'suffers a Clinton-ian crisis of leadership as she tries to impose reforms diplomatically' (Roush 1993).

CONCLUSION

As many analysts have pointed out (including Bell and Bell 1993), Australia has a particularly close tie to the US in terms of a substantially shared commercial orientation in television systems, a strong and long-established US presence on Australian television screens, and some major Australian feature-film breakthroughs in the US that have underpinned an enduring profile for the smaller country in the largest market in the world. Australian television has always paid pre-eminently close attention to US product, and has been amongst the top few foreign markets for US exports since the 1950s (and for US feature films for most of the century).

Australian export, co-production and off-shore hosting of US production intensifies this relationship, even as it marginally balances it. The case of Beyond International's operations, for instance, highlights this: in the words of Russell Kagan (1994), the program consultant who played an important role in facilitating the company's successful entry into the US, 'Sydney is just [like an American] area code – 612, not 61–2–', and 'as far as callers like Discovery were concerned, they were calling a production company somewhere off the Santa Monica pier in the ocean'. Maximised transparency to the US is the condition for greater export success.

Feature films overcome the barrier to entry more easily than television, but there is, especially in the US, no guaranteed 'follow-through' from features to television. The synergies seem to operate more between tourism advertising and features, with Paul Hogan's dual US profile in the 1980s the obvious example, but also there was the flow-through from *The Piano* that led to the young actress Anna Paquin's fronting the very successful advertising campaign by MCI in 1993–4. The example of Kennedy Miller illustrates the lack of synergy between film and television clearly: although many features directed by Miller have had a high profile in the US (*Twilight Zone, Witches of Eastwick, Lorenzo's Oil*), and Terry Hayes is scripting there, there has been negligible follow-through to the company's mini-series. *Bangkok Hilton* was one of the only Kennedy Miller mini-series sold into the US (it sold to the Turner Broadcasting Service). *Vietnam*, the company's outstanding mini-series on the national experience of the Vietnam war, was screened far less internationally than *Sword of Honour*, a routine, formula-based treatment of the same theme. Kennedy Miller was not prepared to enter into any compromise arrangements to smooth the mini-series' passage into the US market (Gidney 1994).

Their reluctance was understandable. The historical mini-series, the high-quality flagship of Australian television in the 1980s, had a particularly poor passage. Nelsa Gidney pointed out that distributors couldn't sell many at all; their historical specificity, or 'parochialism', defeated them. The strongly political *Waterfront* wasn't sold in 1984 and *Captain Cook* had to be totally re-edited from 10 hours down to manageable US formats, whereas *Dunera Boys* worked because of Bob Hoskins, a recognisable international actor, and a very strong, 'universal' story.

However, the promising formats, other than magazine infotainment, remain children's and nature programming. Moves to open up the US market to non-violent, pro-social children's material have occurred since the Children's Television Act (1990) for the first time made it mandatory that broadcasters serve the informational and educational needs of children in their community. In 1993–4, in the wake of this move, the British *Thomas the Tank Engine* and the US *Barney the Dinosaur* were programmed successfully and provided a climate for the success of Yoram Gross' *Blinky Bill*. Before that, programs like *Christmas in Australia* and other Australian programming were the strongest performing in a PBS series 'Wonderworks' in 1991 (Ashley 1994), while HBO, Showtime and, most consistently, Disney, have acquired material as well as co-produced in a few instances with the ACTF. Both up-market natural-history programming, in which the large public broadcasters and US National Geographic channel are the major players, and popular nature documentary, are growing strongly in the US and internationally. The ABC and a wide range of Australian independents have established minor track records in volume terms in this area. Such formats are truly international and are easy to re-version for different territories.

In sum, there has been some marginal specialty penetration of television (in some cable outlets), as there has been for speciality video and the theatrical market, but it is difficult to disagree with international sales agent Tony Ginnane when he argued that there is 'no perceptible Australian presence on US television and probably will never be' (1994). US breakthroughs will remain a symbolic 'Mecca' for many Australian producers, but Mecca, as for most Muslims, is a long way away.

CANADA

Australia enjoys strong similarities with Canada and shares some common elements of political and historical heritage. Both have been UK dominions and settler societies; they have fought beside each other in successive wars. They are not dissimilar in population size; while Canada is a member of the Group of Seven major industrial nations and Australia is not, they nevertheless have many similarities in terms of economic resource base. Both have been historically staples and minerals suppliers to major industrial powers. The structure of each country's polity exhibits many parallels: both accord a high place to the public sector in stimulating and guiding economic activity and achieving socially desirable outcomes, while remaining thoroughly mixed economies, with a dominant capitalist private sector.

More specifically, the broadcasting and the general audiovisual histories of the two countries have run along remarkably similar lines. Their approach to the audiovisual sector is also thoroughly mixed, with high levels of public-sector participation in industries that strive to be commercial in ethos. The state film-production bodies (the National Film Board and Film Australia), state funding bodies (Telefilm Canada and the Australian Film Commission and the Film Finance Corporation), public broadcasting (Canadian Broadcasting Corporation, CBC, and the Australian Broadcasting Corporation) and the regulatory agencies (Canadian Radio-Television and Telecommunciations Commission, CRTC, and the Australian Broadcasting Authority) all share similar histories and inter-relationships. There are broadly shared models across the range of the arts, heritage, film, broadcasting and wider social and cultural policies such as multiculturalism. It is curious therefore, that despite these series of close links, Canada is in some respects the strangest and least promising of all major territories for Australian product – and the reverse trading situation is also minimal.

The ecology of Canadian television is structured around the powerful, popular and substantial presence of US programming in the country. To a significant extent, the history of the development of both Canadian infrastructure and local programming can be viewed as a series of responses to the long shadow extending from the south. The cabling system which grew more quickly than in the US and today reaches considerably more homes than in the US (approximately 80 per cent and in urban areas in excess of 90 per cent, compared to 60 per cent overall in the US) was prompted as much by demand for US channels as by national infra-structure development.

Equally, the development of Canadian content regulation, which requires substantial commitment of both general transmission hours as well as prime-time hours to nationally-produced programs, must be seen in large part as a defensive response to the availability and popularity of US product in the country. Thus, the Canadian television market's potential interest in Australian product is affected by more than the domination enjoyed by US signals in the country. The effects of Canadian regulatory policy – in placing strong emphasis on relatively high levels of local programming in response to this dominance – mean that very little foreign material (other than that from the US) finds its way onto Canadian screens. Thus, while Canadian television is, in its larger markets, an even wider multi-channel environment than the US, and offers a more complex tiered system of pay services and liberal access to US signals, it is actually a market that is more closed than that of the US itself to non-US foreign product outside prime time.

Any non-US foreign product taken is 'screened' through horizons of expectation dominated by US models of mainstream programming, at least with respect to programming for the three Anglophone broadcast networks (CBC, CTV and Global) and most of the pay and specialty services. (The exceptions to this are the educational networks – TV Ontario pre-eminently, but also Access Alberta, the Knowledge Network in British Columbia and Radio Quebec – which operate as low-cost, low-budget public-service-style programmers.) This means an expectation of production values, in prime time, of at least the equivalent of $US1 million per hour, and an American genre-based approach to suitability for prime-time access. Thus, the Canadian situation resembles many other minimum-penetration scenarios for Australian product. There is virtually no scope for prime-time appearance, apart from the rare prestige short-form, high budget co-production (*Black Robe*, *Golden Fiddles*), which satisfies content regulations. Other drama material finds its way without fanfare onto the least-watched segments of the networks' schedules, pay movie channels, or sub-national broadcasters. There is scope for inter-national formats, such as children's and nature programs, but considerable reserve about any other mainstream television fare. The possibilities for varying this situation reside at the margin of volume television, in co-production development.

There is little precedent for stripped serial drama. While French Canadian television is well known for its successful productions in this genre – (the *téléroman*) for access prime time (late afternoon or early evening) – English-Canadian television has no such production tradition and thus there is an even smaller chance of an underdeveloped format such as this being represented by a foreign product (Marshall 1994). (Exceptions to this rule were *Degrassi High* and *Degrassi Junior High*, which were screened weekly and in prime time.) Also, industry analyst Paul Attallah (1992) argues that the production values of Australian serials and series make it impossible to contemplate their making the transition to access prime time, let alone prime-time slots in Canadian network schedules, given Canadian expectations of very high production values. The lower-budget production values of Australian series and serials are not suitable for Canadian access prime time, which emulates US practice, with its stripped re-runs of US high-budget soap and its general commitment to the 4–7 pm period for local-access programming.

The programming of *Home and Away* on YTV (Youth Television) or *The Flying Doctors* on Global during 1992–3 does not constitute a major refutation of this general rule. YTV is a speciality channel, available to about 6–7 million homes, with a reach of around 20 million viewers. Characteristically for foreign long-form drama, *Home and Away* was shifted around the schedule. It started in prime time, then was moved to early evening, then stripped at 5 pm. Another program acquisition of note was *Mother and Son* for Vision TV, a religious network for which the successful comedy series would have been a gentle and conservative addition to the schedule. TV Ontario, a large educational broadcaster, which has substantial co-production agreements with Japan's NHK and the PBS, has taken occasional social documentaries such as *Philippines My Philippines* and quality mini-series like *Vietnam*. In the last ten years, virtually the only Australian drama programs taken by CTV, the principal commercial network in Canada, were *The Paperman* (which screened in the summer of 1991) and *Paradise Beach* (which lasted somewhat longer than in the US during 1993–4). As is the case in several countries, current-affairs segments can be exchanged between Canada and Australia. The SBS' *Dateline* has used segments from the *CBC Journal*, while the speciality news and current-affairs channel Newsworld (a subsidiary of the CBC) has used excerpts from *Four Corners*.

The CBC, subject to radical downsizing and fundamental questioning of its future place in an increasingly commercialised and user-pays system, has never been able to cement major associations with related Commonwealth and other public broadcasters. Its PacRim co-production arrangements (which have included the PBS, TVO, NHK, the ABC and TVNZ) have not resulted in much more than the exchange of segments among current-affairs magazine programs and occasional innocuous nature documentaries. The hoped-for 'cultural coalescence' among the public broadcasters of the Pacific has been a disappointment, according to Bill Morgan, CBC ombudsman (1992). A defensive alliance for financial rather than coherent cultural reasons, it has been unable to exert much influence to redress the tide turning away from public-interest initiatives.

The CBC has always taken advertising and programmed directly against US competition. According to Morgan, Canadian audiences, even for the CBC, show minimal tolerance for anything that is non-Canadian or non-US. Even British material, the traditional brand name in quality television, enjoys little audience response. Like most public broadcasters world wide, the CBC screened British historical dramas in the 1970s. However, the arguably unique pressures on public broadcasting in Canada brought about by the multi-channel environment meant that such up-market foreign programming has not occurred since, according to Morgan, who was program director at CBC-TV in the 1970s and head of news, current affairs and information during 1982–9. And, as evidence of how Americanised the English-Canadian audience is, he cited accent as a significant obstacle to Australian material. He suggested that the PBS has taken more Australian material than the CBC, even though the US, on social and historical indicators, is more of a foreign market than Canada for Australian television.

Canada has been an international leader in striking official co-production treaties, as it has long considered this method a major way to articulate a place for itself in costly drama production. Its first treaty, with France and for film only, dates back to 1963 (Hoskins and McFadyen 1993, p.222). As of 1993, it had agreements with 24 countries; these invariably include feature film and almost always television. Australia's co-production treaty with Canada, signed in 1990, has produced very few results – the only completed projects by 1994 were *Golden Fiddles* and *Black Robe*.

Australia is a late starter and a very small player in international official co-productions, and the divergent definitions of what counts as an Australian program for the purposes of certification (the route to finance for official co-productions, which is accommodating of foreign input), and for broadcast (the TPS14 regulation, which is much tighter), means that official co-production may never be a major item in the Australian audiovisual portfolio. Canadian producers, along with many others, are critical of Australian regulatory inconsistencies, which mean that official co-productions do not automatically qualify for full domestic quota, as they do in Canada. This, however, will change when the effects of the new ABA Australian content standard, which addresses this inconsistency, are felt in the industry.

9

East Asia

Australian television is internationalising and at the same time, Australia as a whole is realising that at a political, economic and cultural level it must integrate more effectively into the Asia Pacific region. This is a trend that can be dated in its most recent phase from the publication of the Garnaut report, *Australia and the North Asian Ascendancy* (Garnaut 1989). In the 1990s, Australian public debate and public policy are undergoing rapid, perhaps fundamental, paradigm shifts through discourses of 'enmeshment' with Asia. Six out of the ten largest markets for Australian trade are in the regions of Asia, while Australian trade with Japan is now equivalent to the whole volume of trade with the European Union. These trends are set to consolidate strongly in the years ahead.

It is plainly impossible in one chapter to consider adequately the television ecologies of the main east-Asian countries, and the cross-cultural issues that trading television within them raises. Rather, this chapter will focus on areas of Australian program and service activity, together with predominantly political–diplomatic aspects of cultural exchange. The main case study will concentrate on a major service initiative, which is Australia's most substantial ongoing programming presence in the region. This service initiative is the Australian Broadcasting Corporation's Australia Television (ATV), launched in February 1993 as a single-channel television service carried on Indonesia's Palapa satellite.

TELEVISION ECOLOGIES OF THE REGION

The east-Asian region is not only extremely diverse politically, economically and culturally; large parts of it, for example Japan, China, Malaysia and Vietnam, have also been traditionally more resistant than most to the 'free flow' of cultural and information product from outside. The reasons for this have included language, political and cultural screens (Hoskins and

Mirus 1988), government policies resistant to Western influence, and the fact that less-developed economies are unable to support large information (including audiovisual) sectors.

However, the rates of economic growth in the region significantly outstrip all others in the world, and the emergence of world-leading Asian media conglomerates and the explosion of television capacity mirror this general economic expansion. Japan, and to a lesser extent South Korea, have assumed greater control of international audiovisual exchange in recent years, by vertical investment in the industry. Major audiovisual hardware manufacturers such as Sony have taken over software manufacturers in the US, notably some of the the Hollywood studios. East Asia is the world's greatest new television market of the future: a potential of US$3 trillion revenue based on two-thirds of the world's population by the turn of the century (Karthigesu 1993). Between 1988 and 1993, there was a 70 per cent increase in the number of television households in the region, compared with growth of 4.3 per cent in the UK and 6.7 per cent in the US. However, market liberalisation and expansion in the region have not followed the model of Western Europe and elsewhere. Asian media have not so much commercialised from within as from without. There is a greater diversity of cultures and political systems, and a far greater retained role for state direction and control than is evident in Western nations (Hamilton 1992). Paralleling this, Australian initiatives in audiovisual export have been as much in the public sector as in the commercial sector.

More than perhaps anywhere else in the world, the television ecologies of the region exhibit a two-tiered structure, with a wide variety of national terrestrial and mostly public services overlaid, as it were, by the strong growth of trans-border services that are typically commercial. If every announced business plan came to fruition, by 1996–7 there would be an estimated 900 new channels available (Cawthorne 1993). This growth is spectacular and is fed by the perception that economic expansion in the region can support exponential increases in information and entertainment services.

The national terrestrial and new trans-border services are bound together in a volatile *pas de deux*. The models of response to the challenge of trans-border services range from 'virtual suppression' (a policy of active restriction of satellite reception for ideological reasons); to 'suppressive openness' (trans-border reception is banned and penalties are severe in theory but enforcement is difficult in practice); to 'illegal openness' (reception occurs by default because there is little attempt to enforce restrictions); to 'regulated openness', where government allows reception (Man Chan 1992). Using this typology, the eastern regions of Malaysia fit the model of suppressive openness, western Malaysia that of virtual suppression, Thailand regulated openness, Brunei virtual suppression, Indonesia a recent mixture of regulated openness and illegal openness, and China a mixture of virtual suppression and suppressive openness. On the other hand, countries like the Philippines and Japan practice un-regulated openness and regulated openness respectively.

Many Asian governments are reasserting national-development and cultural-maintenance strategies alongside a marked increase in Western interest in the media industries of the region. One decisive indicator of this is the decision by Rupert Murdoch to invest in 1993 in Star TV, the new satellite service uplinked on AsiaSat 1 based in Hong Kong and reaching 38 countries from Pakistan in the west to the Philippines in the east. While such a service develops apace, with a footprint encompassing half the earth's population, the governments of Malaysia and China have banned domestic satellite reception, and the government of Malaysia is attempting to allow liberalised entertainment services while restricting information flow from Western sources (Karthigesu 1993).

The more general response of national governments, particularly those that perceive a threat to cultural and political 'stability' from the impact of trans-border flows, has been to improve and increase state terrestrial services, and provide legislative, regulatory and financial incentives for private services to begin or increase in order to provide competition for the blandishments of trans-border television. These strategies will have to cope with huge satellite over-capacity and increased pressure for market liberalisation. AsiaSat 1's already massive capability will be overshadowed by the greater coverage of AsiaSat 2 and China's Apstar series, as well as many others.

Australia's enmeshment policies cannot avoid being influenced by these rapid changes, which seem to offer great trade opportunities for the audiovisual industries but which also raise major questions that strike at the heart of cross-cultural 'transfer of meaning' through information and entertainment. The Australian Film Commission comments that 'while the relative importance of Asian markets escalates for industries such as engineering, shipping, education, tourism and telecommunications, the film and television production industries face significant cultural and economic barriers to entry' (AFC 1994a, p.73). These questions are even more pressing when we consider Australia's bid to become a player in satellite television in the region.

DYNAMICS OF PROGRAM TRADE

From the vantage point of Western-world program trade, there has been a historical lack of attention to the east-Asian region. This has been based on cultural distance, but other factors include very low rates of return from trade, since copyright violations, particularly piracy, remain a considerable problem in certain countries. In addition, censorship and differing cultural values place obstacles to transparent dealing and there is sharp conflict between selling rights to programs for satellite coverage versus territory-by-territory selling. The most financially lucrative territories, such as Japan and Hong Kong, are also the most difficult because they are centres of strong local production. Japan is as insular a television market as the US – barely 3 per cent of total program time is occupied by foreign material, and most of that is consigned to the dustbin of the early hours of the morning. On TVB, Hong Kong's strongest network, the figure is about 10 per cent.

International flows of programming need to contend with a wide variety and changing set of import policies in the region. It contains the hermetic television culture of Japan, as well as one with among the lowest levels of indigenous programming in the world (the Philippines, which imports about 70 per cent). As well, most territories in the region pay some of the world's lowest prices for programming. The trade paper *Television Business International* estimates that approximately 90 000 hours of foreign programming were sold into South East Asian markets in 1992 at an average cost of less than A$1500 an hour (Grantham 1992). This underscores why it took until December 1994 for the first MIP Asia trade convention to be held (in Hong Kong). Many countries, like China, have tended to barter the importation of programming by offering large amounts of advertising time to distributors in lieu of cash payment (Lull 1991).

Program trade is complicated by the way new trans-border services are being overlaid across established territories. Selling program rights to a trans-border service may obviate the possibility of selling on a territory-by-territory basis, a particular issue when the low prices paid by Star TV are considered. The reality of program demand in the region is, that like in all others, domestic programming is most popular. A recent survey of viewer preferences in Indonesia, the Philippines, Singapore, Thailand, South Korea, Malaysia and Hong Kong conducted by Frank Small and Associates found that in the first five, over 90 per cent of the top 20 programs were local, while in Hong Kong it was 100 per cent. In Hong Kong, TVB's Jade

(Cantonese) channel is ten times more popular than its Pearl (English) channel (although Pearl's audience increases by 50 per cent when bilingual broadcasts take place (AFC 1994b, Vol.1, p.7)). The popularity of domestic programming sees acquired programming mostly relegated to outside prime time.

For small traders like Australia, the fact that the US majors already have a strong foothold in the region, supplying much of the non-Asian programming bought by most countries, is a significant obstacle. (There is little opportunity to substitute for US programming, as we have seen in some European territories.) The demand for US programming is based not only on its competitive pricing, but also on the fact that it provides the kind of hard-action productions that resemble the region's most popular indigenous programs (ibid., p.11).

In China, program and technical exchanges are becoming more common as the country seeks to manage its increasing international links. More companies are acquiring programming directly from suppliers rather than working through the state apparatus; the state, in turn, seems to tolerate such exchanges so long as the material maintains 'ideological neutrality' (ibid., p.17). Shanghai Television, operating two channels (the second running an English-language service in the evenings), runs between 40 and 50 per cent foreign programming. Much of this is sourced from the US, Japan and Hong Kong and costs between US$5000 and US$30 000 for drama and around US$500 for documentaries (ibid., p.29). In 1991 the station ran a week of Australian programming in association with the Queensland–China Friendship Association. It sees Australia as a natural partner in co-production according to station editor, Huang Ming Xin (ibid., p.29).

China's 500 cable stations, reaching approximately 30 million households, have shown themselves willing to take foreign programs into their systems (although they do maintain editorial control). However, technical obstacles defeated what promised to be a breakthrough for Australia Television in being re-transmitted on Guangdong province's GZTV, a cable service operating 20 channels and reaching 5 million viewers in southern China.

Indonesia, which had banned foreign television programs up until 1985 in the interests of preserving national culture, now imports a significant proportion of its programming. This has been, in part, a response to the success of its Palapa satellites in attracting international business. For example, Televisi Republik Indonesia (TVRI), which broadcasts in both

Indonesian and English, imports up to 40 per cent of its programming. (In 1991 it purchased the bulk of the Beyond International catalogue, from mini-series to documentaries. Southern Star International has also had similar success with the station.) New services import even more – Rajawali Citra Televisi Indonesia (RCTI) imports between 70 and 90 per cent of its programming. Indonesia leads the region in direct-to-home reception, following the legalisation of this means of television consumption in 1985. SMATV systems redirecting signals through apartment buildings are also very common in the largest cities.

Malaysia's main stations, Radio Television Malaysia (RTM), operating channels TV1 and TV2, and Sistem Televisyen Berhad (STB) with TV3, together with new stations Subscriber News Service (SNS) and TV4, all rely significantly on imported programming. TV1 imports 40 per cent and TV2 60 per cent; sources include the US, Hong Kong, Japan, Indonesia, India, Latin America, Germany, France and the Arab nations. There are government initiatives in existence to improve the nation's English-speaking skills, but opportunities for the increased sales of English-language programming are tempered by government policy and the National Censorship Board's February 1992 ban on all scenes depicting sex, violence or horror, which is expected to reduce the level of imported programming substantially. This move complements the government's plans to introduce an 80 per cent domestic quota by the year 2000 (*Television Business International*, May 1992), and by 1994 TV1, TV2 and TV3 expect to have 70 per cent of their programming produced locally (AFC 1994b, Vol. 7, p.34).

Star TV

Star TV is one of the only major trans-border multi-channel satellite-distributed television services in the world today. It has been operating since 1991. Since mid-1993, it has been owned partly by Rupert Murdoch's News Corporation (63.6 per cent) and partly by the powerful Hong Kong businessman Li Ka-shing (36.4 per cent). It is due to 'migrate' from AsiaSat 1 to AsiaSat 2, which will extend the service's reach much further, 'from Melbourne to Moscow'. The Star service in 1994 comprises a package of five channels. Prime features a mixture of major world sports events; 29.5 hours (approximately 4 per cent) of Australian sporting events including rugby league, yachting and car racing, featured during May 1994. Channel V (previously MTV) is an Asian version of the international music channel produced under licence from the US parent company, Viacom. Chinese is a general information and entertainment channel broadcasting in Mandarin. Star Movies provides a mixture of Western (usually US) and Hong Kong productions.

Star Plus, an English-language general entertainment channel, screens mostly foreign re-run series and serials. Much of the programming is US in origin, with significant Australian serial drama also in evidence. It is this channel that schedules the same episode of *Neighbours* three times a day, Monday to Friday (based on the 1993 deal to buy several hundred episodes of the serial, the greatest single Australian program deal in the Asian region). During May 1994, the channel was screening several Australian programs (*Neighbours, The Flying Doctors, Richmond Hill, Carsons Law* and *Holiday*), and one movie, *Sunday Too Far Away*, constituting 65.5 hours of air time (approximately 8.8 per cent) for the month. Play times were generally outside prime-time viewing hours.

There are other Australian elements in the Star constellation. Murdoch has shifted some of his Australian lieutenants from his other interests such as BSkyB in the UK and News Limited in Australia to Star in Hong Kong. His strategic stake in the Seven Network in Australia has led to the organisation seeking distribution, production and investment options within the Asian region (*Adelaide Advertiser*, 18 August 1993). This network, along with Murdoch's Australian pay-television options, will form a node of an emerging global network of software and delivery platforms, of which Star TV is a major link.

Like all trans-border television services that seek general audiences across many countries and cultures, Star TV faces the challenge of local-ising its service sufficiently. In Star's case, this is even more important because it has the additional challenge to 'Asianise' its mainly Western material for countries and audiences that are vocal about the imposition of Western values. For instance, Rupert Murdoch's 1993 remarks about satellite technology posing 'an unambiguous threat to totalitarian regimes everywhere' was answered by the Chinese government with an attempted ban on the sale of receiving dishes, and continuing attempts to block transmission of Western news sources such as CNN. It also resulted in Star controversially removing its 'News and Information' channel (a 24-hour channel supplied by BBC World Service Television) from its offer in 1994. News Corporation's acquisition of Star has also met other strong political resistance. Dr Mahathir, the Malaysian prime minister, claimed that this was just another attempt by the West to dominate Asian media: 'Why has Murdoch bought 64 per cent of Star TV ... if it is not to control the news that we are going to receive?' (*Age*, 6 August 1993).

The music channel has undergone considerable change to Asianise its offering, and has been successful in doing so. Star also purchased the Golden Harvest and Golden Princess libraries of Chinese feature films. It intends to further regionalise its service, offering different schedules and content for its Chinese, Indian and Indonesian service. This highlights the difficulties confronting a pan-Asian service, where political, cultural and linguistic differences impede the emergence of a truly regional audience, and recalls the problems of pan-European satellite broadcasters, such as Eurikon and Europa, and the early attempts by Rupert Murdoch in the 1980s to establish his Sky service as Western European in coverage (Collins 1993).

AUSTRALIAN PROGRAM TRADE: VARYING MODELS

It will remain the case for the immediate future, as it has to the present, that Europe offers the major territories for Australian film and television export and North America for feature films. The region of east Asia embraces a series of territories that are inescapably relevant to Australia's economic and political future and yet have few established cultural synergies with Australia. There are varying models of program exchange. We shall consider first some problematic precedents – examples of Australian audiovisual material that received sharp negative response in the region – and also look at straight program sales and their positioning in schedules and territories, and at co-productions, especially Film Australia's participation in *Mini-Dragons*. Finally, we shall audit the performance of Australia Television in its first 18 months of operation to late 1994.

The Australian audiovisual presence in east Asia has had a limited and not entirely distinguished recent history. The cases of high-level Malaysian government response to the perceived orientalist racism of the Grundy/ABC drama series *Embassy* (Kessler 1991; Mitchell 1993; Perera 1993) and to the independent feature film *Turtle Beach* indicate the degree to which cultural difference, and the great political sensitivity of some neighbouring governments, are crucial issues for Australian television trade that have yet to be factored sufficiently into production. These cases are examples of particular strategies of explicit ideological resistance to Western representation, strategies which have by no means been confined to Australian productions. While *Embassy*, a 1990–1 series based at an Australian diplomatic post in Ragaan, a fictional country, was never screened in Malaysia, it provoked Dr Mahathir, that country's prime minister, to assert that the program was an attack on Malaysian customs and politics and to threaten dire diplomatic and trade consequences. Since then, Dr Mahathir has on several occasions reminded Australia that its economic, cultural and political relations in the region are by no means assured, and has been joined in this by figures such as former Singapore prime minister Lee Kuan Yew.

Not surprisingly, the major Australian companies have a varied presence in the region. Village Roadshow has moved to invest in cinemas. Grundys has followed its practice of parochial internationalism in establishing an office in Singapore. It has development deals with Star TV to complement its back catalogue sales, and in 1994 began to produce two game shows for Indonesian terrestrial television. Grundys was able to sell its 24-episode children's adventure series, *Mission Top Secret*, to Japan's NHK in 1993 after including a Japanese character. This was Grundys' first pre-sale in Japan, and may lead to closer development links with the major broadcaster (*Encore*, 22 July–4 August 1993). Beyond Distribution claims to have sold 95 per cent of its drama and documentary catalogue throughout the region (AFC 1994a, p.74), securing wide exposure for *Beyond 2000* and *The Great Wall of Iron*. McElroy and McElroy's *Return to Eden* made an enduring impact on Indonesian audiences. Smaller operations, such as the North Australian Film Corporation and Pt Nusantara International Television Productions, an Australian-owned production company based in Indonesia, produce Indonesian-language business and children's programs (ibid., p.77; DITARD 1994).

Co-productions have proved a surer way than completed program sales to establish ongoing relationships with major broadcasters. In October 1993, Japan's Fuji TV launched Film Australia's program for children *Johnson and Friends*. The deal with Fuji involves an agreement for the Japanese broadcaster to represent the program, its music, book publication, merchandising and video publication in Japan. But Film Australia's main connection in Japan has been with NHK, the dominant Japanese public broadcaster, which co-ventured the 13-episode children's series, *Escape from Jupiter*, in 1993. The documentary series, *Mini Dragons* (1990) and *Mini Dragons 2* (1992), co-productions between the PBS Maryland, NHK and Film Australia, were three-part, hour-long documentary series, the first focussing on Singapore, South Korea and Taiwan and the second on Indonesia, Malaysia and Thailand.

The series' theme ('mini dragons') is the intense economic growth experienced by the smaller Asian nations in recent times which, though not rivalling Japan, is a phenomenon of global significance in itself. Episodes are structured around a survey of each nation's policy and

The Girl From Tomorrow (Film Australia) illustrates the general principle that children's science fiction programs travel well across national borders. It has sold well in Europe, America and Asia.
(Film Australia publicity material.)

performance on the ground; selected individuals, who have experienced economic growth differently, are the focus. The general tone of each episode is of balanced criticism – the rapidity and ambitiousness of economic growth has beneficial as well as disjunctive effects on the social fabric. Thus, the Indonesian and Thai episodes focus on the prevalance of militarism, the Indonesian and Malaysian on racial intolerance of Chinese populations in those countries, and many episodes show the dependency for economic growth on foreign multinationals. Social disjunction is typified by narratorial statements such as the comment that Bangkok is 'a city in danger of being suffocated by its own success'.

Subtle differences in emphasis can be discerned in the national origins of each profile. There is a harder edge to the Australian-authored episodes (Singapore and Thailand), due to a stronger journalistic tradition in television documentary, than to either the Japanese or US partners' work (Moir 1994). The international sales version, that is, the version that was marketed outside the three participating countries, contained the US narration, which Bruce Moir described as having a 'light touch', to avoid potential cross-cultural misunderstandings.

Not all 'misunderstandings', however, were avoided. The Singapore episode in the first series was abruptly cancelled in 1991 just as it was scheduled to go to air through the Singapore Broadcasting Corporation. There are differing accounts of this event. Australian/Singaporean journalist Ilsa Sharp commented that the Australian narration of this episode, as distinct from the Japanese and US versions, had acquired a 'hatchet-job' script, and 'Singapore's anger can perhaps be understood' (1994, p.277). However, Bruce Moir, managing director of Film Australia, said that Singapore actually had the PBS narration, but that a Singapore journalist stringer in Melbourne had seen the Australian version and reported back and that this led to the cancellation. The timing was also inauspicious, Moir added; it was about the same time as Australian foreign minister Gareth Evans was attempting to calm diplomatic tensions over *Embassy*. This had the effect of making the second series a markedly more cautious exercise (Moir 1994) and underlines the pitfalls for international television formats that stray outside the bland parameters of nature and children's programming.

However, we must also ask how much this poring over of media texts in the context of regional perceptions of Australia matters. Some of the most sophisticated and informed comment (Kessler 1991; Sharp 1994) suggests that Western notions of media impact and opinion-formation or agenda-setting should not be assumed normative for Asian polities and cultures.

Ilsa Sharp refers to the concept of *Wayang*, or play-acting, as an appropriate form of conduct in public life, and its separation from truth-telling in private life (1994, p.273). This underlines the fact that Western modernist notions of the public sphere may be inadequate to grasp the dynamics of societies which exhibit simultaneously pre-modernist levels of social control (the media are appropriately available to developmental direction) along with subtleties of self-presentation and truth-telling perhaps more appropriate to a post-modernist ethos. This is a conundrum of prime significance for ATV, the new Australian trans-border satellite service, to the performance of which we now turn.

AN ERSATZ ASIAN NATION? ABC SATELLITE TELEVISION

Australia has a long tradition of broadcasting within the east-Asian region. Radio Australia has been an established and respected presence since 1939 in short-wave radio broadcasting. An arm of government policy and wartime propaganda, its origins were markedly geo-political (Hodge 1995). The most significant additional development in Australian public broadcasting within the region is the Australian Broadcasting Corporation's Australia Television (ATV), launched in February 1993.

Australia's new regional television initiative is also overtly driven by geo-political (and now diplomatic rather than overtly propagandist) purposes, and by contemporary economic and trade imperatives. It is, in the words of the service's publicity, 'the only satellite service in the region tailored for the region'. It is a single-channel television service carried on Indonesia's Palapa B2P satellite, uplinked from its production centre at the ABC Darwin studios, and reaches Indonesia, Papua New Guinea, Malaysia, Singapore, Brunei, the Philippines, Taiwan, Burma, Vietnam, Laos, Thailand, Cambodia, Hong Kong and China, as well as northern portions of the Australian mainland.

It was initiated with a direct government allocation of A$5.4 million, matched by the ABC, with a significant portion of its running costs over time expected to be met from corporate sponsorship. The foundation sponsors were major transport and communications players with established interests in the region: Telstra/Telecom, Digital and Qantas. Additional sponsorships came from the major insurance company Australian Mutual Provident Society, Ansett Australia, Foster's Brewing Group, David Jones, Done Art and Design, Amalgamated Wireless Australia, Lincoln Electric, Thai International, Coca-Cola, General Insurance Office, and the Australian Meat and Livestock Corporation.

Advertising exchanges had also been arranged with the leading Indonesian daily *Republika*. In the context of the 'thin' advertising base for satellite television over Asia, Australia Television is a minnow among the big fish. However, it has some advantages over world news providers like CNN and the BBC: a low capital base and programming from the ABC's own portfolio, and potential access to regionally specific sponsorship.

It broadcasts from early morning to late evening (in 1994, 17 hours a day, with the remaining seven hours leased out, thus raising further revenue) across four time zones, and schedules mostly selected ABC domestic programs including children's, language education, drama, documentary, arts and comedy. This amounts to a platform for a major audiovisual initiative that may in time parallel the 50-year-plus presence of Radio Australia as a broadcaster in the region.

The diversity of cultures in the region, together with Australia's marked differences from many of these cultures (Broinowski 1992; Walker 1990), make the task of ATV a pioneering one. What is the nature of the cultural screens, be they political, religious, sexual or racial, filtering the specific adaptations of Western-style material that Australia produces? To what extent will, or should, Australian producers modify their output to accommodate these varying and expanding contexts of reception?

In the words of the government press release for its launch, ATV is 'a key element in the Government's strategy of forging closer relationships between Australia and countries in our region'. This immediately underscores the tensions necessarily arising in the concept of an independent but state-owned and supported broadcaster and its being offered effectively as an arm of government policy. The ABC's *International Editorial Guidelines* attempt a delicate balancing act in relation to these tensions. On the one hand, the guidelines commence with a statement stressing the traditions of independence that have won respect and acceptance for the ABC (though not necessarily in Asia):

> The ABC, through Radio Australia and Australia Television International … is responsible for broadcasting news, current affairs and general programs to international audiences, often to countries whose media are more restricted than in Australia. Occasionally, reports may create difficulties in Australia's foreign relations with another country. This problem is the price of a genuinely independent overseas service and is recognised and accepted by the ABC and the Australian Government (*Editorial Guidelines*, 1992, p.1).

On the other hand, in the diplomatic language of the guidelines, this tradition is distinguished from international broadcasting that is both culturally intrusive and propagandist. Australia Television will be a distinctive international broadcaster by being non-intrusive, 'relevant', 'accessible', 'sensitive' and 'high quality'. It will strive not to be among those broadcasters that 'may still be seen in some quarters as a projection of economic power and of the Western mass media exerting their pervasive influence on values, fashions, tastes, consumer demands and political beliefs' (p.1). There follows a very detailed checklist of potential points of 'cultural sensitivity' in areas of content, style, genre and language. 'However, the ABC recognises ... the overseas services will *not* distort or censor program material, particularly information programs, in order to avoid the possibility of offence to one or other part of the totality of its audience' (p.2, original emphasis).

It is clear and public knowledge that material for the channel as a whole is carefully selected with a view to the cultural sensitivities outlined in the editorial guidelines. These are applicable to all programming, according to Dominic Stone, ATV program scheduler and an acting general manager (1994), who placed the general programming of the channel into a broader perspective. Budgetary considerations have meant that virtually all program content is selected from the domestic ABC service, with some few programs being taken from the SBS. The surge of information programming onto the service over its first year, together with its increasing regional focus, clearly indicates that it is leading with what the ABC believes is its strongest suit. In 1994, one-third of transmission time was occupied by information programming, including the nightly news bulletins, regular updates in Bahasa Indonesian, Cantonese and Standard Chinese, news programs *First Edition* and *The World at Noon*, the business program *The Bottom Line*, and current affairs – *Four Corners*, *Foreign Correspondent*, *Lateline*, and *Asia Focus*. Stone claimed that there is no significant editing (self-censorship) of these programs; among them, only *Foreign Correspondent* is edited – for reasons of length.

Selecting general programming for the service has not posed insurmountable problems; in the words of Bruce Donald, one of its early general managers, 'ABC programming is not extreme' (Walters 1993). However, over its first 18 months, there has been a more adventurous approach, including some domestic comedy and lively satire like *Live and Sweaty* and, more recently, *Frontline*. *Mother and Son* was considered a prime example of a program that potentially has 'universal values' – it has run for most of the channel's history so far. ATV fielded criticism from Chinese viewers that the program was insulting to an old lady who should have been venerated rather than being the butt of many jokes, by introducing the program (and others thought likely to cause offence or incomprehension) through a host, who, in the case of *Mother and Son*, offers a gentle pointer that the genre is comic and that 'the context is of a loving relationship relevant to the Australian way of life' (Stone 1994).

Documentaries have been scrutinised more closely. Several have been edited, or not perceived as relevant to Asian audiences. A documentary on unemployment in Tasmania, *All in A Day's Work*, was put far down the priority list because of 'a lack of relevance' (ibid.). An episode of *A Big Country* titled 'Vinnie and the Revheads', about pub life and bikers, was deleted on the basis that it could give regional audiences the impression that such a life-style was a typical one; while the ABC's groundbreaking March 1994 coverage of the Gay and Lesbian Mardi Gras parade in Sydney was not used for similar reasons.

In the area of drama, the financial cost of clearing rights to screen the many ABC co-productions produced in the 1990s has meant much drama programming has been back-catalogue material (some, like *Rush*, *Spring and Fall* and *Power without Glory*, date from the 1970s and early 1980s). Unsurprisingly, the controversial series *Embassy* was never considered (Walters 1993). However, the serious artistic claims of programs like *Scales of Justice* and *Phoenix* have justified their screening, despite being noted for harsh language and 'difficult' themes. Illustrating the ironies of 'projecting Australia', there is the perception that the often-coruscating criticism and satire levelled at Australian society and institutions by programs such as *Scales of Justice* and *Frontline*, which is worn as a badge of honour by any who advance the importance of freedom of creative opinion and public debate, may contribute significantly to negative perceptions of the country in the region – 'Australia's discussion of herself is ... intensely self-critical' (Sharp 1994, p.277). It is arguable that the only way such programs would ever be screened to Asian audiences is on this kind of service – the parameters of program sales and co-production in the region would definitively exclude them.

A content analysis of *ATV News*, the flagship program of the service (and the only major program made specifically for it), in its first three months and in March 1994 (*see* Cunningham and Ritchie 1994), analysed the occurrence of country coverage and news items in thematic categories: the most significant for our purposes are culture, economics and trade, human rights, politics, and war and civil disorder. The analysis shows a marked emphasis on Australian domestic stories – one-third across all categories. The nearest country coverage in the category of politics was on

Cambodia (which conducted its first democratic election in June 1993). The proportion of items in economics and trade devoted to Australia was far greater than the average, with the closest countries being Japan and China – countries that do not or only marginally receive the service.

There are significant correlations between Australian government policies toward the region and the overall stance of the news. While there may be direct instances of state and internal ABC pressure on ATV journalists (Hodge 1993) and problematic policies of pre- or self-censorship through detailed editorial notions of not offending cultural sensitivities in the region, the stance of *ATV News* is one that seeks to strategically advance Australia's own national development needs to integrate itself diplomatically (in both senses) in the region. It is also structured by the fact that, at least in the medium term, the audience for ATV will be almost entirely elites of the various countries with which Australia seeks enhanced trading, educational, cultural and political ties; in particular Indonesia, Singapore, Taiwan, Hong Kong and Malaysia. They are English-speaking elites for whom positive international presentations of national and regional issues may be of special importance (a fact that is highlighted strongly in the service's promotional publicity). This is a posture we would call 'reverse orientalism'. Edward Said (1991) has shown the degree to which the West constructed a myth of non-Western peoples as the threatening 'other' on the basis of oppositions like rational versus irrational and developed versus undeveloped. Reverse orientalism over-compensates for this history, creating a perhaps premature identification with Asia by Australian Westerners.

Perhaps most interestingly, in the plethora of domestic stories Australia is represented in *ATV News* as being *already* an Asian country. Stories which acknowledge it as a country just beginning to come to terms with the rights of its indigenous population, and as one which is still perceived in Asia in terms of the history of its operation of the White Australia policy, are wholly absent. Australia, rather, is already multi-cultural, willing to assimilate with other cultures, and enjoys religious and racial tolerance. ATV regularly features stories that represent Australia politically as a nation sharing the same interests and goals as its Asian neighbours, particularly the development and health of the Association of South East Asian Nations (ASEAN). While 'Asianisation' may well be an overriding cause of state here, it is hardly reflected in Asian nations' and peoples' perceptions of Australia, as any sample of Asian media coverage will indicate. *ATV News* works to qualify these perceptions, in particular through stories about successful immigration from the region to Australia.

Controversial issues and events concerning Australia–Asia relations go directly to the heart of the tensions between diplomacy, journalistic integrity and cultural difference that structure *ATV News*. One such event was the Bahrin Shah–Gillespie custody case in the first half of 1993. Iddin and Shahira Gillespie were taken to Malaysia in July 1992 by their father, Raja Kamarul Bahrin Shah, without the knowledge or consent of their mother, Jacqueline Gillespie, who was divorced from Bahrin Shah. Rather than simply being a case of a father taking his children, the case has been complicated by a conflict between Australian and Malaysian law on who has the right to lawful custody of the children. On the one hand, Australian law sees Jacqueline Gillespie as the rightful custodian, with Bahrin Shah's actions clearly being a breach of that law. On the other hand, in Malaysia, under Islamic law, Bahrin Shah had the right to take and keep his children. Further, under this law Jacqueline Gillespie is considered a criminal because she had unlawfully taken the children with her when she fled from her marriage to Bahrin Shah and came to Australia. She faced likely prosecution if she returned to Malaysia.

A comparison of *ATV News* with Australian newspaper coverage shows that ATV has considerably rewritten domestic media constructions of the event in the perceived interests of a more balanced coverage – and in the perceived interests of its Asian audience (Cunningham and Ritchie 1994; Loo and Ramanathan 1993). When the Australian prime minister Paul Keating called the Malaysian prime minister Dr Mahathir a 'recalcitrant' for boycotting an Asian Pacific Economic Council (APEC) summit in Seattle in November 1993, the essentially intractable problem this posed for *ATV News* meant that it was accorded very muted coverage and effectively downplayed considerably.

However, *ATV News* has moved toward a more uncompromising journalistic stance in the second part of its first eighteen months of operations. A British documentary covering allegations of much more serious suppression of the East Timorese by Indonesian military forces than either Indonesian or Australian governments are prepared to acknowledge was used on ATV, as well as on domestic ABC, in July 1994. The news coverage of the Indonesian government's closure of leading news magazines *Tempo*, *DeTik* and *Editor* in June 1994 for highlighting divisions within the Suharto regime was very detailed and ran over several days, mirroring almost exactly the extent and type of domestic coverage. Several stories, run within the first four items in the bulletin, were carried over a ten-day period from the announcement of the ban on 22 June. Many featured public protests in Jakarta over the ban, as well as an edited version of an in-depth interview with the Australian correspondent for *Tempo*. The prime minister's visit to Jakarta shortly after the ban was announced was reported to have been 'overshadowed' by the reaction to the ban.

The tensions and challenges faced by *ATV News* and the service generally include the fact that while it is one among several of the signals that could be construed by Asian opinion-formers as 'subverting' their national goals in the region, its rationale for Australia is precisely one of national development. And its ability in the longer term to deliver on a key part of its mission – to 'naturalise' the Australian perspective as regional in its significance – will depend ultimately on establishing its journalistic credentials. These will have to be fashioned in a context of a sponsored service, whose longer-term financial health will depend increasingly on attracting corporate support both in Australia and in the countries receiving the signal. The ABC's marketing document for the service, 'Beaming Across Asia', talks of an audience comprising 'the growing business and government elite in a region providing dynamic export opportunities for Australia'. This projected audience provides more than an attraction for potential sponsors to access an influential market segment, it also nominates those elites that are in a position to influence Australia's integration into the region.

Another tension is that between a public broadcasting ethos and the demands of attracting corporate sponsorship. This was borne out in the criticism the ABC attracted for endorsing results of a survey of the audience for the service, which was primarily an exercise in corporate public relations (PA Consulting 1994). This 'research', by a management consultancy firm, claimed that ATV reaches a 'potential' audience for the full service of 24 million, and 670 million for selected programs. Such an extravagant claim is based only on the number of people under a satellite footprint and within reach of cabling. The reality is that there is, at this early stage in the life of Australia Television, little concrete regional response that can be drawn on to authenticate perceptions of audience reception. However, what little evaluative comment there has been from the region suggests that the service's attempt to position itself as crafted for the region has met with some appreciative response. One international news expert, Kunda Dixit, Asia-Pacific regional director, Inter Press Service (1994) offered his view that *ATV News* is a high-quality service compared to its competitors in the region, especially because of its regional specificity. Children's programming is especially welcome, he said, while the majority of other programming tends to be 'whites only and sports-mad'.

Tensions about sponsorship have continued to hound the service. In the context of the ABC's claim that the service would be self-supporting by 1995, there was a departmental inquiry into its funding viability in 1994. This was the most public outcome of regular concern expressed that David Hill, managing director of the ABC, in initiating ATV and the ABC's involvement with pay television, was taking the national broadcaster outside its core charter activities. This, among several other controversies at the ABC during 1994, precipitated Hill's resignation announcement in late 1994.

On the evidence of its first year of operation, the service exhibits aspects of 'development journalism', but Western-style development journalism; a style characterised by a posture of reverse orientalism. This is not necessarily a result of state direction, but arises from shared intent between media and government elites. By its nature, the service will attempt to provide a broader perspective than that which may be deemed appropriate for domestic consumption. This is welcome, for Australian media have traditionally focussed on European (especially British) and American models, styles and content. However, the challenges it poses for journalists in a volatile cross-cultural mediascape, from the evidence given here, will be significant. Means must be found so that both Australia's economic aspirations in the region and its traditions of independent journalism can flourish.

Tied up with these issues relating to the news, but also relating to wider questions of the whole service, is the challenge to regionalise. By upgrading its use of Asian languages (and possibly its program-supply arrangements with the SBS, the domestic broadcaster with an explicit mission to provide multicultural services to the country), the service might also upgrade its presentation of Australia's populations of Asian origin or heritage, showing the contemporary multicultural face of the country. This cultural undertaking could be a far more fundamental long-range contribution toward projecting Australia in the region, and would widen the hoped-for corporate image of the service from a solid and respected information source to one relaying some of the strengths of a relatively peaceful multicultural democracy.

Such a strategy may perform a crucial cross-cultural function by addressing the ongoing perception in many Asian countries that Australia remains a racist Western country – many still believe that the previous discriminatory government immigration policy, the so-called 'White Australia' policy, is still in place. It would also lend the service a more regional focus without diluting Australian content. If the service can address the considerable cross-cultural challenges it faces, it has the potential in time to become an important voice to project Australia's place in east Asia.

10

New Zealand

GEOFF LEALAND

If one image sums up populist Australian caricatures of New Zealand, it might be the Barry Humphries-created personae of Dame Edna Everage and her bridesmaid Madge Allsop – the large, flamboyant and self-publicising Australian 'superstar' and the much-put-upon, meek and mute New Zealander. New Zealand rejoinders like, 'The immigration flow from New Zealand to Australia raises the IQ level of both countries', and such national-stereotype jokes reveal broader concerns about the power differentials between the two countries. New Zealand and Australia are bound together, not only by historical links as British settler societies, legendary shared military exploits and geographical proximity, but also in formal economic ties through the Closer Economic Relations (CER) agreement and other strategic alliances, and understandings such as common membership of the Cairns Group, a small third force in international trade negotiations. Since CER was signed more than a decade ago, significant liberalisation and harmonisation has occurred in trade in goods and services, aviation, business law, investment, standards, and customs and quarantine procedures. There are now both shared historical experiences and common interests, even though differences emerged over defence alliances in the 1980s.

But at a popular, cultural level there still seems to be much that divides. Recent opinion surveys (quoted in Reid 1992, p.81) confirm that Australians know far less about New Zealand than the other way around. Ian Reid himself opines that '[t]he vacancies and cliche images that constitute New Zealand in Australia's mind have the dissociative function of constructing one's own national identity through a process of distancing it from that which would threaten if acknowledged as too similar' (1992, p.82).

While Australia is currently preoccupied with future constitutional change, which may usher in a republic roughly to coincide with the centenary of federation, enthusiasm for a similar process in New Zealand is lukewarm; a poll in June 1994 showed 64 per cent support for maintaining the constitutional monarchy. As long-time republican and Alliance politician Bruce Jesson pointed out, the main impetus for any change in New Zealand is driven less by a desire for liberation or symbolic independence than by a 'non-sentimental' economic rationalism, which is 'entirely comfortable with a global culture where people, money, goods and services move freely around the world'. In such a world 'New Zealand's British institutions appear quaint and even eccentric' (Jesson 1994, p.82).

It is the same economic rationalism, in place at a national policy level since the mid-1980s, that has swept aside much of the institutional culture associated with a traditional capitalist mixed economy, a culture which Australia retains to a large degree. Radical economic and social change has been the norm for the past decade, through major de-regulation of markets and financial exchange, the disposal of many state-owned assets (most often to foreign ownership), the withdrawal of the state from many services and the dominance of 'user-pays' philosophy, and the entrenchment of New Right concepts of individual responsibility. In return, the New Zealand voter has signaled its desire for radical political restructuring, to a yet-untested system of proportional representation. But given the pace and scale of recent changes, a new political system will not necessarily slow nor reverse the momentum of change.

These changes have given rise to New Zealand's reputation as a 'deregulatory laboratory' and have led, since the 1970s, to a break in New Zealand's traditional trading relationship with Britain. The reorientation is to the Southern Hemisphere, most particularly to Australia – which is now New Zealand's biggest market – and also to the south Pacific. In turn, New Zealand is Australia's third largest trading partner. More than 2000 Australian companies operate in New Zealand and one-quarter of New Zealand's top companies are Australian-owned. This makes the issue of CER, as we shall see later in the chapter, a far more important one for New Zealand's industrial and audiovisual fortunes than for Australia's.

The environmental foci are also different – Australia looks toward a future identity in the South East Asian region, but New Zealand's ethnic, cultural and economic predisposition is more towards the south Pacific. So while New Zealand and Australia are inextricably connected through ties of history, geography and shared economic interests, Ian Reid goes so far as to say that the two countries are oriented to quite different regions and that they are fundamentally unalike in the way each perceives itself and its relation to its immediate external environments (Reid 1992, pp.81–2).

THE NEW ZEALAND TELEVISION ECOLOGY

The New Zealand mediascape has been greatly transformed by the doctrines of economic rationalism. Gone is the centrality of public service objectives, which used to characterise the television ecology of the country. While public-service television organisations in other countries, including the BBC in Britain and the ABC in Australia, mount strong campaigns to justify their continued funding from licence fees or direct government appropriation, such actions would now seem quaint in the New Zealand context. Television in New Zealand is fully commercial, even though a broadcasting fee is still imposed for the right to receive television signals. TVNZ is a state-owned enterprise operating on commercial profit-making principles, while TV3 is a private company, majority-owned by Canadian Issie Asper's Canwest Global Systems.

The broadcasting fee, which totalled NZ$85 million in 1993, goes directly to New Zealand On Air (NZOA, formerly the Broadcasting Commission), which has a brief to distribute it to a number of 'targeted' areas (public radio, Maori radio) but also the discretion to fund television production. In 1993, 60 per cent of collected fees went to production as a direct grant to to the two broadcasters (TVNZ and TV3), to affiliated production houses (for example, South Pacific Pictures, a subsidiary of TVNZ), or to independent producers. Funding is allocated according to NZOA's objectives: 'To foster New Zealand culture and identity ... reflecting NZOA's interest in seeing funding benefits reach the largest number of fee payers via both programs designed for mainstream audiences and those targeted to the special interests of as many New Zealanders as possible' (*NZOA Annual Report*, 1993–4). This brief effectively frees the commercial broadcasters from public interest responsibilities, or at least places these responsibilities second to the primary objective of owning and operating a television system geared to maximise profits.

The limits on NZOA's funds, however, means that it supports only a very small minority of New Zealand-made television. Only 5 per cent of TVNZ's income comes from NZOA, which tends to fund higher-risk drama, documentary and children's programming, while in-house production by TVNZ and TV3 is dominated by sport, news and current affairs. NZOA is testament to the economic rationalist doctrine that direct subsidy rather than public-interest-style regulation (as is in evidence in Australia) is a more transparent and effective, less market-distorting means of delivering social outcomes. NZOA, however, has to reconcile a number of contradictory demands; to satisfy simultaneously mainstream and minority interests, and to counter accusations that it should not be in the business of underwriting commercial successes, such as the nightly soap drama *Shortland Street*.

NZOA intervenes in a small way in a television ecology where TVNZ continues to dominate, with an 82 per cent share of the broadcast audience. TV3 trails behind at 16 per cent. TVNZ has also diversified locally into pay television (a 16 per cent share of Sky Networks) and regional television (a major shareholding in Horizon Pacific Television), and internationally into a Pacific service and the Asia Business News. The financially troubled TV3 is shaped by the controlling interest held by Canwest (which also holds a significant interest in Australia's Channel 10). Sky Networks, the pay television service primarily owned by an American consortium (Ameritech, Bell Atlantic, Tele-Communications Incorporated (TCI) and Time-Warner), had inched its subscription base past 140 000 by 1994.

For a population of 3.09 million, New Zealand appears to be a media-saturated society. In Auckland in 1994, for example, there were 27 radio stations. Television offers three national channels, Sky another four pay channels, there is regional television in major population centres, and a music-video channel in Christchurch and Auckland. But, by international standards, New Zealanders do not seem to be voracious consumers of the electronic media. While there is universal television ownership, and 35 per cent of New Zealand homes have more than two sets, conventional ratings indicate that on average only 38 per cent of the potential audience watch regularly during prime time. As one commentator notes, 'That figure would worry networks elsewhere' (Guy 1994).

There also seems to be a generational split between an older, information-seeking audience for ONE, TVNZ's first channel, and a younger, entertainment-seeking Channel 2 audience. TV3 has attempted to provide for both, with disappointing results. Program preferences seem to follow a similar pattern: ONE schedules are heavy on in-house local content (sport and news) and British drama and often rather elderly sitcoms; Channel 2 features US drama and sitcoms, and more populist local content (infotainment and *Shortland Street*). Most Australian drama imports are scheduled on Channel 2 and TV3.

AUSTRALIAN PROGRAMS ON NEW ZEALAND TELEVISION

The Australia–NZ television relationship is overwhelmingly one-way: Australia sells, New Zealand imports. Simple counts confirm this.

Table10.1:   **Sources of Programming on New Zealand Television (in Percentages)**

	US	UK	Australia	NZ
December 1989	56.9	17.1	5.1	19.8
December 1993	49.8	12.5	12.9	27.3

Source: program listings *New Zealand Listener*, 1989, 1993.

Through the 1980s and into the 1990s Australian programs have contributed in the range of 5 to 8 per cent, or between 80 and 100 hours monthly, of New Zealand television content. On some occasions the contribution has been greater, as in the December 1993 figure above, which included extended Australian coverage of one-day cricket between the two countries. Of course this is usually less than imported content from the two other major sources of programming, particularly that originating in the United States. In contrast, New Zealand-made programs are rarely, if ever, seen on Australian television.

Australian programming has made a consistent contribution to New Zealand television schedules. But mere hours of programming are never as important as where programs are placed in the schedule and the numbers of viewers who choose to see them. In May 1994, for example, there were Australian programs screening at 7 pm across all three channels: the Grundy-produced game show *Wheel of Fortune* on ONE; the Grundy co-produced New Zealand medical soap *Shortland Street* on Channel 2; and the Australian-originated infotainment program *Hard Copy* on TV3. This domination of the very important early-evening lead-in time slots on New Zealand television by Australian-flavoured stripped programming is the residual effect of a period in New Zealand television history when, as noted in a previous study (Lealand 1990), the most direct influence on the shape of television programming and on programmers' notions of the New Zealand viewing audience was Australian.

In the late 1980s, New Zealand television schedules were stage-managed by Australian expatriates from the Australian commercial networks, who crossed the Tasman with aggressive confidence about commercialising the preferences of the New Zealand audience. Kel Geddes, imported from the Nine Network to be the first head of programming at TV3, launched into competition with TVNZ in November 1989 with extravagant claims of a new future in television. But the reality was that TV3 was critically under-financed, scheduling errors were made, and TV3 quickly slid towards insolvency and ownership by creditor–bankers. The immediate 25 per cent audience share promised to TV3 by Kel Geddes in the early days of the channel has never materialised.

There has traditionally been regular cross-Tasman 'trade' in television executives, the imbalance of which is not nearly as severe as that in programming. New Zealand has given the eminent executive Des Monaghan (Seven's Network director of production and program development), Rob Guest of *Man O Man*, and the controversial television host Derryn Hinch to Australia. While some direct influence on New Zealand television programming style persists, its level has declined since the 1980s. However, television culture in New Zealand has grown into a commercial, ratings-dominated media environment; at least part of this can be attributed to Australian influence.

For several years in the late 1980s and early 1990s, Australian programming appeared to dominate the schedules. *Neighbours, Home and Away*, and *The Sullivans* all were stripped across prime slots in the schedule. *The Flying Doctors* was a core, top-rating program in the Channel 2 line-up. Australian programs, according to Channel 2 manager of programming Bettina Hollings:

> have been an important part of television in New Zealand for a long time because of successful programs and close cultural [ties]. Soaps of both *The Flying Doctors* and *Neighbours* types have been a popular genre. *Police Rescue* is worth a mention too. There is not a lot of adult drama being made world wide and this was a very successful addition to Channel 2. Australian programs are generally well sampled when they launch because viewers have a high regard for them. Country of origin doesn't generally determine the level of interest for a program [but] I think that Aussie shows have had a better than average performance record here. Australian programs rate reasonably well and sometimes very well (Hollings 1994).

By 1993 and 1994, however, Australian programming no longer occupied such a central position on New Zealand screens, and has played to more muted success. Hollings argues, 'now Australian programming is seen as just part of the overall imported contribution to television schedules in this country; merely part of the schedule that competes with or complements the local content of our television'. A 'snapshot' of television schedules taken in late March 1994 bears out this suggestion. *The New Adventures of Skippy* was scheduled at the very dawn of the television day (6.30 am on Sundays on TV3); the Grundy detective series *Bony* on Saturday afternoons at 1.00 pm on the same channel; the sitcom *Mother and Son* scheduled on TV3 at 9.45 am on Sundays; *Lion Red Aussie League* in the late-night hours on Channel 2 (at 11.45 pm on Saturdays and 10.45 pm on Sundays); *Paradise Beach* stripped at 5.00 pm and *Neighbours* at

5.30 pm on weekdays on Channel 2 (and repeated on ONE at 10.00 am on weekdays); *Home and Away* on ONE at 4.10 pm on weekdays; *Aerobics Oz Style* at 10.00 am on Channel 2; a repeat of *Chances* at midnight on Channel 2; the 1986 Australian mini-series *Sword of Honour* at 11.05 pm on TV3 ; and a short Australian film *Dance-7 Colours* in the Educational TV slot on ONE at 9.00 am.

In prime-time hours – 6–10 pm for New Zealand television – only a few Australian programs appeared: the populist sci-tech series *Beyond 2000* on Wednesdays at 7.30 pm on TV3; the mini-series *Banjo Paterson's The Man from Snowy River* on Thursdays at 7.30 pm on Channel 2; and police drama *Blue Heelers* on Fridays at 7.30 pm on ONE. A New Zealander had been introduced to front the 7.00 pm stripped tabloid news program *Hard Copy* on TV3, but the program content still appeared to be from Australia (or more correctly, from the United States via Australia). In addition the Australian Steve Irwin fronted the wildlife documentary *Our World* at 6.30 pm on Sundays. The New Zealand version of *60 Minutes* (Sundays at 7.30 pm on Channel 2) typically featured a US-derived story, a local story, and a personality-profile courtesy of the Australian version of the show.

The sense that the presence of Australian programming on New Zealand television appears to be less significant in the mid-1990s than in the late 1980s and early 1990s is supported by the failure of some Australian programs (*Banjo Paterson's The Man from Snowy River* and *Snowy*) as well as a local model (*The Mad, Mad World of Television*) of a long-running Australian variety show, *Hey Hey It's Saturday*. But though Australian voices are no longer heard as often on New Zealand television screens, and success can no longer be guaranteed in the 1990s, Australian names and company logos still feature on the end-credits of a number of important New Zealand programs.

THE NEW ZEALAND EXPERIENCE OF GRUNDYS' PAROCHIAL INTERNATIONALISM

According to Bettina Hollings, 'The time was ripe [in 1992] for a New Zealand soap', which would carry storylines 'that were not soft and fluffy like *Neighbours*'. Starting in May 1992 and stripped across week nights at 7 pm on Channel 2, the medical soap *Shortland Street* rapidly overcame initial misgivings to become a serial with a strong following, critical acclaim (it won the Best Drama Series Award at the 1993 New Zealand

Film and Television Awards), and a central place in contemporary New Zealand life. It has been credited with regenerating writing and production skills in the industry (largely through offering continuous employment), it has spawned a diverse range of personalities for women's magazines, and has initiated widely dispersed and complex television talk amongst viewers.

Even though it owes a large debt to soap operas and to the medical soap in general, it is unlike other specific examples of the genre. The pace and multiplicity of its narratives makes it different from US day-time soaps (such as *General Hospital*). The multi-cultural flavour of its cast (Pakeha, Samoan, Maori, Chinese), and the continual incorporation of social issues (divorce, teenage suicide, multiple deaths, gay relationships, extramarital relationships, drug addiction, the sale of human organs) mark it off from Australian soaps such as *Neighbours* or series such as *The Flying Doctors*. It is constantly testing what can be portrayed in an early-evening serial, to the extent that Hollings argues that 'it deals with the kinds of serious, local issues which would never find a place on Australian television'. While that claim may be debatable in the light of the long tradition of social issues regularly canvassed in popular long-form Australian dramas such as *A Country Practice*, *GP*, and *Heartbreak High*, it does display a new-found, and justified, cultural confidence that the country's audiences can make popular its own prime-time serial drama. But though *Shortland Street* is generally regarded as a thoroughly New Zealand production, Grundys was instrumental in its genesis and retains international distribution rights as half-owner.

The Grundy presence in New Zealand began with setting up the game show *Sale of the Century*, which ran in the 7.00 pm (and in its later stages, 5.30 pm) slot on ONE across week nights from April 1989 to June 1993 (and then reappeared in late 1994). Of the six game shows made locally during this period, three were produced by Grundys – *Sale of the Century*, *Wheel of Fortune* and *Jeopardy*. The Australian-owned Fremantle Group were involved in *The Price is Right* and *Face the Music*. The only wholly New Zealand game show (made by Communicado) was *It's In The Bag*, revived in television form from an earlier and popular radio quiz show. According to Caterina de Nave, who directed a substantial number of early episodes of *Shortland Street* and who was also head of entertainment at TVNZ in the late 1980s, Grundys' early incursions into cross-Tasman television exemplify the way their strategy of parochial internationalism works on the ground:

Deals were negotiated at a very high level within Television New Zealand and TVNZ paid a per program fee to Grundys, which included both the licence fee for the format and the production fee. Grundys also sent over a couple of their producers to produce it and train local people up. Grundys produced the show, which meant that not only were they selling us the concept of the program but they were ensuring that the way the program was made followed approved forms – unlike [in] other places where the sale of rights have resulted in major changes to the format, such as the Americans 'Americanising' game show formats (1993).

Grundys' financial investment in *Shortland Street* was less substantial than that of the other partners. Those costs remaining of the original NZ$10 million investment after NZOA had contributed NZ$3 million and TVNZ NZ$4.5 million were shared with co-producer South Pacific Pictures. Despite this, contractual terms meant that Grundys became half-owner of *Shortland Street* and continue to be a 50 per cent shareholder. The company's continuing equity position in the serial is not only for financial return in the New Zealand market (since the other major shareholders are producer and broadcaster), but to enable Grundys to sell *Shortland Street* to foreign markets as part of its international catalogue.

Parochial internationalism means that the most portable product can, and should, be attractively local in its country of origin but also should have the potential to be delocalised for the purposes of international sales, if that is considered the best way to position it. Grundys' corporate-sales advertising typically will not single out programs as originating from particular countries. In the Grundy Worldwide catalogue of 'Programs That Work', *Shortland Street* is volume product for stripping; that it is a New Zealand program is irrelevant. This strategy of delocalisation probably is based on the fact that New Zealand is a relative newcomer to the international market for long-form drama; marking it by country of origin would not increase its saleability. By late 1994, *Shortland Street* had become popular in late-afternoon slots on seven ITV stations in the UK, attracting estimated audiences of up to 5 million. After a long period of uncertainty about an Australian sale, for reasons we shall consider shortly, it was finally taken by SBS in October 1994 for the lead-out from its evening news, rather than by one of the three commercial networks.

In the spirit of parochial internationalism, Grundys played a crucial part in the creative genesis of the program in addition to the organisation's financial investment and marketing responsibilities. The initial invitation to Grundys came from local producers, said de Nave:

It has been important for us in terms of enhancing ... success to have Grundys on board as advisors – they are experts in the field. When I first started at South Pacific Pictures, one of my important goals was to establish a five-nights-a-week serial on television. SPP and Grundys have put a very strong team together, and the episodes I've seen so far have confirmed my belief that we have a very good series with high production values on our hands (1993).

Ian Bradley, senior Australian-based Grundys executive, and co-producer of *Shortland Street*, talked up the series to its local audience at its inception, predicting that it would be 'bigger than *Neighbours* and the characters would soon become household names' (*Networks* 1992). According to de Nave, Bradley was one of a number of Australians shaping the early days of *Shortland Street*. However his involvement was limited to being there 'just to answers questions about the practicalities of studio set-ups and so on', unlike the two Grundy writers, Jason Daniel and Gavin Strawhan, who were responsible for getting the serial up and running through opening storylines and character development. De Nave says that the contribution of these two writers (both of whom had previously worked on *Neighbours*) was 'fundamental' in the early success of *Shortland Street*, both in terms of creating stories and characters and assisting other writers. But she added 'there was never any intention to make a *Neighbours* clone for New Zealand consumption ... it was never like that because the Australians had never made a serial that even remotely approaches the depth and breadth that *Shortland Street* has' (1993).

The contribution of Daniel and Strawhan could also be explained by the impoverished pool of serial-form writers in New Zealand in 1992. Unlike Australia, where serial television had been thriving for years, it had been quite some time since any New Zealand-produced long-form drama had been on screen (in fact, since the evening limited-duration series *Gloss*, in June 1988). Also, several writers were involved in the TV3 serial *Homeward Bound*, which was up against *Shortland Street* for NZOA funding. *Homeward Bound* eventually went to air as a weekly 22-part series but was dropped after failing to attract a significant following. The input of the Australians, says de Nave, ensured that *Shortland Street* had a greater chance of success.

By 1994, the writing team for *Shortland Street* was headed by New Zealand story editor Rachel Lang, who fronted a team of 15 dialogue writers, six storyliners and three editors. Gavin Strawhan stayed on as script supervisor, the remaining direct link with Grundys. Although the

New Zealand producers of the serial are no longer beholden to an Australian input they do not seem to begrudge a lingering presence. Comments by Tony Holden, producer of *Shortland Street* in 1994, suggest that Grundys still continues to keep a weather eye on the serial. Some concern was expressed about gay storylines in 1993–4 episodes, and it was argued that the proliferating plotlines were breaking 'Grundy rules'; most particularly that *Shortland Street* was 'burning up' stories too quickly and had broken a 'cardinal rule' by killing off a core-cast character. According to Holden, the resistance put up to this feedback meant that 'they now leave us alone' (1994).

CREATING A TRANS-TASMAN AUDIOVISUAL SPACE

There is a belief among some industry figures in New Zealand that the reason why an Australian commercial network might find it difficult to schedule *Shortland Street* is because of its often contentious material, given the normal expectations for early-evening drama on Australian commercial television. This seems unlikely. Far more significant barriers are that Australian programming dominates in the late-afternoon and early-evening schedules, that such programming has an established popularity, and that Australian-content rules currently in force would treat *Shortland Street* as foreign in content.

The Trade in Services Protocol to the CER agreement requires the removal of most forms of domestic assistance and regulation in service sectors, other than those either country might specifically tag for exclusion. It is unclear (possibly because of a lack of foresight) why Australia chose not to 'inscribe' (that is, exempt) local-content quotas in 1988 when the protocol was developed. New Zealand producers now argue that the inclusion of New Zealand programs in the Australian-content quota is a necessary result of that choice but there is considerable opposition to such an outcome within the Australian television production industry and in some sections of the government.

Based on a thoroughgoing New Zealand industry audit, which resulted in a range of strategies for audiovisual industry development, Project Blue Sky was launched in November 1993. This joint venture of public- and private-sector film and television interests has as a primary objective, '[To] develop New Zealand and Australia as one economic market for television and film', which would help 'develop and maintain a strong, viable, and stable domestic base of production' and 'increase the amount of foreign exchange being invested and earned by the industry' (Project Blue Sky 1993). This grand strategy will be in place from 1994 to 1996.

NEIGHBOURS

New Zealand prime minister Jim Bolger, annoyed by the indifference of Australian commercial television stations towards New Zealand productions, in spite of considerable flow the other way, lobs a tape of New Zealand's favourite soap onto the head of the Australian prime minister, Paul Keating.
(Reproduced by permission of *The New Zealand Herald*, Auckland, 6 May 1994.)

As it stood in 1994, TPS14 stipulated 'Australian' programs as the necessary description for inclusion in local-content tallies; advocates of Project Blue Sky argue that it should be re-drafted to read 'Australian and New Zealand programs'. In addition, the requirement that the Australian Broadcasting Authority should perform its functions 'in a manner consistent with Australia's international obligations' embodied in section 160D of the *Broadcasting Services Act (1992)* has given weight to Project Blue Sky. The argument centres on the reconciliation of two apparently contradictory pieces of public policy, one contained in a cross-national agreement and one in a set of regulations of a broadcasting regulatory body. For their part, the New Zealand lobby argues 'firstly that CER is a deal and Australia has not upheld its side of it. Secondly, they stress the benefits to both countries of a larger, single audiovisual market' (Given 1994). Blue Sky executive director Jo Tyndall (quoted in Bell 1994) points to the historical disparity between export figures as the basis for these claims. In the 1990s, Australia has on average earned NZ$13 million annually while New Zealand has earned only NZ$300 000 annually from cross-Tasman program sales, she claims.

New Zealand rhetoric on the issue can be strong. Mark Holman, senior advisor on international communications policy with the NZ Ministry of Commerce, stated flatly that Australia was contravening the CER protocol on Trade in Services and argued that this was limiting New Zealand program production. On *Shortland Street* as a test case, former TVNZ sales representative Marius von Zeppelin attacked Australia's 'protectionist stance' in 1994, arguing that 'the market [should] actually test the product. If they (the Australians) don't like the accents or storyline then we will find out' (Scott 1994). John Barnett, head of South Pacific Pictures, flew in the face of the international acceptability of Australian programs when he argued:

> We see it as a market that goes both ways. Letting New Zealand product into Australia is not going to be some kind of Trojan horse. In New Zealand we live in a de-regulated economy and there is now more production here than ever before. But what the Australians will find with their protectionist rules is that if their product is made by Australians, about Australians and with Australians they should expect the only audience they are going to get is Australian. We are working in a global business and Australia and New Zealand have much more to gain from being with each other than agin each other (Scott 1994).

The debate so far has been shaped by legal and economic rationalist arguments, with debates about cultural sovereignty and shared culture more muted. Nevertheless, there has been some opposition on cultural grounds; quite predictably this has been voiced by Australian interests. The Screen Producers Association of Australia suggested that counting New Zealand programs as Australian local content 'would water down local content on Aussie TV [and] Australian program-makers would fight the move' (Drinnan 1993). Jim Bolger, New Zealand prime minister, joined in the debate in May 1994:

> Attempts to market *Shortland Street* ran slap into another barrier based on the desire to protect jobs for Australian actors. I am making some inquiries on the matter as it seems fair and logical to argue that as New Zealanders have to watch *Neighbours*, the Australian soap, it would be good for Australia to watch our *Shortland Street* (Murphy 1994).

The factor not included in Bolger's argument is that New Zealand has never had a television quota system, which would govern whether they got to see *Neighbours* or not; imported content on Australian screens is subject to a degree of contestability within the Australian quota rules.

Although there is much shared and mutually embraced by Australia and New Zealand, the Tasman Sea does seem to remain both a highly symbolic and tangible physical divide between the two countries. Some differences manifest themselves as occasional arguments over 'ownership', such as whether Jane Campion, director of the Academy Award-winning *The Piano* is a New Zealand or an Australian film-maker. Others are more deeply entrenched, like the strong reluctance on the part of New Zealanders to consider formal political alliance with Australia. Despite the futuristic 'Ausland' in the Spielberg-produced television series *Seaquest DSV*, there seems to be little desire for such confederation at the popular level.

In the case for *Shortland Street* to be counted as an Australian television program, the legal and anti-protectionism arguments are strong. But as one anonymous source in the New Zealand television industry remarked, the moral case is weaker: 'It may be an open-and-shut legal case for those pushing it but it is a case with no emotional or cultural logic.' But such off-the-record dissenting comments are rare in a debate fuelled by a sense of inequity and unfairness. Even though New Zealanders may share the general spirit of the Australian quota rules, namely the protection and fostering of local television identity, the debate is focused specifically on the one-way street of television program flow between the two countries. Most New Zealanders would probably argue that there is a strong case for Australia to show more New Zealand programs but might be unwilling for *Shortland Street* to be co-opted to undercut the general principle of safeguarding cultural sovereignty. In the 1994–5 review of the Australian content regulations the ABA opted to retain the existing rule that treats New Zealand programs as foreign.

CONCLUSION

A contestant on the New Zealand Grundy-produced game show *Wheel of Fortune*, screened in late March 1994, had his answer discounted and his bid for a major car prize discredited because he gave his answer in an 'Australian accent'. Filling in the missing person for the 1960s group Crosby, Stills & Nash, the contestant apparently was heard to say 'Steels', a 'wrong' answer. Some weeks later, after the program had gone to air as live television, all was resolved in a flurry of transparent publicity and the contestant got his car. But the irony remains that the contestant was not a 'real' Australian but an expatriate New Zealander who had lived a little too long in Australia and subsequently picked up a strange accent. At this moment, Australia and New Zealand seemed like two countries forever divided by a common language.

But there is more than just accent. CER is more than 12 years old and there seems little difference in 'the things we buy, the food we eat and the beer and wine we drink, even the sports we enjoy' (Ansley 1994). However, in the audiovisual space bridging the two countries, there is much activity – Sydney-based expatriate New Zealand director Jane Campion is to make a film, *Portrait of a Lady*, with Hollywood export Australian Nicole Kidman. New Zealander Sam Neill plays Australian artist Norman Lindsay in *Sirens* with Australian US-based international supermodel Elle Macpherson, who produces her own line of lingerie with the New Zealand manufacturer Bendon. New Zealand-born comedian Pamela Stephenson and her Scottish husband Billy Connolly make advertisements for Australian food in Auckland. There is a long and growing list of productions built on talent spanning the small pond, by international standards, that is the Tasman. Nevertheless, in respect to cultural relations between Australia and New Zealand – and most particularly the one-way television flow from the bigger country to the smaller – greater reciprocity is yet to be achieved.

11

Papua New Guinea and the South-West Pacific

HELEN WILSON

Of 39 nations identified by UNESCO as without a television service by 1988, 12 were in the Pacific (Sreberny-Mohammadi 1991, p.136). By 1994, over half of these had introduced permanent services, after they had considered offers by Australian broadcasters, among others. In contrast to all other regions surveyed previously, Australia has had a dominating, colonial or neo-colonial, presence in the south-west Pacific. Nations in this region share many characteristics with those of Africa, South America and parts of Asia as they face issues of underdevelopment and neo-colonialism.

While the cultural imperialism thesis offers a well-established and plausible account of the effects of the export of cultural commodities to these regions, the weaknesses of that view are becoming clearer as evidence emerges of the complexities of cross-cultural negotiations of meaning. It is against this unique background that the implications of an Australian program presence in the Pacific must be viewed. In this chapter we canvass many of these issues, while concentrating on one nation – Papua New Guinea (PNG) – where the Australian television industry has exerted its greatest influence in recent decades.

Australia's influence has been primarily political and economic, because of the way television is tied to national political structures and embedded in economic processes of trans-nationalisation and distribution through urban hubs. The social and cultural influences of television are clearly significant but more elusive, since television is merely one aspect of the long process of the expansion of 'the culture of capitalism'. Radio and movies were well established in the Pacific before the widespread consumption of various forms of video began in the early 1980s as a precursor to broadcast television.

Historically, it has not only been programming that has been exported to these regions. Television services — an institutional presence – and Australian-owned transmission technologies have also been established.

As Liz Fell notes (1989), the Pacific nations were seen as a strategic area of expansion by the Australian communication entrepreneurs of the 1980s, such as Kerry Packer, Alan Bond and Kerry Stokes. The most notable examples are the Nine Network's activities in Fiji prior to the Rabuka coups and its present ownership of the only free-to-air television service in PNG; the Newcastle television licence-holder Kevin Parry's former owner-ship of a PNG licence, and the use by several operators in the south-west Pacific region of Australia's domestic satellite (previously Aussat, now part of Optus Communications).

Unlike Australia's presence in other world markets, geographical proximity to these regions might indicate that Australian technology and services are likely to be a continuing presence. However, despite some aggressive attempts in the 1980s to establish other outlets, only PNG had become a successful market for Australian television by 1994. The newer services of the smaller Pacific states exhibited the same characteristic as the established or rapidly expanding multi-channel markets in Europe and North America, where Australian audiovisual product most typically was placed as a marginal supplement. In PNG, by contrast, Australian pro-gramming has a sufficient presence for it to be seen as an imperialising influence, dominating television schedules, introducing what many might argue to be inappropriate cultural values and squeezing out indigenous production opportunities. On that country's EM TV, for example, we find the early-evening schedule consisting of *Skippy*, *Home and Away*, *A Current Affair*, *Sale of the Century* and *Neighbours*, with the line-up of Australian programs interrupted only by local news.

Not only does Australia export entertainment programming to PNG. Australian current-affairs programs are broadcast unmodified and are a prime source of news coverage. It is in this area that the power of Australia to set agendas is especially troubling. *60 Minutes* has given offence, for example, through pushing the government on its military suppression of the secessionist movement in Bougainville, as much as for carrying a notorious segment on Madonna early in 1993.

Australian television's presence in this region cannot avoid being framed within debates about 'development communication' in the Third World. John Lent's 'Mass Media in the Developing World: Four Conundrums', first presented in 1974, provides an outline of the perpetual general dilemmas faced by communications organisations in poor Third World countries that experience neo-colonial underdevelopment. Mass-media services and programming have to be made economically and culturally practicable for newly emergent nations and must better serve the interests of the general population. The conflict between press freedom and 'development communication' must be resolved, and media theory and research appropriate to the Third World must be designed.

In an update, Lent concludes that the conundrums remain (Lent 1993, p.235). On the one hand, new production centres have challenged the US dominance of program supply, critical research in the under-developed world has increased and there are more technological options. On the other hand, there has been disillusionment with the performance of 'big TV' in meeting the development agenda and there is greater reliance now than 20 years ago on the industrialised nations for tech-nology. Local elites still ignore majorities, even to the extent of not using their languages (radio in PNG uses only a handful of the country's 800 languages). And the West condemns rather than supports attempts to develop alternative news values, while enthusiastically exporting the dubious expertise of the 'hucksters of high technology and other machinery and techniques that have failed in the past' (Lent 1993, p.253). Australian interests such as Aussat and the Nine Network have to be included among these 'hucksters' who have for decades promoted expen-sive and inappropriate equipment for telecommunications and broad-casting in the Pacific.

TELEVISION IS INTRODUCED TO THE PACIFIC

Stewart Firth (1989) divides the Pacific nations into those that enjoy sovereignty and those that do not. The fully sovereign states are PNG, Fiji, the Solomons, Vanuatu, Western Samoa, Tonga, Kiribati and Nauru. Tonga is a kingdom which has never been truly colonised; the others are former colonies of the UK, Australia and New Zealand. Britain was always a reluctant coloniser in the Pacific Basin, a stance inherited by Australia and New Zealand. These three powers have either willingly followed United Nations de-colonisation pressures since the 1960s, or have had little choice in doing so, unlike the US and France, whose territories remain constitutionally dependent on their colonial rulers. The total population of the Pacific states is about 5.5 million, over three-quarters of whom live in PNG and Fiji.

Australia's former colonies are PNG, in the Melanesian sub-region of the south-west Pacific, which gained independence in 1975, and Nauru (Micronesia), which gained full independence in 1968. While Australia might have preferred to secure its strategic interest in PNG, this was not politically possible; the advantages were outweighed by a fear of

Melanesian immigration (Firth 1989, p.93). Unlike the many Polynesians who have chosen to settle in New Zealand, Papua New Guineans do not have the option of migrating to Australia; this would have issued from a continuing colonial status, as with Puerto Ricans in the US. The PNG state and infrastructure were basically set up in the Australian image, although Australia's involvement since independence has been of a different kind.

Australia has seen its commitment to the Australia, New Zealand and United States alliance (ANZUS) including an obligation to keep transport channels open and governments friendly in the south-west Pacific. Australia is the largest donor of aid to the region, which is the most aid-dependent per capita region in the world, and Australian investment is encouraged. On the face of it, Australia and New Zealand are givers and helpers, supporting the development agenda of the Pacific states, which fosters national identity, autonomy and growth. However, the two countries are also the dominant forces in trade and industry, finance, transport and communications, and their aid and investment is greatly outweighed by the returns on these commercial activities (Hau'ofa: 1987, p.9). The fact that New Zealand opted out of ANZUS in the mid-1980s and therefore was seen as a more neutral and potentially sympathetic regional power may have helped to promote an easier way for its investments than some Australian companies, including television interests, have experienced.

Though aid-dependent states can hardly be called sovereign, the South Pacific nations nominally have been free to choose sources of aid and investment. That television was not provided by their former colonists was 'for reasons that probably owed more to parsimony than to policy' (Johnstone 1984, p.4). Introducing television, courtesy of a Western provider, has been a popular gesture governments have been able to make since the mid-1980s, and the coverage of international sports events is often offered as a lure. For example, the French and US territories of the Pacific have had services and programs supplied by their colonial rulers since the 1960s.

The strategic agenda of Western governments and their entrepreneurs was in many respects out of step with the development agenda of the Pacific states and their aid providers, who favoured small-scale, local and educational television; some states had moved to instigate a video infrastructure. In 1984 Media Niugini, a community video company, began its operations in market-places, playing videotapes containing one hour per day of recycled popular programs and some local announcements and advertising. These tapes were bicycled around PNG and shown repeatedly in 23 market-places. This, ironically, served to introduce the country to commercial television, as opposed to development video. Similarly, the Fiji government established a national video production centre. This was thought an appropriate way to go, for local production capacity would grow slowly until a broadcast operation was feasible (Molnar 1993, p.301).

Though the states were free in a sense to choose when and how to introduce television, some technological developments were out of their control and forced their hand. Various 'hucksters of high technology' were providing audiovisual entertainment in the form of videos and improvised cable services, which were eagerly accepted. Videos for rent consisted largely of recordings from Australia and New Zealand, pirated and re-copied many times so that the technical quality diminished. The acceptance of low-quality recordings of a wide range of broadcast programs undermined the developmentalist stance of Pacific governments and forced them to reconsider their position on national television services.

While no studies of cross-cultural reception in PNG exist, Nii-K Plange (1993) studied the reception of videos in Fiji, including many pirated off-air recordings from the US and Australia, just after a broadcast service was introduced in 1991, and found that they had had an enormous influence in restructuring family relations and use of time. He raises well-established but intransigent issues about the lack of cultural fit between the official values of the Fijian authorities and the appeal of Western, secular, sexualised, consumerist dramas. Plange reports that there were about 100 000 video players in Fiji in a population of 750 000 people. Thus television was already a significant presence, although not in broadcast form.

By the mid-1980s, the south-west Pacific presented an unusual situation in which television tastes were acquired solely through the free market of video rentals. Western programs such as soap opera established followings that became very difficult for governments to deny. The outcomes seem not to please many groups, including conservative policy makers, prone to anxiety about the loss of traditional values. Horsfield (1990) argues that as a result of the previous exposure to video and other media, television's effects in PNG could not be as dramatic as this cultural-protectionist discourse would have it. She sees the discourse as a projection of developmentalist models effectively operating as a means for bureaucrats to protect their privileged position.

Despite widespread concern and controversy about the cultural dangers of popular Western programs, recent criticisms of the cultural imperialism framework stress the importance of not assuming that such material is inherently destructive (Tomlinson 1991). Doing this can result in alliances between critical scholars and conservative forces in terms of pre-judging television's effects. In a study of Trinidad, for example, the evidence forced one cultural anthropologist to look at the enormously popular soap opera *The Young and the Restless* in its specific articulations with local cultural categories, and to conclude that 'authenticity has increasingly to be judged *a posteriori* not *a priori*, according to local consequences not local origins' (Miller 1992, p.181). The popularity of *Neighbours* in PNG, for example, may well call for a similar account. On the other hand the 'active audience' school may be blind to the unbalanced political and economic forces inherent in television's presence (Sreberny-Mohammadi 1991).

Although still officially regarding television as a low priority, Pacific leaders now had reason to upgrade it, so that some control could be exerted over the consumption of Western programs and messages. Pacific states effectively sought to restrict access to the medium by setting up controlled broadcasting systems, in the belief that these could not be a greater cultural danger than video already was (Varan 1994), and could be turned to political and cultural advantage. Political leaders recognised opportunities to be associated with the introduction of television, as Western broadcasters sought new markets in the region.

A related development was the utilisation of the increasing number of satellites above the Pacific and South East Asia as trans-border program feeds for private and unregulated cable systems. This was happening in PNG before broadcast television began. HiTron, later to become the major cable television supplier in the country, was started in 1983 as a contractor to instal public address, security, alarm and closed circuit TV systems. Television services began in 1986, with neighbourhoods connected by cable in order to defray the costs of satellite reception from Aussat, Intelsat and Palapa. HiTron runs its own movie channel and bulletin board and carries NBC, CNN and ESPN from the US, TV3 (Malaysia), RCTI (Indonesia), a Philippines service, the North Queensland commercial channel QTV and two ABC signals from Australia: the new international service, Australia Television (ATV), and the Queensland domestic service. The cable services are available basically in the areas of expatriate enclaves: the towns and mining, forestry and other resource developments. Wealthy Papua New Guineans and expatriates (perhaps 25 000 people, a small but powerful minority) thus have access to a wide choice of television services, though much of the drama content is recycled American fare.

Little information is available about program schedules. The *Papua New Guinea Post Courier* publishes listings of ABC and QTV only among the satellite services. *The National* also carries the schedule for the SBS, a recent addition. Neither is there much television criticism. The *Post Courier* recycles publicity material for *Neighbours* and *Home and Away* in its television and radio guide, but does not comment on the programs. The more consciously PNG-oriented weekly, *The Times of Papua New Guinea*, gives far more attention to local music than to television.

Two new satellites were expected in 1994, with wide Pacific capacity, PanAmSat (US) and Apstar (China), so programming choices would then increase again, with Star TV a likely inclusion. The trans-border flow of satellite signals has been an intractable issue in international communications, and poor tropical countries are likely to bear the brunt of it, as their location gives them easy access to satellites in geo-stationary orbit (Wilson 1993). This fact may, however, be to the Pacific nations' advantage as availability increases and prices come down, but this will depend on genuine choice in program supply and some local programming, preferably with the capacity to uplink to elsewhere in the region.

AUSTRALIAN RULES: PAPUA NEW GUINEA AND EM TV

In the mid-1980s, both Australia's Nine Network and the New Zealand government broadcaster, TVNZ, made unsuccessful bids to run a satellite television service to the Pacific, in light of the increasing awareness of satellite delivery both as a threat to their areas of established influence and as an opportunity to expand themselves. Australia had advantages. Its program industry was beginning to have some overseas success, and it had decided to have a domestic satellite system that looked to be under-used and, following regional manoeuvres and pressures, contained south Pacific capacity (Fell 1989). It had northern reaches within the tropics, which made for easy access to international satellites. Packer's vision of satellite-supplied television to the Pacific continued to be in line with the government's strategic agenda, given the threats of increased supply from outside the region.

Policy controversies surrounding the Aussat satellite and the financial crisis in the Australian television industry in the late 1980s (O'Regan 1993b, p.40ff.) complicated Australia's involvement in Pacific television and, despite getting very close in Fiji before the Rabuka coups, ultimately it was only in PNG that Australian entrepreneur Kerry Packer succeeded in gaining a foothold. The model proposed by Packer's company

Publishing and Broadcasting Limited (PBL) was to have a station originally serving the capital city only, much like a regional station in Australia, using standard broadcast equipment and employing a staff of about 50, most of whom would be local. Though undertakings were made to produce local content, it was never assumed that this would involve sacrificing metropolitan production values. Molnar sees PBL's view of indigenous content as 'quaint, unprofessional and a necessary evil, preferably in small doses' (Molnar 1993, p.307). In PNG, as in Fiji, the aspiring commercial broadcasters assumed that public-service television would follow, and would have the mandate for local content.

The process leading to the licensing of a commercial operator in PNG was a protracted, complex and controversial one (ibid.). Rival Australian operators were vying for the licence and the process became embroiled in inter-party and intra-party conflicts in PNG. Two licences were allocated - one to a subsidiary of the licensee of the Newcastle, New South Wales, television station NBN, and the other to Media Niugini. In the early stages, PBL was a consultant to Media Niugini, but this situation developed ultimately into PBL's full ownership of EM TV, the only licence to survive. This chapter in the history of television in the Pacific, and of Australian relations with its neighbours, is not looked on with approval in those countries.

EM TV has become the de facto national television broadcaster of PNG as it has tried to develop local expertise and national reach. Its existence has put a stop to any further discussion about the introduction of public-service broadcasting. Without the capital investment by its parent company, however, it would long ago have folded, for advertising revenue took many years to build to the level of an operating profit (J. Stewart 1993, p.4). Though EM TV was making money by 1993, 'millions' were still owed to the Nine Network (*Islands Business Pacific*, October 1993, p.40). Despite the attempts to develop local programs, such as a current-affairs program based on the Nine Network's *A Current Affair*, it has remained basically an Australian operation. Its local production is mainly manifested in its news program, entirely staffed by Papua New Guineans but often criticised for being too centred on Port Moresby and not critical enough, although its sources have been expanded by stringers with home-video cameras around the country. One glaring shortcoming is the coverage of local sport, which usually features only as highlights on the news. Yet because of the abundance of Australian television in the country, Australia's footballers are well known in PNG despite the popular enthusiasm for local rugby league.

The network input is clearest in its news, information and sports programs. PBL's ownersip of EM TV means that the latter has access to Nine Network material and facilities at reduced rates, although regional rights still have to be negotiated. Some Nine Network programs, such as *A Current Affair*, *Today*, and *60 Minutes* are broadcast live from Australia via Optus satellite, while others are stored off the satellite for later replay. The reliance on Nine Network current-affairs programs is partly in order to educate Papua New Guineans in the genre, but there can be unexpected problems for the government in the way the country is represented. The *Post Courier* (23 May 1994) carried a front-page headline 'Wingti storms over PNG media image', reporting the prime minister's protest to some Australian business people about the exaggerated portrayals of PNG's law-and-order problems by the Australian media.

PNG sensitivities about political and sexual representations have resulted in other cases of censorship of Australian programs. Phil Hayward (1993) documents the involvement of EM TV in the making of the documentary *Tabaran*, which is about the collaboration of Australian band, Not Drowning, Waving, and some Rabaul-based musicians, and notes that even this positive case of cross-culturalism was marred by a request from the Australian High Commission not to include the song 'Blackwater', a lament for the annexation of West Papua by Indonesia and for the continuing conflict along PNG's western border. Though the song was played in the locally compiled music program, *Mekim Music*, the chief censor subsequently required that all overseas clips be previewed by his office. This was, in fact, the result of the banning of *60 Minutes* for some weeks early in 1993 because of a segment on Madonna, which had caused offence for its sexual content, but the ruling made it easy for political content to be censored as well.

Other program sources, including Australian networks, are also used, and programs are generally available for EM TV purchase. There is no particular priority given to the latest and best; *Neighbours*, for example, was begun from the first episode some time after its Australian beginnings, although current episodes are available via satellite on QTV, the North Queensland broadcaster. Older programs like *The Young Doctors* and *Bonanza* are cheaper to buy, and John Taylor, EM TV's chief executive, saw them as a cultural investment, to allow new audiences to catch up (Taylor 1992). He makes programming decisions cautiously, resisting *Beverly Hills 90210*, for example, with its 'blatant' sexual content.

Neighbours was enormously popular in the early 1990s, regularly winning the station's audience competition for most popular program.

The program's popular appeal is still clear, but how are people reading it and how varied are the readings? Though local intellectuals may dismiss it as 'not PNG life', Taylor saw this as precisely its value, for it is 'teaching people a lifestyle'. Furniture dealers told him *Neighbours* was showing people what sorts of beds and tables Western houses have (Taylor 1994). This illustrates one of the major economic roles scholars identify for television in underdeveloped nations. Particularly through advertising, demand for Western products is created and, along with the technical infrastructure, television's promotion of consumerism can exacerbate imbalances in national economies.

Television also has powerful political implications, for example, in the rise and legitimacy of the modern state and the new dominance of national as opposed to village or provincial concerns. Varan is concerned about the power of elites to shape the forums where cultural and national identities are formed (1994, p.305). Along with other national machinery such as parliament, the public service, schooling and other national media, television contributes to the creation of national identity from diverse groups. It can also be used by national leaders as a political tool and as a way to demonstrate and personalise their performance and achievements. Horsfield comments on 'the perceived value that television might be to hegemonic nationalism from which these elites would undoubtedly benefit' (1990, p.100). At the same time, in a country like PNG, with its 800 language groups and complex colonial history, 'hegemonic nationalism' is an understandable policy goal, with the construction of a new Papua New Guinean identity superseding the many differences among the populace.

Conscious of television's role in contributing to urban migration, early in 1993 EM TV began to deliver its signal nationally via Palapa, chosen over Optus because of cost. Although committed to extending coverage through assistance with the construction of school and village-based receivers, Taylor estimated that of a population of 3.5 million, there was an audience for EM TV of only about 500 000 in the early 1990s, because of the lack of mains electricity. This lack of reach was a big problem, as there were large populations, for example one million people in the densely populated Highlands, which could not constitute a market without the technological infrastructure (Taylor 1992). Reaching into the countryside was a political rather than an economic priority, as the government tried to redress the imbalance between the towns and the rural areas by bringing a desired form of modern culture to the villages, and thus persuading people to stay there rather than migrating to the towns.

EM TV has been criticised from many quarters for being too much of an Australian operation. Helen Molnar sees this model as quite inappropriate for the Pacific, with its attachment to Western notions of professionalism and program standards, and its stifling of local expression (Molnar 1993, pp.290ff.). Amos Thomas (1994) analysed EM TV's output over six months in 1990–1, and found that viewing time divided into 21.5 per cent sitcom or soap opera, 20.8 per cent crime or western and 18.8 per cent children's programs or cartoons. By source, 54.1 per cent was of US material, 24.7 per cent Australian, and 15.5 per cent Papua New Guinean. He concludes that multinational providers of commercial television dominate the policy agendas of small Third World countries, so that states such as PNG lose control over programming. Taylor's reply is that expertise is slow to develop in people not raised on television.

FIJI: AUSTRALIA'S LIMITED PRESENCE

New Zealand broadcaster TVNZ has become active in the broader Pacific region (Wilson 1994). TVNZ's program-supply and consultancy arm, the Pacific Service, was operating in six Pacific states, including Fiji, by 1993, arguably providing a more appropriate service for small, isolated nations. It was low cost, involving Super VHS technology, perhaps influenced by the 'small TV' calls of a decade earlier asking for locally manageable systems, in light of the reception accorded the Australian operators in PNG and Fiji. It also recognised the clear enthusiasm from audiences for popular Western programs. The service was supplied by TVNZ and run by the local state-owned radio broadcaster, so that decisions about programs chosen and local content production were in principle in local hands, though the broadcaster's finances, very low advertising revenue and the lack of training provided by TVNZ allowed for very little such production.

The Pacific Service's clients included Australia's former territory of Nauru, where we might have expected the history of Australian involvement and its larger television industry to have meant that an Australian broadcaster provided the service. However TVNZ has perhaps been a smarter operator and helped by New Zealand's longer experience and greater credibility in the Pacific. The Australian entrepreneurs only showed interest in large markets and/or economies of scale. The rise of the Pacific Service may have had the effect of blocking out Australian operators such as the ABC from the region, because of the exclusivity of TVNZ's distribution arrangements, and their unwillingness to approach most Australian distributors.

Part of the unofficial agreement in Fiji was that TVNZ would not broadcast soap operas, which it did not do until 1994. The exact causes of this moral panic and its relationship to the politics of Christian evangelism are obscure, and would need to be investigated, for indications are that Pacific people love Western soap opera, including old serials still broadcast on radio in Fiji. While generally expressing anxiety about the potentially damaging effects of Western culture, and advocating that television in the Pacific 'be given the chance to support development not dependency', Pamela Thomas had earlier acknowledged the challenge of a comment by some Samoan villagers that far from being irrelevant to their lives, *Days of our Lives* was their favourite program.

> When I asked them why they liked it, they said 'Because it is just like us. That is just like our lives here in Samoa.' I couldn't have imagined lives more different – until I sat down and thought about it. Indeed it was just like their lives. They identified with what they recognised and they recognised human emotions – love, hate, power relations, jealousy, marriage, adultery. The trappings were immaterial (Thomas 1987, p.20).

Variants of this story are heard, and they recall Liebes and Katz's (1990) study of the reception of *Dallas* by culturally dissimilar groups in Israel. Yet there was a denial of the possibility of comparable cultural response by Fiji's supremacist and developmentalist leaders, and the unquestioned popularity of Australian soaps in PNG was a challenge TVNZ had to meet as viewers turned back to video or to the new satellite services to receive programs available free to air elsewhere.

The New Zealand soap *Shortland Street*, in which Grundys had a 50 per cent production stake, was for a long time an obvious omission from Pacific schedules. With its Polynesian and Maori characters and occasional cross-cultural storylines, *prima facie* it would have been a more acceptable daily ritual for young Pacific people, as it was in New Zealand, than *Neighbours*, frequently criticised for its Anglo-Saxon world view. On grounds of relevance also *Shortland Street* would seem to pass, although its stories of adolescent sexual exploration would probably have displeased the moral guardians. However, to its credit, TVNZ tried *Shortland Street* on Fiji One in 1994, and it quickly gained popular favour.

Christine Fenby (1994), in charge of acquisitions for the Pacific Service, saw soaps as inherently low in quality and had not challenged the views of Pacific authorities that 'quality' was what was demanded, so she sought nature programs, other documentaries and British dramas. The Australian 'quality' drama *Brides of Christ* was played, and *Police Rescue* was well received. Beyond International had proved to be such a rich Australian source of documentary, information, and increasingly drama programs for the service that other Australian distributors were not even approached. Fenby's gatekeeper role of being slow to promote popular New Zealand- and Australian-made programs seemed oddly inappropriate, given their international success and TVNZ's concerted efforts to position itself as an international operator. The cautions and compromises began to loosen, however, as the strategy of the Pacific Service succeeded.

CONCLUSION

Television has been readily accepted throughout the Pacific, despite a long history of procrastination on policy due to its perceived negative effect on national development and traditional cultures. Although Pacific policy makers and Western aid-providers might prefer to see television develop in small, local ways, this has not met with popular acceptance. However, because video and international satellite signals have become pervasive and impossible for nation states to prevent, Pacific governments have been pressured to introduce a service which includes popular Western programs. The results are most significant in the political and economic domains, in terms of building and supporting the nation-state and con-tributing to the restructuring of national and international relations. In the south-west Pacific, television has taken one of two major forms: the regional Australian model of EM TV and the more modest and flexible Pacific Service of TVNZ.

Lacking anthropological research, it is difficult to reach a clear con-clusion about the social influence of Australian television programs in the region. While they are a dominant presence in PNG, there is little documented evidence of specific cultural influence or even critical recep-tion of the kind relied on elsewhere in this book. There is a general anxiety evident in various policy stances by Pacific governments, including PNG's 1994 National Communication Policy, that the medium undermines Christian and other conservative values (Centurion and Philpott 1994). Notwithstanding development discourse and political rhetoric, close observation draws attention to the 'extraordinary resilience' which Pacific people have demonstrated in the face of the long process of the im-position of Western culture begun by nineteenth-century missionaries (Crocombe 1972).

PART

4

Conclusion

12

Benefits and Drawbacks of Internationalisation

Neighbours is about to move to the US. *Prisoner* is titillating Thailand's housewives. *Richmond Hill* is being resuscitated in Canada. Pat the Rat of *Sons and Daughters* is still conniving in Barbados. *The Young Doctors* is providing melodrama in Monaco while *The Flying Doctors* is number one in the chilly lounge rooms of The Netherlands ... *A Country Practice* is one of the few Australians welcome in Indonesia. And *Skippy* ... well, *Skippy* has been hopping around the world for two decades and was last seen leaving Italy bound for early-morning British TV (Macken 1989, p.25).

... in one sense the Australian film and television industry has made almost no progress at all in the thirty years it has existed in its new life in terms of it having become a significant export achiever. The markets that have been penetrated by Australian television have either been very small, or those where product ... just gets sold by weight. The UK is the one market where one can see a substantial growth ... and industry people there can be positively aggressive about its middle-to-lowbrow nature. Beyond that, and beyond the Grundy games shows ... the amount of penetration is very small indeed (Tony Ginnane 1994).

Australia is a small but significant international trader of television programming and an even smaller player in trans-border satellite television. However, it exerts a presence on the world's film and television screens that is disproportionate to its population base, geographical position and market size. The underlying reasons for this have been outlined in the early parts of this book. In assessing these reasons, we have seen that a middle-range approach, between macro-level political economies of global communications and micro-level audience-response studies, captures the variability of conditions best. These conditions include the nature of the media landscape a program is entering; the attitudes and perceptions of viewer preferences held by gatekeepers; the regulatory

245

culture; perceptions that Australian programming is like or, on the other hand, unlike US programming; and a variety of other cultural and even mythic factors, which come into play in countries like Britain and New Zealand that are culturally proximate to Australia. Summing up, what are some of the benefits and drawbacks of internationalisation, and the effects of increased internationalisation on the domestic policy and industrial landscape?

There is a sense in which a relatively 'new' society, a Western nation perched on the edge of the Asia-Pacific, placing itself increasingly within a global economy and increasingly rapid flows of communications, has an especial need to attend to outside perceptions of itself. Richard Woolcott, former Australian ambassador to the United Nations and former secretary of the Department of Foreign Affairs and Trade, argues that Australia's still-evolving definition as a society that is multicultural and Asia-oriented, its small power status, and greater aloneness in the world than at any previous time in 'our brief history' make such attention imperative (1993, p.17). It is also clear that hardware platforms and globalising flows of information have meant that the demand for and the supply of images of international cultures are circulated ever more rapidly and widely without necessarily an improvement in the quality of the information provided. Mackenzie Wark (1994b) has shown how imperatives of simultaneity, visuality and reach over-ride depth and understanding in global information flows.

These issues have been noted at many points throughout this book. We have seen how the structure of international information flows concerning Australia is dominated by London as a staging post for colonial/post-colonial perceptions (Chapter 6) and that the most sustained televisual impacts have occurred in Britain. We have seen also how any concerted and substantial projection of a positive image of Australia (rather than this projection occurring as a contingent by-product of market transactions), such as the ATV initiative (Chapter 9), is necessarily a fraught and complex undertaking. Booster rhetoric – like the lists of territories into which programs have been sold that regularly feature in journalistic commentary, or the quote beginning this chapter from an article titled 'Invasion of the Aussie Soaps' – barely conceals a proto-nationalist delight in the reverse imperialism that such 'invasions' indicate, and elides the great unevenness of cultural acceptance or impact that Australian programs may have achieved in world markets. This can lead to seemingly opposite conclusions about the track record of Australian television export, as the comments by Tony Ginnane also show.

Film has been by far the medium that has had most attention in terms of cultural ambassadorship. While the old adage 'trade follows the film' was invented by, and has really only been appropriate for, the US, there is a sense in which the externalities or intangibles accruing to Australia as a result of overseas acceptance of audiovisual product are manifold, even as they are enduringly difficult to assess empirically. It became part of the core folklore of the 1980s that what tourism marketing theory calls 'hallmark' events, such as the *Crocodile Dundee* films (which followed the highly successful Australian Tourism Commission campaigns featuring Paul Hogan), had a significant impact on international tourism to Australia. Inward-bound tourism from the US to Australia increased 20.5 per cent between 1981 and 1988 and, in 1989, an American Express study identified Australia as the most desired single destination for travel out of the US. An Economic Intelligence Unit study estimated that hallmark events that had given Australia a high profile in the US were worth $50 of publicity for every dollar spent on tourism advertising (Riley and Van Doren 1992, pp.18–19 and *see* AFC 1993). The downside to the search for the hallmark event (the blockbuster) is that it tends to have an inherently conservative effect on industry and culture. The extraordinary resilience of the 'crocs and rocks' image in the US freezes the image of Australia within a limited repertoire (Clark 1994) and there is a danger of returning to the well (of a now outdated image of the Australian character) too often – as the reception of Hogan's film *Lightning Jack* shows (*see Daily Variety*, 16 March 1994).

The same specifiable multiplier effects cannot be evinced for television programs, mainly because of the far more diffuse means of their circulation. Nevertheless, they are certainly assumed by the tourism industry and cultural officials to have similar effects, and this is borne out by various surveys of opinion on Australia carried out in several parts of the world. And while hallmark Australian film events are rare, with only the exception reaching beyond up-market niche audiences into a broad viewing public, television exports are the opposite, typically being of broad middlebrow appeal. *Return to Eden* has been the single most quoted source of positive understanding of Australia in Indonesia (Milne 1993). A 1991 study of provincial French adolescents' perceptions of Australia (de Jabrun 1993) showed that the prime source for general information about Australia was film and television, and that teen music and *Neighbours* personalities Kylie Minogue and Jason Donovan far outscored all other mentioned Australian figures. *Neighbours* and *Return to Eden* were as often mentioned as films, pre-eminently *Crocodile Dundee*.

Television programs usually do not have the status of hallmark events (with the possible exception of *Neighbours* in the UK) because almost by definition, such events are shortlived and dramatic, whereas from an economic point of view, the best sort of television must go on week after week, year after year. However, television programs can play a role in reinforcing images generated by films and other hallmark events, as well as serving to modify them. As we have seen in Chapter 6, although the most popular Australian films seem to have projected the outback as a metonym for Australia, *Neighbours* constructs an image of Australia as suburbia. In 1991 the Australian Tourist Commission (ATC) studied the impact of soap opera running in Europe, looking for ways to broaden and renovate predominant images of Australia as an outback adventure location. They found significant preferences among Germans for meeting small-town locals (influenced by *A Country Practice* or *The Flying Doctors*), while Italians liked beaches (*Home and Away*) (McCathie 1991). Conversely, a similar tracking study by the ATC in Britain in 1993 produced some evidence that deeper engagement with a succession of soap operas, as only British audiences have had opportunities to per-form, can produce images of a less-friendly destination, with responses about 'suburban Australia as a place of high drama and conflict' (Collins 1994, p.4).

An increasing international orientation has led the industry and commentators to question whether the 1990s has borne tidings of the 'end of the national project' in higher budget drama. Graeme Turner has argued that signs in the policy, criticism and production climates indicate that decision-makers, cultural intellectuals and industry personnel now all doubt the contemporary viability of cultural nationalism as a binding rhetoric and policy frame for the industry, even though it has undoubtedly served as the intellectual glue holding together state support and audience response (Turner 1994). For Tom O'Regan, the industry's financial troubles of the late 1980s meant that a country 'capable of producing not simply more, but better quality, television, well placed to manage *on its own terms* the popular audience-oriented "internationalization" taking place in the more profitable parts of the international television system' had missed the boat (1991b, p.107, original emphasis).

However, it is possible to see a greater international orientation, com-bined with social policies of multiculturalism, recasting traditional cultural nationalism but by no means abandoning it. To be sure, this is an ambivalent project, influenced to a considerable degree by the *force majeure* of international co-production and sales. The only way high-end

Australian production can prosper is through increased international linkages. But, at its best, internationalisation facilitates this redefinition, rather than fudging it in imprecise trans-national cultural artifices. Whereas feature film co-productions are often characterised by no on-screen sense of the participation of one or more of the partner countries (for example, *Black Robe*, *The Prisoner of St Petersburg*), most television co-productions entered into by Australian participants do achieve some degree of on-screen partnership, caused no doubt by the need for all partners to engage popular audiences domestically.

This recasting means that the key interpretative categories used to analyse Australian drama production in the 1970s and 1980s (*see* Dermody and Jacka 1987; 1988a; 1988b) have to be remodelled. The key oppositions – which approximate the modernist and post-modernist elements of audiovisual culture outlined in Chapter 3 – are no longer between what Dermody and Jacka called Industry-1 (cultural nationalism, art cinema and social realism, government protection) and Industry-2 (commercialism, international appeal at all costs, Hollywood imitations), but largely between those forms of internationalism that advance local cultural development and those that do not.

The earlier phase of greater international orientation in the mini-series in the 1980s, for example, relied on either fairly standard Australian ethnocentrism, using Asian-related stories as backdrops for Western characters (*Barlow and Chambers: A Long Way From Home* in 1988, *Bangkok Hilton* in 1989), or took the much-worn route of importing an American star to bolster potential sales for an Australian-based story (*The Last Frontier* in 1986). More recently, some major television events in the 1990s such as *The Leaving of Liverpool* (1992) and *The Magistrate* (1989) have shown the degree to which international co-production can advance an organic and critically revisionist, yet popular, sense of a multicultural contemporary Australia.

Overall however, it is clear from the foregoing chapters that the programs that travel best, and that have the best potential for export, are not necessarily the most innovative or most searching of Australian society. This only confirms the truism that television is fundamentally a local medium. Humour, and thus comedy formats, most drama, relying as it does on some unavoidable specificities of character and place, and of course the vast bulk of news and current affairs, remain stubbornly resistant to exploitation in a multiplicity of markets. What international acceptance such formats do find cannot be predicted with any degree of accuracy (and thus are resistant to policy and strategic settings).

The international market-place of discrete program trade is, unavoidably, a levelling arena, while trans-border television has before it the considerable challenge of creatively overcoming cultural screens as a central aspect of scheduling and marketing. It is in the areas of sport, nature documentary/natural history, some children's programming, and magazine-style science and sci-tech, that global television seeks sufficient purchase in universal thematics (the 'neutral' common values, settings and aspirations Roland Barthes (1973) analysed in his 'Family of Man' essay) to offset the discount of cultural screens. It is in these formats, along with those serial-drama forms that have established long-term acceptance internationally – what we have called 'volume television' – that the bulk of Australian trade is accomplished.

While Australian television program makers have engaged in significant export, increasingly so over the last decade and the trend is set upward, there are dangers in turning such activity over to a policy-led export drive, as current signs in the Australian policy environment indicate. These were canvassed in Chapter 3. One of the laws of international trade is that the most harmonious relationships tend toward equilibrium, with imports and exports balancing out. Embracing globalisation can mean greater industrial as well as cultural reasons to import as much as export. This is not necessarily a cultural or industrial negative, but it does underline that much rhetoric about the export thrust is narrow and one-sided. The current Australian focus on export to Asia, for instance, should be viewed in the light of the converse situation – Australia's growing population originating from Asian countries (6–7 per cent or about 1 million first or second generation) is the basis for as much if not more imports from the region as there has been previous scope for export into it. Audiovisual import, mainly in the form of Hong Kong movies and videos, other Chinese-language material, and SBS imports, and the pay rates for them at present, would probably outweigh export figures significantly.

Australian broadcasting policy, particularly in the area of providing a regulated safety net for local television production, has been based explicitly on the central *cultural* rationale of ensuring that Australians see themselves, their lives and society, reflected on their screens in reasonable amounts, and that this reflection take account of the pluralistic nature of the society. Now it is arguable that when we put these two principles together, we get a rationale for more imports, for instance the perfectly reasonable assumption behind the importation by the SBS of a wide range of non-Anglo television material that speaks to the growing multicultural complexion of Australian society (though this of course has nothing to do with regulation per se). An *industry* policy of enhancing export will not necessarily match up with this, or rather is not designed to do the same job. The current emphasis on industry policy has the potential to eclipse the original reasons for having a cultural policy for broadcasting.

Strong arguments have been mounted, both within the country and internationally, that Australia should change its strong local television regulation to a Canadian-style system, because of the industry benefits resulting from off-shore production that could count as local quota. There are, indeed, powerful reasons to underpin these developments with un-equivocally supportive industry policies and initiatives, but these should not be confused with, or allowed to eclipse, a cultural policy for broad-casting. There are also in-built limits to growth of the industry, at least in the areas of traditional program production; in general, a program needs to have secured a local network licence before or while it seeks overseas markets. If the only objective was industry growth (irrespective of whether increased program production found an audience here) then the argument for loosening content regulation would be hard to resist. But most overseas buyers look to local cultural resonance and viewer acceptance as a litmus test when they consider the program for their own market.

It is important not to exaggerate the export record and potential of the industry. By world standards it is of small-to-medium size and its export record slight in comparison to other Australian service-industry exports. For example, education services netted Australia A$1 billion in 1992 compared with an estimated A$65 million for total audiovisual industries (film, television and video). In 1992–3, the figure increased significantly to A$98 million, the highest figure for royalties received from overseas since 1987–8 when reliable aggregate figures for the industry first became available. A recent government report (BIE 1994) says that in all audiovisual industries (which include music industry inputs), export is only 4 per cent of total revenue. But this information needs major refinement. Until 1994, there had been no specific data collection for audiovisual industries and the methods by which the available figures have been captured – as part of an overall industry survey – severely under-estimate the dollars earned from export. They do not take account of the presence of foreign companies' investments in Australian programs, which accounted, in 1992–3, for the largest single source of investment in Australian audiovisual product (Given 1993). Nor do they factor in revenues from off-shore production, which have put audiovisual indus-tries in a leading bracket of export-oriented industries in Queensland (Richard Stewart 1993), nor the earnings of Australian companies producing programs outside Australia (which would exclude the majority of Grundy material); nor the developments in new media products, which are being exported increasingly (DITARD 1994). With these lacunae in mind, many industry representatives have claimed, with justification, that the figures should be closer to A$200 million (more than treble the official figures).

While the dollar amounts involved in export and co-production should not be slighted, the audiovisual sector will never be a pied piper leading the way out of Australia's endemic balance of payments deficits. As we have argued earlier in this chapter, its function as a platform for greater international cultural understanding, profile and acceptance will continue to be as important, in the widest sense of Australia's national interest as an internationalising society, as the actual dollars earned as export income. Ultimately the arguments for audiovisual export will continue to be the same as arguments for support for audiovisual domestically – cultural first and then economic.

There are also some specific threats to the domestic industry arising from export. It may be that one of the factors leading to decreased licence fees from the networks for drama production is precisely the increased

FIGURE 12.1:   Total Credits and Debits for Overseas Royalties Income on Films and Videos 1987–8 to 1992–3

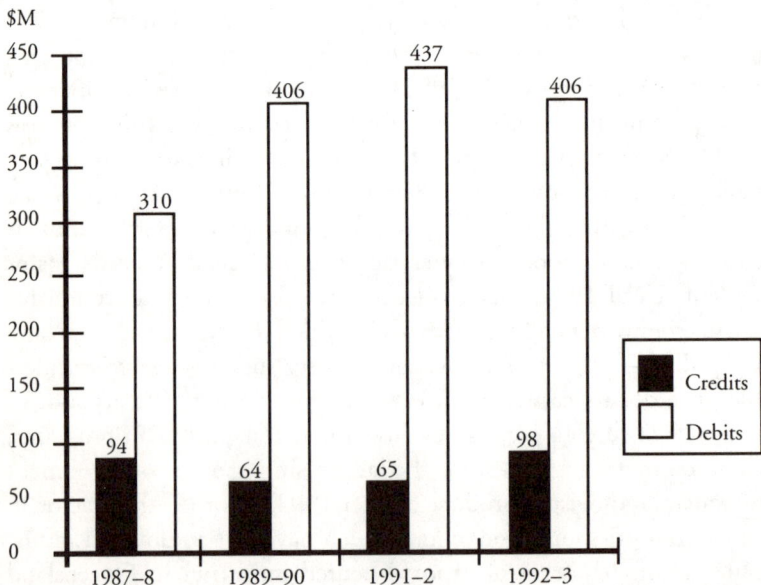

Source: *AFC News*, February 1995.

export success of Australian television, on the assumption that producers can top up with foreign earnings. And as Australian export activity becomes an expected norm, we might even see the re-emergence of the old 'infant industry' argument used against continued government support: because the industry has matured into an international player, it does not need the iron lung of taxpayer support any longer. On balance, Australia's export profile is both unavoidable (for financial reasons) and welcome (for cultural reasons), but there can be clouds within every silver lining.

The implications for Australia in developing a cultural and industrial strategy for this new multi-channel world would seem to be that we should continue to produce largely for the home market and with local cultural relevance to the fore, but at the same time be aware of some of the strengths of Australian program styles and production methods in the international arena. Any wholesale attempt to compromise cultural aims in the audiovisual sector in favour of pursuing the chimera of international fame and fortune first and foremost would seem to be doomed for television as it was for film before it. (The same principle, we would suggest, applies to multimedia development.) The internationalisation of television, and with it both opportunities for Australian program export and a greater impact on local industry by global imperatives, will develop apace in the near future. Australian audiovisual exchange, particularly within the region of which we are part, is still in a formative stage. How far this transforms the television we customarily take for granted will be of signal importance in years to come.

References

ABA (Australian Broadcasting Authority) 1994a. *Australian Content Standard Review Working Paper*. Sydney: ABA

ABA (Australian Broadcasting Authority) 1994b. *Broadcasting Financial Results 1992–3*. Sydney: ABA

ABT (Australian Broadcasting Tribunal) 1977. *Self-Regulation for Broadcasters? A Report on the Public Inquiry into the Concept of Self-regulation for Australian Broadcasters*. Canberra: Australian Government Publishing Service

Acheson, Keith and Maule, Christopher J. 1992. 'The business side of an international television festival', *Journal of Arts Management, Law and Society*, 22 (2), pp.118–33

ACTF (Australian Children's Television Foundation) 1993. *Annual Report 1992–3*. Carlton: ACTF

AFC (Australian Film Commission) 1987. *Film Assistance: Future Options*. Sydney: Allen & Unwin

AFC (Australian Film Commission) 1992. *Get the Picture: Essential Data on Australian Film, Television and Video*, 1st edn. Sydney: AFC

AFC (Australian Film Commission) 1993. 'A Bibliography on film, television and tourism'. Sydney: AFC, October

AFC (Australian Film Commission) 1994a. *Get the Picture: Essential Data on Film, Television and Video*, 3rd edn. Sydney: AFC, October

AFC (Australian Film Commission) 1994b. *South East Asian Television Study*, 7 Vols. A report prepared for the AFC by KPMG Peat Marwick. Sydney: AFC

Allen, Bill (Director of Sales, Central Television Enterprises) 1992. Interview with Elizabeth Jacka. London, November

ALP (Australian Labor Party) 1993. *Cultural Policy 1993 Election. Distinctly Australian: The Future for Australia's Cultural Development*. Canberra: ALP

Amdur, Meredith 1993. 'A European programming pass to NATPE', *Variety*, January, p.82

Ang, Ien 1985. *Watching Dallas: Soap Opera and the Melodramatic Imagination*. London: Methuen

Ang, Ien 1991. *Desperately Seeking the Audience*. London: Routledge

Ang, Ien 1994. 'Globalisation and culture', *Continuum*, 8, No. 2, pp.323–5

Ansley, Greg 1994. 'To CER with love', *New Zealand Herald*, 15 January

Appadurai, Arjun 1990. 'Disjuncture and difference in the global cultural economy', in Featherstone (ed.)

Appleton, Gil 1988. 'How Australia sees itself: The role of commercial television', in *The Price of Being Australian*. Sydney: ABT

Ashley, Stephen (Director, Scheduling and Planning, PBS) 1994. Interview with Stuart Cunningham. Alexandria, Virginia, March

Askoy, Asu and Robins, Kevin 1992. 'Hollywood for the 21st century: Global competition for critical mass in image markets', *Cambridge Journal of Economics*, 16, pp.1–22

Attallah, Paul (Carleton University) 1992. Interview with Stuart Cunningham. Ottawa, February

Bailey Johnson, Brooke (Senior Vice President, Programming and Production, Arts and Entertainment Network) 1994. Interview with Stuart Cunningham. New York, March

Baker, Matt and Busfield, Steve 1994. 'BBC gets commercial nod', *Broadcast*, 8 July

Barlow, Helen 1994. 'Crew stability the key to Polish shoot', *Encore*, 12, No. 17, 31 October–13 November

Barrios, Leoncio 1988. 'Television, *telenovelas* and family life in Venezuela', in Lull (ed.)

Barthes, Roland 1973. *Mythologies*. London: Paladin

BBC (Broadcasting Research Department) 1989. *Annual Review of BBC Broadcasting Research Findings*. London: John Libbey

BBC (Broadcasting Research Department) 1990. *Annual Review of BBC Broadcasting Research Findings*. London: John Libbey

BBC (Broadcasting Research Department) 1991. *Annual Review of BBC Broadcasting Research Findings*. London: John Libbey

Belet, Annie (Quartier Latin) 1992. Interview with Elizabeth Jacka. Paris, November

Bell, Cathie 1994. 'Aussies shut out NZ film industry', *The Dominion* (Wellington), 30 November

Bell, Philip and Bell, Roger 1993. *Implicated: The United States in Australia*. Melbourne: Oxford University Press

Bell, Philip and Boehringer, Kathe 1989. 'Publicising Progress: Science on Australian television', in John Tulloch and Graeme Turner (eds), *Australian Television: Programs, Pleasures and Politics*. Sydney: Allen & Unwin, pp.103–19

Bennett, Tony 1982. 'Theories of the media, theories of society', in Michael Gurevitch, Tony Bennett, James Curran and Janet Woollacott (eds), *Culture, Society and the Media*. London: Methuen

Berkman, Marcus 1992. 'Strewth, a good Aussie drama', *Daily Mail*, 24 January

Bianchi, Jean 1984. *Comment comprendre le succès international des séries de fiction à la télévision? – Le cas 'Dallas'*. Lyon: Laboratoire CNRS/IRPEACS, July

BIE (Bureau of Industry Economics) 1994. *Audiovisual Industries in Australia: a Discussion Paper*. Canberra: BIE, April

Bland, Judith (Managing Director) and Cook, Liz (Director International Sales, Eaton Films) 1992. Interview with Elizabeth Jacka. London, November

Breig, James 1993. 'Drama examines nuns in '60s', *The Evangelist*, 10 June

Bright, Greg 1994. 'Blinky's rolling in it across US market', *Encore*, 23 May–5 June, p.11

Broinowski, Alison 1992. *The Yellow Lady: Australian Impressions of Asia*. Melbourne: Oxford University Press

BTCE (Bureau of Transport and Communications Economics) 1991. *Economic Aspects of Broadcasting Regulation*. Canberra: Australian Government Publishing Service

Buckingham, David 1987. *Public Secrets: Eastenders and its Audience*. London: British Film Institute

Carcy, James 1989. *Communications as Culture: Essays on Media and Society*. New York and London: Routledge

Carrington, Michael 1993. Speech by Manager, Discovery Europe, Documentary Conference. Sydney, December

Castles, Stephen 1990. 'Global workforce, new racism and the declining nation state', *Occasional Paper No. 23*. Centre for Multicultural Studies, University of Wollongong

Caughie, John 1990. 'Playing at being American: Games and tactics', in Patricia Mellencamp (ed.), *Logics of television: Essays in Cultural Criticism*. Bloomington and Indianapolis: Indiana University Press, pp.44–58

Cawthorne, Russell 1993. Speech by Managing Director, Golden Harvest Productions, Hong Kong, to Screen Producers' Association of Australia Conference, Canberra, November

Centurion, Diosnel and Philpott, Malcolm 1994. 'Papua New Guinea's new communications policy'. *Media Information Australia*, No. 71

Christopherson, S. and Storper, M. 1986. 'The city as studio; the world as back lot: The impact of vertical disintegration on the location of the motion picture industry', *Environment and Planning D: Society and Space*, Vol. 4, pp.305–20

Clark, Pilita 1994. 'Agents of change', *Sydney Morning Herald Good Weekend*, 23 July, pp.44–7

Collins, Carolyn 1994. 'Soapies hurt our friendly image', *Australian*, 6 January, p.4

Collins, Richard 1989a. 'The language of advantage: Satellite television in Western Europe', *Media, Culture and Society*, 11, No. 3

Collins, Richard 1989b. 'White and green and not much re(a)d: The 1988 White Paper on broadcasting policy', *Screen*, 30, Nos 2, 3

Collins, Richard 1990. 'Language, culture and global information markets: The hardware–software relationship in television', *Policy Research Paper No. 5*. Melbourne: CIRCIT

Collins, Richard 1993. 'Public service broadcasting by satellite in Europe – Eurikon and Europa', *Screen*, 34, No. 2, pp.162–75

Commonwealth of Australia 1994. *Creative Nation: Commonwealth Cultural Policy*. Canberra, October

Cooper-Chen, Anne 1993. Goodbye to the global village: Entertainment TV patterns in 50 countries. Paper delivered at the Association for Education in Journalism and Mass Communication Annual Convention. Kansas City, August

Copley, Jason 1991. The Road that leads to Ramsay Street: Towards the study of soap opera's popularity in its imported context. BA Hons dissertation, Goldsmiths' College, University of London

Cox, Peter 1994. 'Switch to Bonanza when it's money for the box', *Weekend Australian*, 16–17 July, p.23

Craven, Ian 1989. 'Distant neighbours: Notes on some Australian soap operas', *Australian Studies*, No. 3, December, pp.1–35

Crocombe, R. 1972. 'The future of Pacific cultures, part 2: Customary behaviour'. *Pacific Perspectives*, Vol. 1, No. 2

Crofts, Stephen 1993. 'Why the *Neighbours* phenomenon in Britain?', *Metro*, No. 95, Spring

Crofts, Stephen 1995. 'Global *Neighbours*?', in Robert C. Allen (ed.), *To Be Continued... Soap Opera Around the World*. London and New York: Routledge

Crystal, Tammi (Program Scheduling, Discovery Networks) 1994. Interview with Stuart Cunningham. Bethesda, MA, March

Cunningham, Stuart 1988. 'Kennedy-Miller: "House Style" in Australian television', in Dermody and Jacka (eds)

Cunningham, Stuart 1992. *Framing Culture: Criticism and Policy in Australia*. Sydney: Allen & Unwin

Cunningham, Stuart and Jacka, Elizabeth 1993. 'Australian television – an international player?', *Media Information Australia*, No. 70, November, pp.17–27

Cunningham, Stuart and Ritchie, John 1994. 'An ersatz Asian nation? The ABC in Asia', *Media Information Australia*, No. 71, February, pp.46–54

Curtin, Michael 1993. 'Beyond the vast wasteland: The policy of global television and the politics of the American empire', *Journal of Broadcasting and Electronic Media*, Vol. 37, No. 2, Spring, pp.127–46

DASET (Department of the Arts, Sport, the Environment and Territories) 1992. *The Role of the Commonwealth in Australia's Cultural Development*. Canberra: DASET, April

de Bens, Els, Kelly, Mary and Bakke, Marit 1992. 'Television content: Dallasification of culture?', in Karen Siune and Wolfgang Truetzschler (eds for the Euromedia Research Group), *Dynamics of Media Politics: Broadcast and Electronic Media in Western Europe*. London: Sage.

de Nave, Caterina (New Zealand television diector) 1993. Interview with Geoff Lealand, Auckland, December

de Swann, 1991. 'Notes on the emerging global language system: Regional national and supranational', *Media Culture and Society*, 13 (3), pp.309–24

de Jabrun, Mary 1993. 'French adolescents' perceptions of Australia', in Grant and Seal (eds), pp.102–07

de la Garde, Roger, Gilsdorf, William, and Wechselmann, Ilja (eds) 1993. *Small Nations, Big Neighbour: Denmark and Quebec/Canada Compare Notes on American Popular Culture*. London: John Libbey

Dermody, Susan and Jacka, Elizabeth 1987. *The Screening of Australia, Volume 1: Anatomy of a Film Industry*. Sydney: Currency Press

Dermody, Susan and Jacka, Elizabeth 1988a. *The Screening of Australia, Volume 2: Anatomy of a National Culture*. Sydney: Currency Press

Dermody, Susan and Jacka, Elizabeth (eds) 1988b. *The Imaginary Industry: Australian Film in the Late Eighties*. North Ryde: Australian Film Television and Radio School

DITARD (Department of Industry, Technology and Regional Development) 1994. *Media Developments in Asia and Implications for Australia: A Discussion Paper*, Canberra: DITARD, March

Dixit, Kunda (Regional Director, Asia-Pacific, Inter Press Service, Manila) 1994. Email correspondence with Stuart Cunningham, May

Drinnan, John 1993. 'Aussie TV with a Kiwi accent', *Dominion*, 17 December

During, Simon 1992. 'Postcolonialism and globalization', *Meanjin*, 51 (2), pp.339–53

Encore 1990. 'ABC forms distrib arm and appoints UK's Telso', 8 (19), 15 November–5 December

Featherstone, Mike (ed.) 1990. *Global Culture: Nationalism, Globalization and Modernity*. London: Sage Publications

Fejes, Fred 1981. 'Media Imperialism: An assessment', *Media Culture and Society*, 3, pp.281–9

Fell, Liz 1989. 'Space communication: Australia in the South Pacific', in Helen Wilson (ed.), *Australian Communications and the Public Sphere*. Melbourne: Macmillan

Ferguson, Marjorie 1992. 'The mythology about globalization', *European Journal of Communication*, 7, pp.69–93

Film Australia (1992). *Annual Report*

Film Australia (1993). *Annual Report*

Firth, Stewart 1989. 'Sovereignty and independence in the contemporary Pacific', *The Contemporary Pacific*, Vol. 1, Nos 1–2

Freeman, Jane 1994. 'Crawfords sacks staff in new TV drama', *Sunday Age*, 20 September

Fuller, Chris 1993. 'Top Dutch Indies join', *Variety*, 27 December

Gardella, Kay 1993. 'A dramatic test of faith', *New York Daily News*, 11 June

Garnaut, Ross 1989. *Australia and the North Asian Ascendancy: Report to the Prime Minister and the Minister for Foreign Affairs and Trade*. Canberra: Australian Government Publishing Service

Gellner, Ernest 1983. *Nations and Nationalism*. Oxford: Basil Blackwell

George, Sandy 1991a. 'Making a buck meaningfully', *Encore*, 9 (17), 1–14 November, p.20

George, Sandy 1991b. 'On all fronts, name builds abroad', *Encore*, 9 (17), 1–14 November, p.23

George, Sandy 1994. 'Quality programs reap good returns at MIPCOM', *Encore*, 12 (18), p.15

Gerrie, Anthea 1992. 'Teaching the US to suck soap', *Bulletin*, 9 June, pp.98–100

Gidney, Nelsa (Senior Program Buyer, American Program Service) 1994. Interview with Stuart Cunningham. New York, March

Giles Consulting 1992. *Film Industry Opportunities for the Gold Coast Albert Region: An Economic Perspective*. Report for the Gold Coast Albert Regional Development Committee and the Department of Business, Industry and Regional Development, April

Gillespie, Marie 1991. 'Soap viewing, gossip and rumour among Punjabi youth in Southall'. Paper presented to the Fourth International Television Studies Conference, London, July. Reprinted (1993) shorter version in P. Drummond, R. Paterson and J. Willis (eds), *National Identity and Europe: The Television Revolution*. London: BFI Publishing, pp.25–42

Ginnane, Anthony I. (International Sales Agent, Fries Distribution) 1994. Interview with Stuart Cunningham. Los Angeles, March

Given, Jock 1993. Australian content, broadcasting and export opportunities. Paper for the 1993 Australian Broadcasting Summit, Sydney, 11 November

Given, Jock 1994. 'New Zealand shoots for the sky', *Media Information Australia*, No. 71

Golphin, Vincent 1993. 'Series challenges the image of nuns', *Syracuse Herald-Journal*, 5 June

Gomery, Douglas 1989. 'The Reagan record', *Screen*, 30, Nos 1–2, pp.92–9

Goodwin, Peter 1991. 'A comfortable arrangement', *TV World*, December, UK Liftout, pp.4ff.

Goodwin, Peter 1993. *TV World Guide to the UK*, December, pp.12–13

Gordon, Bruce 1993. TV programming update: Current scheduling strategies. Presentation to Screen Producers' Association of Australia, 8th Annual Conference, Canberra, November

Graham, J. 1992. 'Post-fordism as politics: the political consequences of narratives on the left', *Environment and Planning D: Society and Space*, Vol. 10, pp.393–410

Grant, Don and Seal, Graham (eds) 1994. *Australia in the World: Perceptions and Possibilities*. Papers from the Outside Images of Australia Conference, Perth, 1992. Perth: Black Swan Press, Curtin University of Technology

Grantham, Bill 1992. 'Far Eastern promise', *Television Business International*, October, pp.48–54

Greaves, William 1989. 'Down under on the up and up', *Radio Times*, 11–17 March

Greer, Germaine 1989. 'Dinkum? No bunkum', *Radio Times*, 11–17 March

Guback, Thomas 1969. *The International Film Industry*. Bloomington: Indiana University Press

Guback, Thomas 1984. 'International circulation of US films and television programs', in G. Gerbner and M. Siefert (eds), *World Communications: A Handbook*. New York: Longman

Guy, Camille 1994. 'Boxed in', *New Zealand Herald*, 14 May

Halberstadt-Harari, Simone (President and Director General, Tele-Images) 1992. Interview with Elizabeth Jacka. Paris, November

Hall, Stuart 1977. 'Culture, the media and the "ideological effect"', in James Curran, Michael Gurevitch and Janet Woollacott (eds), *Mass Communication and Society*. London: Edward Arnold

Hallam, Wendy 1992. Interview with Elizabeth Jacka. London, November

Hamilton, Annette 1992. 'The mediascape of modern Southeast Asia', *Screen*, 33, No. 1, Spring, pp.81–92

Hamilton, Peter and Mathews, Sue 1986. *American Dreams: Australian Movies*. Sydney: Currency Press

Hartley, John 1992. *Tele-ology: Studies in Television*. London: Routledge

Harvey, David 1989. *The Condition of Postmodernity*. Oxford: Basil Blackwell

Harvey-Sutton, Donna 1994. ABC TV drama in the 1990s: Culture and commercialism. Master of Arts thesis in Film and Television, Faculty of Humanities, Griffith University

Hau'ofa, Epeli 1987. 'The new South Pacific society: Integration and independence' in A. Hooper *et al.* (eds), *Class and Culture in the South Pacific*. Centre for Pacific Studies, University of Auckland and Institute of Pacific Studies, University of the South Pacific

Hawker, Philippa 1988. 'Ian Bradley does his sums'. *Cinema Papers*, 69, May, pp.18–19

Hayward, Phil 1993. 'After the Record: The *Tabaran* documentary, Papua New Guinea and inter-cultural relations', *Perfect Beat*, Vol. 1, No. 3

Hjort, Anne 1985. 'When women watch TV – how the Danish female public sees *Dallas* and the Danish serial *The Daughters of War*', in *Medieforskning*, Denmark Radio

Hodge, Errol 1993. 'Editorial Integrity and Australia Television', *Australian Journalism Review*, 15, No.2, July–December, pp.91–100

Hodge, Errol 1995. *Radio Wars: The Struggle for Radio Australia*. Melbourne: Cambridge University Press

Holden, Tony 1994. Presentation to Film & Television Studies Course, University of Waikato, 10 June

Hollings, Bettina (Programming Manager, TVNZ Channel 2) 1994. Interview with Geoff Lealand. Wellington, February

Holmes, Ian (Managing Director, Grundy Organisation) 1992. Interview with Stuart Cunningham. Sydney, June

Holmes, Ian (Managing Director, Grundy Organisation) 1994. Broadcast programming speech at IIR Conference, Sydney, June

Horsfield, Julianne 1990. *The Introduction of broadcast television into Papua New Guinea: a case study in the sociology of mass communication*. Master of Arts thesis, Sociology Department, University of Melbourne

Hoskins, Colin and McFadyen, Stuart 1989. 'Television in the new broadcasting environment: Public policy lessons from the Canadian experience', *European Journal of Communication*, 4, pp.173–89

Hoskins, Colin and McFadyen, Stuart 1991. 'The US competitive advantage in the global television market: Is it sustainable in the new broadcasting environment?', *Canadian Journal of Communication*, 16, No. 2, pp.207–24

Hoskins, Colin and McFadyen, Stuart 1993. 'Canadian participation in international co-productions and co-ventures in television programming', *Canadian Journal of Communication*, 18, pp.219–36

Hoskins, Colin and Mirus, Roger 1988. 'Reasons for the US dominance of international trade in television programs', *Media, Culture and Society*, Vol.10, No.4

HRSCERA (House of Representatives Standing Committee on Environment Recreation and the Arts) 1992. *Report of the Moving Pictures Inquiry*. Canberra: Australian Government Publishing Service

Jacka, Elizabeth 1991. *The ABC of Drama: 1975–90*. North Ryde: Australian Film Television and Radio School

Jacka, Elizabeth 1993. 'The production process: film', in Stuart Cunningham and Graeme Turner (eds), *The Media in Australia: Industries, Texts, Audiences*. Sydney: Allen & Unwin, pp.180–92

Jesson, Bruce 1994. 'Jim Bolger, Republican', *The Republican*, No. 82

Jezequel, Jean-Pierre and Pineau, Guy 1992. 'French television', in Silj (ed.)

Johnstone, Ian 1984. 'Television in the South Pacific', *Pacific Islands Communication Journal*, Vol.13, No.2

Jones, Ross 1991. *Cut! Protection of Australia's Film and Television Industries*. St Leonards: Centre for Independent Studies

Kagan, Russell J. (International Program Consultants) 1994. Interview with Stuart Cunningham. New York, March

Kalo, K. 1987. *Report of the Board of Inquiry into Broadcasting (including Television) in Papua New Guinea*. Port Moresby: Government Printer

Karthigesu, Ranggasamy 1993. Where does television fit in the Asian cultural map?'. Paper presented to the Post-Colonial Formations Conference, Griffith University, July

Katz, E. and Liebes, T. 1985. 'Mutual aid in the decoding of *Dallas*: Preliminary notes from a cross-cultural study', in P. Drummond and R. Paterson (eds), *Television In Transition: Papers from the First International Television Studies Conference*. London: British Film Institute

Keating, Paul 1989. Partial transcript of launch of Australian Film Finance Corporation. Sydney, 3 February

Keating, Paul 1992. Speech by the Prime Minister, The Hon. Paul Keating, MP, at AWGIE Awards Presentation Dinner, Melbourne, 10 July

Keller, Julia 1993. 'Religious life treated with wit, reverence in *Brides of Christ*', *Colombus Dispatch*, 13 June

Kessler, Clive S. 1991. 'Negotiating cultural difference: on seeking, not always successfully, to share the world with others – or, in defence of *Embassy*', *Asian Studies Review*, 15, No.2, pp.57–73

Kilborn, Richard 1993. '"Speak my language": current attitudes to television subtitling and dubbing', *Media Culture and Society*, 15, pp.641–60

Kingsley, Hilary 1988. *Soap Box*. London: Papermac

KPMG Management Consulting (1992). *A History of Offshore Production in the UK: A Report for the Australian Film Commission*. April.

Kreutzner, Gabriele and Seiter, Ellen 1991. 'Not all "soaps" are created equal: Towards a crosscultural criticism of television serials', *Screen*, 32, No.2, pp.154–72

Langenstein, Gottfried (Deputy Director, International Affairs, ZDF) 1992. Interview with Elizabeth Jacka. Mainz, October

Lealand, Geoff 1990. '"I'd just like to say how happy I am to be here in the seventh state of Australia": The Australianisation of New Zealand television', *Sites*, No 21, Spring, pp.100–12

Lee, Chin-Chuan 1980. *Media Imperialism Reconsidered: The Homogenizing of Television Culture*. London: Sage

Lent, John 1993. 'Four conundrums of Third World communications: A generational analysis', in K. Nordenstreng and H. Schiller (eds), *Beyond National Sovereignty; International Communication in the 1990s*. Norwood NJ: Ablex

Leonard, Hugh 1993. 'Asian broadcasting: the changing scene', *Media Asia*, Vol.20, No.3, pp.123–6

Leonard, John 1993. 'Television', *New York*, 11 June

Lewis, Daniel 1994. 'Europeans troppo over Grundy soap', *Sydney Morning Herald*, 13 August

Lewis, Glen 1987. *Australian Movies and the American Dream*. New York: Praeger

Liebes, Tamar and Katz, Elihu 1990. *The Export of Meaning: Cross-Cultural Readings of Dallas*. New York: Oxford University Press

Loo, Eric and Ramanathan, Sankaran 1993. 'Coverage of the Terengganu Prince affair by Australian and Malaysian print media: A study of cross-cultural communication'. Paper presented at the Australian Communication Conference national conference, July. Version published in *Media Information Australia*, No.70, November 1993

Lowry, Brian 1993. 'Producers caught between Regs, Studios', *Variety*, 17 August

Lull, James 1991. *China Turned On*. London: Routledge

Lull, James (ed.) 1988. *World Families Watch Television*. Newbury Park: SAGE Publications

Lumby, Catherine and O'Neil, John 1994. 'Tabloid television', in Julianne Schultz (ed.), *Not Just Another Business: Journalists, Citizens and the Media*. Marrickville: Pluto Press and Ideas for Australia, pp.149–66

MacBride, Sean 1980. *Many Voices, One World: Report for the Study of Communication Problems*. Paris: Kogan Page/UNESCO

MacDermott, Doireann 1993. 'As We See You', in Grant and Seal (eds), pp.86–91

Macken, Deirdre 1989. 'Invasion of the Aussie soaps', *Sydney Morning Herald Good Weekend*, 8 April

Maddox, Gary 1991a. 'Crawfords opens two new studios', *Encore*, 9 (15), 27 September–10 October, pp.ii–iii

Maddox, Gary 1991b. 'Still flying after 200 episodes', *Encore*, 9 (15), 27 September–10 October, pp.viii–ix

Man Chan, Joseph 1992. Satellite television and the infosphere: National responses and accessibility to Star-TV in Asia. Paper presented at the Ninth World Communication Forum, November

Mann, Virginia 1993. 'Sisters are people, too', *The Bergen Record*, 13–19 June

Mansoufis, Marena (Head of Program Sales and Acquisitions, ABC International) 1993. Interview with Stuart Cunningham and Elizabeth Jacka. Sydney: September

Marin, Minette 1989. *Daily Telegraph*, 10 March, 18, quoted in Wober and Fazal 1994, pp.78–87

Mars, Gerard 1992. 'The Flying Doctors: een plattelandspraktijk in het groot (a country practice on a large scale)', *VARA TV Guide*, September

Marshall, David (University of Queensland) 1994. Interview with Stuart Cunningham. Brisbane, March

Martin, John 1993. 'Brides of Christ', *The Providence Journal-Bulletin*, 11 June

Martz, Carol (Program Manager, KCOP LA) 1994. Interview with Stuart Cunningham. Los Angeles, March

Mattelart, Armand 1979. *Multinational Corporations and the Control of Culture*. Brighton: Harvester Press

McCathie, Andrew 1991. 'Europe tunes in to "new-look" Australia', *Financial Review*, 3 September, p.32

McElvogue, Louise 1989. 'AFS negotiates Crawfords bid', *Encore*, 7 (12), 3–16 August

McLuhan, Marshall 1964. *Understanding Media: The Extensions of Man*. London: Routledge & Kegan Paul

McLuhan, Marshall and Powers, Bruce R. 1989. *The Global Village: Transformations in World Life and Media in the 21st Century*. New York: Oxford University Press

McMahon, Nick (Managing Director, Village Roadshow Pictures) 1992. Interview with Stuart Cunningham and Elizabeth Jacka. Sydney, June

McNamara, James (Chief Executive Officer and President, New World Entertainment), Diserio, Thea (Senior Vice-President, New World International), and Oldham, Phil (Executive Vice President, Genesis Entertainment) 1994. Interview with Stuart Cunningham. New York, March

Michael, James 1990. 'Regulating communications media: from the discretion of sound chaps to the arguments of lawyers', in Marjorie Ferguson (ed.), *Public Communication: the New Imperatives*. London: Sage

Michaels, Eric 1991. *For a Cultural Future*. Sydney: Artspace

Miller, Daniel 1992. '*The Young and the Restless* in Trinidad, a case of the local and the global in mass consumption', in R. Silverstone and E. Hirsch (eds), *Consuming Technologies: Media and Information in Domestic Spaces*. London: Routledge

Miller, J. D. B. 1987. *Australians and British: Social and Political Connections*. Sydney: Methuen

Miller, Toby 1991. 'Splitting the citizen', *Continuum*, 4 (2), p.197

Miller, Toby 1994. 'When Australia became modern', in Review of *National Fictions*, 2nd edn, *Continuum*, 8 (2), pp.206–14

Milne, John 1993. 'Overcoming Australia's regional image problem: A personal view', in Grant and Seal (eds), pp.283–90

Milner, Andrew 1991. *Contemporary Cultural Theory*. Sydney: Allen & Unwin

Mitchell, Gary (Sales Manager, Richard Price Television Associates) 1992. Interview with Elizabeth Jacka. London, November

Mitchell, Tony 1993. 'Orientalism in Ragaan: *Embassy*'s imaginative geography', *Meanjin*, 52, No. 2, Winter, pp.265–76

Moir, Bruce (Managing Director, Film Australia) 1993. Address to the Screen Producers' Association of Australia Annual Conference, Canberra, November

Moir, Bruce (Managing Director, Film Australia) 1994. Interview with Elizabeth Jacka. Sydney, September

Molloy, Simon and Burgan, Barry 1993. *The Economics of Film and Television in Australia*. Sydney: AFC

Molnar, Helen 1991. 'Communication technology in the Pacific: in whose interest?', *Australian Journalism Review*, Vol.13, Nos 1–2

Molnar, Helen 1993. *The Democratisation of communications technology in Australia and the South Pacific: Media participation by indigenous peoples, 1970–92.* PhD thesis, Department of Politics, Monash University, Melbourne

Monaghan, Des (Network Program Development Director, Seven Network) 1994. Interview with Elizabeth Jacka. Sydney, August

Moran, Albert 1985. *Images and Industry: Television Drama Production in Australia.* Sydney: Currency Press

Moran, Albert 1991. *Projecting Australia: Government Film Since 1945.* Sydney: Currency Press

Moran, Albert 1993. *Moran's Guide to Australian TV Series.* North Ryde: Australian Film Television and Radio School

Morgan, Bill (Ombudsman, Canadian Broadcasting Corporation) 1992. Interview with Stuart Cunningham. Toronto, February

Morley, David and Robins, Kevin 1989. 'Spaces of identity: communications technologies and the reconfiguration of Europe', *Screen*, 30, No. 4, Autumn

Mulgan, Geoff and Warpole, Ken 1986. *Saturday Night or Sunday Morning? From Arts to Industry – New Forms of Cultural Policy.* London: Comedia Publishing Group

Murphy, Tim 1994. 'Bolger goes to bat for TV soap opera', *New Zealand Herald*, 5 May

Murray, Sue 1994. 'The International Perspective', *ABA Update*, No. 17, March, pp.18–20

Naficy, Hamid 1993. *The Making of Exile Cultures: Iranian Television in Los Angeles.* Minneapolis and London: University of Minnesota Press

Networks, 74, 1992. '*Shortland Street*: a new era in television', 15 May

Nicholson, Paul 1991. 'A nervous new order'. UK Special Report in *Television Business International*, November, pp.iii–vi

Nieuwenhuis, A. J. 1992. 'Media policy in the Netherlands: beyond the market?', *European Journal of Communication*, 7 (2), pp.195–218

Nordenstreng, Kaarle and Varis, Tapio 1974 *Television Traffic – a One Way Street.* UNESCO Reports and Papers on Mass Communication, No. 70

O'Regan, Tom 1988. '"Fair dinkum fillums": The *Crocodile Dundee* phenomenon'. In Dermody and Jacka (eds), pp.155–76

O'Regan, Tom 1991a. ' From piracy to sovereignty: international videocassette recorder trends', *Continuum*, 4 (2), pp.112–35

O'Regan, Tom 1991b. 'The rise and fall of entrepeneurial television, Australian TV 1986–1990', *Screen*, 32, No. 1, pp.94–108

O'Regan, Tom 1993a. 'The international, the regional and the local: Hollywood's new and declining audiences', in Elizabeth Jacka (ed.), *Continental Shift: Culture and Globalisation.* Sydney: Local Consumption Publications

O'Regan, Tom 1993b. *Australian Television Culture*. Sydney: Allen & Unwin

Ohlsson, Terry and Samulenok, Don (Managing Director and Director of Sales, Crawfords Australia) 1992. Interview with Marie Delofski and Elizabeth Jacka. Melbourne, August

Oliver, Chris 1993. Address to the Screen Producers' Association of Australia Annual Conference, Canberra, November

Oliver, Robin 1993a. 'Suffering Paradise', *Sydney Morning Herald: The Guide*, 31 May, p.15s

Oliver, Robin 1993b. 'Paradise pumped up to a new low', *Sydney Morning Herald: The Guide*, 9 August, p.15s

Ostergaard, Bernt Stubbe (ed. for the Euromedia Research Group) 1992. *The Media in Western Europe: The Euromedia Handbook*. London: Sage Publications

PA Consulting 1994. *Australia Television: Market Development Profile*. February

Papandrea, Franco 1994. Effectiveness of Australian content regulation for television programs. Paper presented at the Media Futures: Policy and Performance Conference, Surfers Paradise, July

Perera, Suvendrini 1993. 'Representation wars: Malaysia, *Embassy*, and Australia's *corps diplomatique*', in John Frow and Meaghan Morris (eds), *Australian Cultural Studies: A Reader*. Sydney: Allen & Unwin, pp.15–29

Plange, Nii-K 1993. 'Video, TV and Fiji's society: Fast-forward into the future or pausing for a closer look', *Pacific Islands Communication Journal*, Vol. 16, No. 1

Prisk, Tracey 1990. 'Ohlsson aims to double Crawfords' TV output', *Encore*, 8 (4), 29 March–11 April

Project Blue Sky 1993. Publicity material, New Zealand Film & Television Conference, Wellington, NZ

Pusey, Michael 1991. *Economic Rationalism in Canberra: A Nation-Building State Changes Its Mind*. London, New York and Melbourne: Cambridge University Press

Reid, Ian 1992. 'Fog over the Tasman: New Zealand attitudes to Australia', in Grant and Seal (eds), pp.78–83

Riley, Roger W. and Van Doren, Carlton S. 1992. 'The "Crocodile Dundee" paragon: Justifying a film commission's existence', *Locations*, Fall, pp.14–19

Robertson, Roland 1992. *Globalization: Social Theory and Global Culture*, London: Sage Publications

Robertson, Roland 1994. 'Globalisation or glocalisation?', *Journal of International Communication*, 1 (1)

Rogge, Jan-Uwe and Jensen, Klaus 1988. 'Everyday life and television in West Germany: An empathic-interpretive perspective on the familiy as a system', in Lull (ed.)

Roush, Matt 1993. 'Heavenly "Brides"', *USA Today*, 11 June

Rowe, David 1994. 'The federal republic of *Sylvania Waters*', *Metro Magazine*, No. 98, Winter, pp.14–23

Said, Edward 1991. *Orientalism: Western Concepts of the Orient*. London: Penguin

Schembri, Peter and Malone, Jackie 1994. 'Paradise Beach reconsidered', *Cinema Papers*, Nos 97–98, April, pp.30–3

Schiller, Herbert 1976. *Communications and Cultural Domination*. New York: M. E. Sharpe

Schiller, Herbert 1991. 'Not yet the post-imperialist era', *Critical Studies in Mass Communication*, 8, pp.13–28

Schmidel, Michael (Production Department, Taurus Films) 1992. Interview with Elizabeth Jacka. Munich, October

Schutze, Manfred (Head of Acquisitions, ZDF) 1992. Interview with Elizabeth Jacka. Mainz, October

Scott, Rebecca 1994. 'Screen protectionism', *Sunday Star*, 6 February

Seiter, Ellen *et al.* 1989. 'Introduction', in Ellen Seiter *et al.* (eds), *Remote Control*. London: Routledge, pp.1–15

Sharp, Ilsa 1994. 'Looking beyond the *Wayang*: Perceptions and coverage of Australia in Southeast Asian media (with special reference to Singapore/Malaysia)', in Grant and Seal (eds), pp.273–9

Shawcross, William 1992. *Rupert Murdoch: Ringmaster of the Information Circus*. Sydney: Random House

Sheridan, Greg 1994. 'Stereotypes trap our image in Asia', *Australian*, 28 June

Shoebridge, Neil 1993. 'Village goes Global with Low-Risk TV', *Business Review Weekly*, 7 May, pp.10–11

Shoesmith, Brian 1993. 'Technology transfer or technology dialogue: rethinking Western communications values', *Media Asia*, 20 (3), pp.152–6

Shohet, Rachel 1993. 'Life's a beach in Paradise', Brisbane *Sunday Mail Magazine*, 16 May

Silj, Alessandro 1988. *East of Dallas: The European Challenge to American Television*. London: British Film Institute

Silj, Alesandro (ed.) 1992. *The New Television in Europe*. London: John Libbey

Silverstone, Roger 1991. Television, ontological security and the transitional object. Paper presented to the Fourth International Television Studies Conference, London, July

Silverstone, Roger 1994. *Television and Everyday Life*, London and New York: Routledge

Sinclair, John 1990. 'Neither west nor third world: the Mexican television industry within the NWICO debate', *Media Culture and Society*, 12, pp.343–60

Sinclair, John, Jacka, Elizabeth and Cunningham, Stuart (eds) 1996. *New Patterns in Global Television: Peripheral Vision*. London: Oxford University Press

Skovmand, Michael and Schroder, Kim Christian (eds) 1992. *Media Cultures: Reappraising Transnational Media*. London and New York: Routledge

Smith, Anthony D. 1990. 'Towards a global culture?', in Featherstone (ed.)

Smith, Roff 1992. 'I am 68. I live in the Bahamas. I am Australia's biggest TV star. Who am I?', *Sunday Age*, 26 July, Agenda 1–2

Sreberny-Mohammadi, Annabelle 1991. 'The global and the local in international communications', in J. Curran and M. Gurevitch (eds), *Mass Media and Society*. London: Edward Arnold

Stewart, Adrien 1994. 'Know your product: *Paradise Beach*', *Exposure*, Issue 1, January, pp.6–7

Stewart, Julianne 1993. 'EM TV: the first six years of broadcast television in Papua New Guinea', *Pacific Islands Communication Journal*, Vol. 16, No. 1

Stewart, Richard (Executive Director, Film Queensland) 1993. Address to Screen Producers' Association of Australia Conference, November

Stone, Dominic (Program Scheduler and Acting General Manager, Australia Television) 1994. Interview with John Ritchie. Sydney, May

Stratton, Jon and Ang, Ien 1994. '*Sylvania Waters* and the spectacular exploding family', *Screen*, 35, No. 1, Spring, pp.1–21

Swoch, James 1993. 'Cold war, hegemony, postmodernism: American television and the world-system, 1945–1992', *Quarterly Review of Film and Video*, 14 (3), pp.9–24

Tariff Board 1973. *Tariff Board Report into a Tariff Revision for Motion Picture Films and Television Programs*. Canberra: Australian Government Publishing Service

Task Force 1993. 'The Report of the Twentieth Century Fund Task Force on Public Television, with Background Paper by Richard Somerset-Ward', *Quality Time?* New York: The Twentieth Century Fund Press

Taylor, Catherine 1993. 'Squeaky-clean soap, export quality', *Australian*, 28 May

Taylor, John (Chief Executive Officer, EM TV) 1992. Interview with Helen Wilson. Port Moresby, October, supplemented March 1993

Taylor, John (Chief Executive Officer, EM TV) 1994. Interview with Helen Wilson. Port Moresby, February

Thomas, Pamela 1987. 'Mass media—mass dependency', *Pacific Islands Communication Journal*, Vol. 15, No. 1

Thomas, Amos 1994. 'Broadcast policy versus commercial imperative: television programming in Papua New Guinea', *Media Asia*, Vol. 21, No. 1

Tolen-Worth, Louise (Head Program Purchasing, Nederlandse Omroepprogramma Stichting) 1992. Interview with Elizabeth Jacka, Hilversum, October

Tomlinson, John 1991. *Cultural Imperialism: A Critical Introduction*. Baltimore: Johns Hopkins University Press

Tracey, Michael 1985. 'The poisoned chalice? International television and the Idea of dominance', *Daedalus*, 114, No.4, Fall, pp.17–56

Tracey, Michael 1987. 'European viewers: what will they really watch?'. *Columbia Journal of World Business*, Fall, pp.77–85

Tracey, Michael 1988. 'Popular culture and the economics of global television', *Intermedia*, 16, No. 2, March, pp.9–25

Tunstall, Jeremy and Palmer, Michael 1991. *Media Moguls*. London and New York: Routledge

Turner, Graeme 1994. 'The end of the national project? Australian cinema in the 1990s', in Wimal Dissanayake (ed.), *Questions of Nationhood in Asian Cinema*. Bloomington: Indiana University Press

TV World 1993. 'Guide to the UK'. December, pp.1–12

TV World 1994. 'TV World special report: Game shows'. January–February, pp.17–21

Unger, Arthur 1986. 'Three TV specials go head to head Sunday', *Christian Science Monitor*, 3 October, pp.23–4

van Essen, Ria (Head of Programming, VARA Televisie) 1992. Interview with Elizabeth Jacka, Hilversum, October, supplemented by written communication, June 1994

Varan, Duane 1994. 'Television, culture and state: new forums for negotiating identity in the Pacific', *Continuum*, Vol. 8, No. 2

Varis, Tapio 1974. 'Global traffic in television', *Journal of Communication*, 24, No. 1

Varis, Tapio 1984. 'The international flow of television programs', *Journal of Communication*, 34, No. 1

Vecera, Kim (General Manager, Business Affairs, Roadshow, Coote and Carroll) 1994. Interview with Elizabeth Jacka, Sydney, July

Vincent Report 1962–3. The Parliament of the Commonwealth of Australia, The Senate, *Report From the Select Committee on the Encouragement of Australian Production for Television, Part I*

von Bochove, Hedy (Director Acquisitions and Development, Joop van den Ende TV – Produkties BV) 1992. Interview with Elizabeth Jacka. Aalsmeer, October

Walker, David (ed.) 1990. 'Australian perceptions of Asia', Special issue of *Australian Cultural History*, No.9

Wallerstein, Immanuel 1991. *Geopolitics and Geoculture: Essays on the Changing World System*. Cambridge: Cambridge University Press

Walters, Conrad 1993. 'The latest news on Asia', *Sydney Morning Herald: The Guide*, 17 May, p.5s

Wark, McKenzie 1994a. 'Vectoral perception', *Journal of International Communication*, 1 (1), pp.60–87

Wark, McKenzie 1994b. *Virtual Geography: Living With Global Media Events*. Bloomington: Indiana University Press

Weinstock, Neal 1994. 'Watch this space', *TV World Guide to the US*, January–February

Wichtel, Diana 1993. 'Ain't it a Beach', (New Zealand) *Listener*, 28 August, p.7

Wildman, Steven S. and Siwek, Stephen E. 1988. *International Trade in Films and Television Programs*. Cambridge, Mass.: Ballinger Publishing Company

Williams, Raymond 1974. *Television: Technology and Cultural Form*. London: Fontana

Wilson, Helen 1993. 'Television in Papua New Guinea: Policy challenges in the satellite age'. *Media Information Australia*, No. 68, May

Wilson, Helen 1994. 'TV for Fiji: A dangerous undertaking'. *Media Information Australia*, No. 74, November

Wober, J. M. and Fazal, S. 1994. 'Neighbours at home and away: British viewers' perceptions of Australian soap operas', *Media Information Australia*, No. 71, February, pp.78–87

Woolcott, Richard 1993. 'Advance Australia where?: The continuing search for an Australian identity and for our place in a changing world', in Grant and Seal (eds), pp.17–21

Wroe, Martin 1992. 'Soap that cleans up all over the world', *The Independent*, 17 October

Index

271